Moral Disquiet and Human Life

NEW FRENCH THOUGHT

SERIES EDITORS
Thomas Pavel and Mark Lilla

Monique Canto-Sperber

Moral Disquiet and Human Life

Translated by Silvia Pavel

 NEW FRENCH THOUGHT

PRINCETON UNIVERSITY PRESS · PRINCETON AND OXFORD

Originally published in French as *L'inquiétude morale et la vie humaine* by
Presses Universitaires de France, 6 avenue Reille,
Paris 75014, France; copyright © 2001; this translation is made from the second edition,
published 2002 by Presses Universitaires de France. The English translation is
copyright © 2008 by Princeton University Press

Published by Princeton University Press, 41 William Street,
Princeton, New Jersey 08540
In the United Kingdom: Princeton University Press, 6 Oxford Street,
Woodstock, Oxfordshire OX20 1TW

Library of Congress Cataloging-in-Publication Data

Canto-Sperber, Monique.
[Inquiétude morale et la vie humaine. English]
Moral disquiet and human life / Monique Canto-Sperber;
translated from French by Silvia Pavel.
p.   cm. — (New French thought)
Includes bibliographical references (p. 181) and index.
ISBN 978-0-691-12736-1 (hardcover : alk. paper)
1. Ethics. 2. Humanism. 3. Philosophy—France—History. I. Title.
BJ1063.C3613   2008
170—dc22   2007038758

British Library Cataloging-in-Publication Data is available

Publication of this book has been aided by the French Ministry of Culture

This book has been composed in Bauer Bodoni

Printed on acid-free paper. ∞

press.princeton.edu

Printed in the United States of America

10 9 8 7 6 5 4 3 2 1

For Bernard Williams

Contents

Part Two: HUMAN LIFE

Acknowledgments

MY SPECIAL THANKS to all those who have read the manuscript and provided good advice and constructive criticism, including Jean-Pierre Dupuis, Claude Habib, Charles Larmore, Ruwen Ogien, Philippe Coulomb, Anne Fagot-Largeault, John Elster, Michel Horps, Marcela Jacub, Pierre Livet, Patrice Maniglier, Bernard Manin, Philippe Raynaud, Paul Ricoeur, Dominique Terré, David Wiggins, and all my friends from the seminar on moral philosophy.

PART ONE

Moral Disquiet

CHAPTER 1

Ethics and the Challenge
to Moral Philosophy

ETHICAL DISCOURSE is so fashionable these days that people tend to forget how much it owes to moral philosophy for its main concepts, claims, and topics. This book therefore serves as a reminder that without moral philosophy, there is no such a thing as ethical deliberation and that without ethical deliberation, there is no ethics worthy of consideration.

My analysis deals mainly with France, where ethics' privileged status remains unchallenged. Could the present situation be taken as an indication that moral philosophy is a blooming garden in the intellectual landscape of French philosophy? Or that our understanding of moral reasoning and ethical deliberation is now deeper, more refined, and more nuanced than ever before? Are there any good reasons to rejoice that rational deliberation has regained its vigor or that it has become multifaceted and unbiased?

My answer to each of these questions is negative.

No, French moral philosophy is not blooming. True, ethics is being treated better than logic or the philosophy of mind, but moral philosophy—as a philosophical discipline with its own history, rigorous concepts, and systematic approaches—is as ignored today as it was a generation ago. Ethical thinking and moral philosophy arise both from the same kind of intellectual endeavors: an unprejudiced understanding of a question's scope, premises, and consequences; a fair assessment of possible action or lack thereof; and deliberations and decisions supported by justifications, whether partial or multiple, complete or not. Due to this common intellectual core, ethical deliberation may be applied successfully to a whole range of concrete, present-day questions, whereas moral philosophy concerns itself with more traditional issues that are sometimes revisited by contemporary thought. The essential point is that ethics and moral philosophy are closely linked by their common ways of reasoning.

Ethics is no doubt more fashionable today in France than at the end of the 1980s, but its success will be rather precarious and at risk of being misunderstood so long as moral philosophy remains ignored. It does not help that moral philosophy is actually attacked, led astray, dogmatized, or broken up in self-help moral lessons by so-called friends more harmful than its open enemies. In the face of excessive recycling and multiple attacks, there is only one conclusion to be drawn: among professional French philosophers, only a few are truly trying to find out what is moral philosophy, what are its concepts and methods.

The first proof of it being so is that the teaching of philosophy in our high schools and universities—with one or two exceptions—lacks a modern moral philosophy component. The same could be said of other branches of philosophy. The fact is that a general characteristic of all philosophy courses taught in France—at least to the level of *aggregation*, that is, the state examination that certifies secondary school teachers—is the almost total lack of reference to the twentieth-century history of philosophy and the very scarce mention of the state of philosophy in other countries or of any topics debated among contemporary philosophers. It is as though one resolved to teach a scientific discipline—or, for that matter, any discipline in natural affinity with clarity and argumentation—by vaguely alluding to its history in the past twenty-five years, ignoring its developments in other countries, and leaving one's students in total darkness as to contemporary debates in that field. As for moral philosophy, the gap between educational and intellectual reality is even greater, because this discipline (as defined in the twentieth century) is nowhere to be found in today's French universities. The contrast with ethics could not be greater: in France, the teaching of modern moral philosophy has no recognized place whatsoever.

Another proof comes from the nature of publications claiming to belong to the realm of ethics. Here again, one is bound to notice that almost every author who tackles the subject of morality goes about it in his or her preferred idiom—be it postmodern, Kantian, or materialistic—but very rarely treats moral philosophy as a rational and critical discipline. Most authors start from scratch, often dealing zealously with the work of their favorite philosopher, but remaining oblivious to everything written before them on its subject and rarely mentioning anybody else's relevant contributions in the matter. In stark contrast, all reflexive disciplines share in a common pool of research topics and methods, as well as a whole range of viewpoints and debates that it would be unthinkable not to mention, and without which new contributions make no sense whatsoever. When recently published works of ethics are avoiding all reference to the state of contemporary philosophical thought on morality, I doubt that happens because their authors are following Rousseau's famous call to "Leave all books behind." Rather, it happens because these authors are blissfully unaware of the actual thinking going on in their discipline.[1]

The root cause of both the absence of moral philosophy from university curricula and the lack of interest shown by French philosophers for contemporary issues in this field lies in our philosophical community's inability to distance itself from its own, mainly historical, training and ossified certainties, such as "Good philosophy can only be found in France," "Morality can only be Kantian," "The history of an issue is all one needs in order to properly understand it," "ancient, modern, and present-day philosophy are well-defined divisions in the history of thought," "The Moderns are superior to Ancients in everything," "Science and technology are the enemies of philosophy," "A formal argument is worse than superstition." This is how our philosophers, suspicious of science and non-French thought but sure of having a good grasp on the future of the human mind, delude themselves. Yet, the reality is markedly different. Philosophical studies are excellent elsewhere; the Kantian approach is only one among many; the history of human thought does not follow a predetermined path (that would just happen to coincide with chronological divisions widely adopted in the teaching of philosophy in France); philosophy is universal because its theses are intelligible and its developments rational. More tellingly, the history of moral philosophy shows no discernible linear progression toward truth or goodness, and rational arguments, including formalized ones, are at the heart of ethical thinking. Any serious and informed study of moral philosophy could have delivered a decisive rebuttal to every delusional certainty that afflicts contemporary philosophy in France, but, alas, none has been forthcoming. The old conceptual frame still shapes the teaching of philosophy in our universities and any component of moral philosophy that does not fit in is simply ignored. For all these reasons, it cannot be said in fairness that moral philosophy—as a rigorous discipline—is blooming in France today.

No, there has been no research or analysis attempting to grasp the significance of moral thought. The meaning of the term "moral code" remains loose and mostly arbitrary. All of a sudden, everybody has awakened to the urgent need of dealing with ethics. The once sparsely inhabited field is now crowded. Until recently, any attempt to reinvigorate moral thinking was looked upon with mistrust and scorn. Nowadays, the label "ethics" confers respectability to almost any statement. Its present celebration could however be as harmful as was its past neglect. But, while the neglect was entirely due to ignorance, the actual tendency of indiscriminately using the term "moral" makes the concept unrecognizable, and therefore useless. Both neglect and celebration come from the failure to grasp the essence of moral thought. Stigmatizing or trivializing a research object seems to be the easiest way of exempting oneself from analyzing its specificity.

Let us consider the scenario of a philosophical debate on a moral question. In the absence of a well-argued exchange, each participant would advance his or her own philosophical beliefs and, instead of a principled dialogue highlighting the rigor and sophistication of each point of view, one would witness a thunderous clash of irreconcilable opinions. Generally speaking, philosophical exchanges about ethics are still viewed as a confrontation whereby each side would rather defend its beliefs and state its viewpoints than strive to clarify concepts, to qualify its positions, to detect its own vulnerabilities, and to try to fully understand a point of view contrary to its own. This being the case, it cannot be said that French philosophers are today any better at grasping the essence of moral thought than their predecessors.

Lastly, practical reasoning is still not a privileged subject of tolerant or pluralist discussion. Rhetorical accusations and denunciations can be found on both sides of the debate. By the end of the 1980s when ethical thought again became important, the return to moral codes of conduct and raising moral standards was angrily denounced as moralizing. It goes without saying that no philosopher would favor a reign of moral prejudice or conformism. Excessive moralizing was therefore properly criticized at that time. The problem was that the criticism had started before anyone knew what its object was. Moral thinking has little in common with moral conformism. On the contrary, it may often become the best way of avoiding conformism. This is a topic that I take up again and again in this book, but it should be clear from the start that if moral thinking can be easily defended against any criticism of moral conformism, it does not follow that it is above all criticism. It is all right to criticize the pretensions of moral philosophy, to be suspicious of its hegemonic tendencies, or to question its premises, concepts, or methods. No body of thought can grow and mature if made into a constant object of reverence. The best way to test its value is by exposing it to criticism and questioning. There is, however, a limit beyond which criticism outweighs its usefulness: this happens when it takes on poorly conceived conclusions and doubtful caricatures about its object, or when it deliberately ignores the true nature of its object or willfully confuses the issues.

To illustrate this point, an imaginary conversation could better serve our purpose than a lengthy development of the subject.

—One cannot look for moral standards everywhere. In politics, for instance, it is useless to do so.
—No doubt, but it all depends on what the meaning of "moral" is. If you mean by it "moral lessons," then I agree, they are pointless in politics. However, politics can be a valid object of ethical or normative analysis.
—Not so. Ethics is a matter of commitment and conviction. The morality of convictions, which is the only one out there, has nothing to do with political thought, which deals with power, complex hierarchies, and consequences.

At this point, allow me to interrupt the conversation so as to contest the stealthy definition it gives of "moral." Moral analysis and political analysis are both part of practical philosophy, also called philosophy of human action. But it would be erroneous to say that moral philosophy is limited to conviction and commitment. Moral philosophy is not limited to defending opinions. It may be inspired by a conviction, but this is not always the case. Mainly, it is a reflexive approach, and there is no reason for it to replace political analysis entirely. But neither is there any reason for arbitrarily detaching it from such an approach, confining it to the realm of personal convictions—or, in more modern terms, treating it as a kind of secular religion or complacent humanism.

Moral philosophy is not politics, a religion, or a general philosophy about human beings; rather, it is a mainly intellectual, rational field of research. Only in a limited sense can it be said to be a repository of commitments, yearnings, or convictions. The value of moral thought is gauged first by its reasons, not by the grandiloquence or emotional appeal of its premise. The freedom of thought is the first precondition of any thought process. Thus, one should feel free to evaluate a point of view, criticize a given thesis, suggest counterexamples, or make objections without being spooked by gloomy overstatements (as in "saying this shows that in fact you mean . . ." or "talking about this, even in critical terms, shows your readiness to accept it") and by the conjuring up of horrible consequences such as the loss of all human dignity, the inescapable genocide, or various combinations thereof, and, to cap it all, by alluding to Hitler and the Nazis.[2]

Many a criticism of moral philosophy is built on a deliberate misreading of its specificity. Such a misreading is deliberate not only because it is intentional but also because no attempt is ever made to correct itself. This is the main reason that such criticism has failed to this day to achieve a true pluralism. It is undoubtedly difficult to spot the fine line between, on the one hand, pluralism and nuanced debate aiming to reach the best possible explanations and, on the other, unrestrained antagonism. Be that as it may, I still feel that antagonism and the lack of fair exchanges have left their sorry mark on the philosophical debate in France. The propensity for veneration that begets dogmatism and stifles open and lively debate goes hand in hand with an excess of criticism and denunciation that has a sterilizing rather than an enriching effect on intellectual debates. It is precisely this mixture of blind veneration and stubborn misconception that makes me doubt the existence of conditions conducive to open and lively debate in France.

In 1992 I wrote an article about the state of research in moral philosophy for the French review *Le Débat*.[3] The article points out the near disappearance of moral philosophy from the French intellectual landscape. It mentions the absence of publications, research, and debates on the subject and deplores the denunciation of morality and the disregard if not disdain for the idea that philosophers can have a valid contribution to the debate on

society's issues. Eight years have passed since, and I have to admit that
the situation has changed in certain cases, at least on the surface. Books,
articles, and special issues have been published that give the public, including university students, a general idea of what contemporary moral
philosophy is about. I have myself tried to bring to their attention the
continuous history of moral ideas, the main topics, the basic principles,
and even the style of current debate in this field.[4] Among other signs of
change, one notices the creation of a few discussion groups and a small
community of philosophers interested in the normative aspects of moral
thought.

If so, then what justifies the doubts I now express? In my view, these
changes have not really affected the status of moral philosophy in France.
The discipline is still mostly absent from university curricula, and very
few philosophers are aware of it. People interested in philosophy have no
means of evaluating or criticizing what is published under the heading
"moral philosophy." Worse still, professional philosophers remain largely
unaware of moral philosophy as a discipline, while thoroughly infatuated
with ethics. A world in which people understand the importance of ethics
is surely preferable to one in which they do not. But this only underlines
the urgency of the following questions: What are the reasons of this public
omnipresence of ethics? Is it grounded in solid intellectual reality? It is
precisely on this point that I have the greatest doubts and fears. If ethics
is not rooted in philosophical reflection, then the term could be used indiscriminately to impress, intimidate, or blame instead of being restricted to
thinking and reasoning.[5]

In writing this book, my main purpose has been to thoroughly examine
moral philosophy, to scrutinize its current reality, and to explore the role
it can play in the community of philosophers and French society in general.
I aim to show that moral philosophy is the foundation without which concerns with ethics and moral claims lack seriousness, and that concern for
ethics is not in itself a guarantee of relevance. To this day, there is no
permanent link between appeals to ethics and moral considerations. Moreover, the state of moral reflection itself is not entirely satisfactory. The
doubts and fears expressed earlier arise from a double acknowledgment:
moral reflection is often inconsistent, and ethical activism in the form of
proclamations of virtue, commitments, or rebukes shows in most cases no
connection whatsoever with the intellectual undercurrent of moral philosophy. The major source of legitimacy resides in thought. The development
of moral philosophy and the awareness of the links binding it to concrete
ethical deliberation are the principal preconditions for the ability of our
society to carry out successfully an ethical reflection that is informed, judicious, fair, and as objective as possible. This is the only way to secure
a critical role for moral philosophy in helping to better understand and

appreciate important aspects of the human condition and contemporary thought. A critical approach is particularly useful today, when the infatuation with ethics—facilitated by the specificity of our world—could be seen as a taste for ready-to-use answers. Such answers could easily be found in what I call moralizing. Moral philosophy is altogether different.

Hence, the topic of my book: Is there such a thing as a moral philosophy in France? What tasks is it called to perform? What are its pathways and dead ends? How could it define its main issues, challenges, insuperable obstacles, goals? Drawing up a reflexive and critical approach is a difficult and precarious task in philosophy. Success is not assured in advance. Ten years ago, at the rebirth of moral philosophy, the main intellectual task was to help rebuild it as a discipline by reopening the debate on a set of issues, methods, and concepts that had been forgotten for thirty years and by placing them again at the core of philosophical scrutiny. Today, moral philosophy must also rid itself of superfluous claims and ambitions that are incompatible with this task.

If moral philosophy is to play a legitimate role in modern critical thought, it must answer a few challenging questions. Some of those deal with its history, its neutrality, and its connections with political philosophy and with the real world. They are typical expressions of the need for introspective reflection in a discipline intent on rigorously defining itself. Others, though, are intentionally stuck in misunderstandings and misconceptions. Questions raised in this connection usually attack imaginary targets that reveal bias more than anything else. Still, they too deserve answers for seeking some clarifications and explanations. This exercise in refutation and rebuttal can sometimes lead to a better understanding of the issues under consideration. Between stimulating criticism and unfair attacks, there is, however, a third kind of questions. These are of the "dangerous friend" type. Their harm lies in attempting to assign a role to moral philosophy that it cannot and should not fulfill, that is, the role of a modern religion or a science of all things human. Let this be a reminder that no moral philosophy worthy of its name should ever aspire to become a secular religion or a philosophy of modernity.

A few requisites have been set up arbitrarily as necessary preconditions of relevance for contemporary moral thought. I intend to introduce them one by one and offer a detailed critical analysis for each. First, though, I want to warn the reader against all of them by recalling some examples of these allegedly self-evident preconditions for accurate and legitimate moral thinking: the certitude that moralizing intentions or power struggles are always the hidden motivating factors of moral thought; the doctrinaire assertion that moral thought and ethics are opposites, the former representing the law and the latter, the good behavior; the stubborn belief that, modern ethics being rational and autonomous, it has left behind religion, which is seen as authoritarian and not autonomous; the mistaken belief that only atheists can legitimately engage in moral thinking; the unrealistic conviction that modern man is the product of a necessary and univocal process of emancipation; the illusion that modernity is a singularity and, as such, is homogeneous and could not have evolved differently from what it is today; the deluded notion that a phenomenon such as Kantian philosophy has generated a new kind of reasoning, that Kantian formalism and universalism define by themselves the relevance criterion for modern moral philosophy as a whole, and that everything preceding the Kantian approach, particularly the thought of Ancients, is therefore out-of-date.

However strongly held, these philosophical beliefs are as open to questioning as any other substantial commitment to a stated position. They are acceptable as long as they remain subject to discussions, counterevidence, and arguments but become ossified dogma when taken as indisputable and unconditional truths. As articles of faith, though, they are at best unwarranted and at worst misguided approximations of ethical thinking. They encourage philosophers and their readers to accept passively comforting illusions and to misunderstand completely the complex intellectual tasks that our world faces today. To me, it seems impossible to preserve a plausible and realistic image of our moral experience without criticizing such beliefs and their pretension to be the sole yardstick for valid moral reflection.

If my analysis appears to be critical, it is so because it inevitably reflects at least part of what is presently being said, written, or thought in France. When criticism is used fairly, without libel or abuse, it can become an intellectual duty—all the more so when bias and dogmas threaten to stifle dynamic thought.

Critique of "Ethical Ideology": Truths and Falsehoods

Having deplored the quasi disappearance of moral philosophy, should we also be worried by the omnipresence of the term "ethics"? Charles Péguy thought that the trivialized use of a term heralds its near demise. When a term becomes widely used in all kinds of contexts with all kinds of meanings, it will soon lose all meaning. Many have rightfully criticized the abusive usage of "ethics." In so doing, they helped undo the cocoon of easy certitudes and complacencies in which this term is often wrapped. When, by such abusive usage, the term "ethics" becomes unavoidable in all discourse, there is a point beyond which a reversal of such a situation becomes inevitable. The inflated use of "ethics" can only become distasteful. Seeing its damaging effect on moral reflection, one almost wishes it would become so.

Unfortunately, those who are denouncing "ethical ideology" are themselves often making false representations of contemporary ethics. Unlike their predecessors of the sixties, such so-called defenders of ethical thought are uncertain whether to stop or continue discussing it. So, while proclaiming that ethics is worth nothing, they hasten to add that there is an authentic ethics nonetheless. An assertion such as "the ethics (suggested by others) is worthless, but the ethics (that I will reveal) is worthy" tries to present a hotchpotch of confused ideas and declarations of intentions as valid arguments in the debate. Such rhetorical denunciations do not allow for an answer to the only philosophically valid question: What is truly ethics, once the surrounding chatter is removed? Why should we not follow the example of any other subject field and consider ethics to be a body of knowledge, a conceptual network with a set of principles that remain valid regardless of the semantic deviations and arbitrary redefinitions to which it is exposed?

The little book entitled *Ethics* that Alain Badiou published in 1993 illustrates quite well this swing motion of denunciation and rehabilitation. In it, the author describes ethics—the dominant philosophical trend at that time—as a stabilizing influence on the discussion of political, social, or scientific events. Thus, ethics is backed up by institutions (the famous French State Committees on ethics) and enjoys an authority of its own that the author leaves unspecified.[6] The distinctive characteristic of this stabilizing influence is the concern for propriety and the obsession with conventionality. In his view, ethics is an outline of opinion guided by the motto "You should like only what you have always strongly believed."[7]

Alain Badiou criticizes that "object" of ethics, which, according to him, amounts to an abstract, statistical consensus that lacks forcefulness: we recognize evil by the suffering it inflicts on its victims. As for the general and abstract "subject" of ethics, Badiou declares that the victims themselves are its subject.[8] The current obsession with evil and fondness for victims provide ethics with a unique program: the defense of human rights. The tearful concern for the suffering of others can only be understood as the expression of a fascination with death—typical for our world—based on the conviction that the only thing that will inevitably happen is death. According to Alain Badiou, the contemporary ethics of a "proper life" comes down to a decision about who dies and who does not.[9] He believes that this explains the infatuation for bioethics and the obsession with euthanasia. In this sense, the inordinate predilection for ethics exhibited by our contemporaries is seen as a manifestation of nihilism.

On this topic though, Badiou's sound-and-light display does strike a right note: an inflated ethical discourse, fed on the fetishism of human rights and aggrandized by the rhetoric of an abstract, universal subject, often stiffens moral reflection instead of yielding a better understanding of its own specificity. Human rights cannot constitute a morality in and of themselves.[10] But Badiou's criticism displays the same self-righteousness as its target. For a fleeting moment, the certainties of this demystifier seem as unshakable as those of ethical conservatism. Yet soon enough he too returns to that which he has always liked and—for this reason—believes to be true. The main point of his criticism is to proclaim once more what he considers to be a universally known truth, that is, that the main actor in ethics is the public opinion—a universal, nondescript, resigned, and submissive victim that a semblance of democracy misleads into believing that it still has a free will and the power of decision. One might ask: to what is public opinion submissive? To the economy, of course, comes the answer. In Badiou's words, public opinion is submissive to "the logic of capitalism," stating that "our parliamentary systems are satisfied with a public opinion subjectively constrained to ratify whatever is beforehand deemed necessary."[11]

Here, it seems to me, we can recognize the familiar logic of self-proclaimed radical discourse. We are nothing but heedless slaves, subdued by necessity, addicted to powerful opiates that give us the illusion of being free. Ethics is such a drug. It has the same power as parliamentary institutions to lull us into a trance wherein we move as little as possible and want to change nothing in spite of sporadic convulsions that can sometimes lapse in spiteful anger. Badiou asserts that the main cause of "subjective resignation and contentment with the existing state of things" is the shared annoyance at the very possibility of future atrocities.

Let us examine the last statement more closely. What is Badiou attacking? Is it the fact that most of us react with either horror or compassion to the suffering of others? But who would wish that suffering leave everybody unmoved? Does he condemn the kind of indignation that easily makes one feel self-righteous yet somehow indifferent? Is it the indignation itself that leads to inaction? Badiou does not give any answers, his intention being not to explain but to condemn, not to enlighten but to sentence. As a matter of fact, there is nothing wrong with the feeling of annoyance; one would rather wish that it were more widely shared. It is also entirely plausible that such a feeling would not incite people to act. It could very well become a product for general consumption or foster an attitude of smug but inconsequential bewailing. What should be criticized for leading to indifference or inaction is not the annoyance at somebody's suffering or it being a shared feeling, but the inability to act, the decision to do nothing, or any number of related factors.[12]

In order for Badiou's analysis to have any relevance, the reader has to agree that we are the victims of an illusion. Only then would Badiou's radical solutions put us right, give us back our lucidity, and reconnect us with reality. But there is no reason to agree or disagree that such is indeed our condition. His statement belongs to the class of beliefs that can be neither proved nor disproved. However, all beliefs are not equally able to help us better understand the world, or foresee or influence it. This kind of intellectual task could benefit from the lesson of American pragmatism: "one can assess a belief by the extent to which it helps us understand."[13] Badiou's idea than we do not think what we want to think, that we do not do what we want to do, does not help improve our understanding of reality, tighten our hold on it, or increase our ability to influence it. Such an idea can certainly deny all possibility of knowledge or action, but it has never thrown the slightest light on what we are. This does not prove that the idea is false; it just furthers our claim that it does not amount to much.

With such radical demystification often comes prodigious naiveté. If we accept the idea that we form collectively a great "subject" that is manipulated and victimized, formal and at the same time empty, then Alain Badiou's injunction—to detach ourselves, to move off center, to become somebody else, some kind of "nonsubject"—might seem justified. However, there is a classical objection to this thesis—that is, if we were indeed distancing ourselves from the subject, then would this not entail renouncing also all notion of responsibility, project, or action?[14] Yet Badiou rejects this objection. As Gilles Deleuze had declared before him, "Contrary to received opinion, it is not necessary to claim one's belonging to the human race in order to resist it."[15] Badiou shares the idea that commitment does not need a subject. He finds positive proof of its validity in the fact that Michel Foucault, who denied all pertinence to the concept of subject, had nonetheless "vigorously involved himself in the cause of the imprisoned" and Louis Althusser, an advocate of "theoretical antihumanism," "was simply aiming to define anew a true emancipation policy." As for Jacques Lacan, who believed that the subject was dependent on history's contingency laws and on the objects of its desires, he passed "most of his life listening to people."[16]

This amounts to mistaking anecdote for proof and juxtaposition for causality. There is absolutely no indication that Foucault, Althusser, or Lacan had acted as he had because he was applying his own, antihumanist philosophy. Furthermore, signaling the compatibility of a theory with a worthy commitment has never been considered sufficient proof of that theory's truth or superiority. Alain Badiou tells us that these thinkers were able to distance themselves from the idea of "subject" and to defend "their rebellion against established order, their radical dissatisfaction with it, while remaining deeply involved in real situations."[17] Yet rebellion, resistance, protestation, dissatisfaction, rejection, even commitment are all mental states, attitudes, or actions with no moral value in and of themselves.[18] True, the ability to distance oneself from reality in order to better criticize it is often a sign of practical rationality and, as such, is linked to moral philosophy. Nevertheless, the moral value of rebellion resides essentially in that to which it is opposed, and that for which it is opposed. Human reality plays a fundamental role in the ethical evaluation of rebellion. And this reality is not a manipulated human being, subject to subconscious desires or social infrastructures, but a human individuality embodied in a single being that has its own thoughts, desires, and expectations. Rebellion against an unjust state of affairs is morally justified only if it occurs in the name of the respect due a given person. Conversely, the idea of "antisubject" and the expectation to transcend the subject bring by themselves no moral justification to any kind of rebellion. Therefore, if the rebellion of the antihumanists or their criticism has any ethical value, it comes from something wholly unrelated to their philosophy, that is, from their fight for the rights of the oppressed. This only shows that the thesis claiming the extinction of the subject, so fashionable in the sixties, is acceptable as a descriptive and historical claim (there is no subject anymore) but not as a normative one (there should be no subject). For this reason alone, such a thesis is compatible with the kind of actions that require the existence of a subject and which would be impossible under a normative conception of the nonsubject as found in works by Antoine Artaud or Georges Bataille.

Alain Badiou defines the human being as "a particular kind of animal brought about by circumstance" and states that, in addition to being able to exceed his own limits, this creature's mind is crossed by various truths and summoned by transcendence to immortality.[19] The nature of the summon remains ill-defined; however, it is quite clear that his description leaves no place for the protection of individual rights. If the human being is a mere product of interacting mechanisms and primary forces, and if various truth processes cross his mind but their meaning is found beyond him, then what justification would there be for opposing his elimination when a higher calling is hindered by the contingency of his existence? Who would assess or protect the right of human beings to oppose the success of rebellion or the attainment of "transcendence"?

Badiou insists that the source of such legitimacy is collective, not individual, and that ethical ideology is misleading on this very point. It limits reflection to a schematic concept of the abstract individual and makes us "renounce initiative, any politics of emancipation, and all valid political causes."[20] This is too fuzzy a thesis to be either proved or falsified. If he means that only a collective can attain goodness and truthfulness, then one would be hard put to find a single actual collective realization that would historically illustrate this thesis. On the other hand, there are many instances of collective emancipation inspired by the hope "to organize collective powers and work toward reaching undreamed of possibilities" that ended in untold death and destruction of human beings.[21] As Isaiah Berlin used to say in this respect, we have always seen the broken eggs but never the omelettes. For his part, Badiou likes to prophesize that "the rights to Immortality assert themselves; the rights to Infinity exercise their sovereignty over the contingency of suffering and death."[22] One can only tremble at his conclusion that "the contingency of suffering and death" could legitimately be imposed on a particular human being in the name of "the rights to Infinity." The choice of the term "rights" to qualify a sovereignty that goes mostly *against* individual autonomy is an abuse of language. For now, those are only a philosopher's delusions. But they can easily become worrisome when their author proudly reveals his admiration for one of the most sinister episodes in the history of mankind: "During the Chinese cultural revolution of 1967, when some of the Red Guards announced the abolition of egoism, they were envisaging a society cleared of individual interests, in which they would replace personal opinions with their own truth."[23] And what was that truth? Who has the right to decide what interests are to be suppressed, without considering the persons whose interests are to be suppressed?

Too attractive a subject to be left alone, ethics catches the eye of Alain Badiou, who then endeavors to explain what true ethics should be about. This firmly puts a kind of gigantomachy in place. On the one side, one finds the "ethical" ideology fed on conformism and fascination with death. On the other, there is Alain Badiou's "ethics of truth" based on an ontology of events capable of creating a new way of being.[24] His ethics of truth considers the subject as the bearer of loyalty to events. It welcomes the new configurations of meaning and the gaps created by singular or situational truth processes.[25] It is always opened to some form of transcendence and has a genuine capacity for goodness. Badiou's ethics of truth advises us to go beyond our limits and to answer the call of immortality. It celebrates reality as a chance encounter.

Some of the features that Badiou assigns to his "ethics of truth" are no doubt those of ethical reasoning. This seems to be the case when he states that his ethics should feed on moral dissent and pluralism, that it should stick to the singular reality of situations, and that it should stay closely attached to goodness. But he fills each of these requisites with a mixture of invective and excess so noxious that it leaves them devoid of all meaning.

When he speaks of moral pluralism, Badiou declares that it belongs exclusively to the discourse on the death of man, whereas what he calls "ethical ideology" needs only a soft consensus.[26] This could be true of the caricature of ethics that his essay attacks, but certainly not of what is commonly understood by moral reflection. Pluralism is a basic component of ethical rationality. Moral reflection thrives indeed on dissent and dilemmas. If, by what Badiou calls "the division in two," he means the ability to seek the pro and con of a moral issue in order to have a better access to the truth, then such an approach is part and parcel of ethical debate.[27] But taking pluralism seriously means always being ready to consider beliefs that seem contrary to those that one considers true for the best of reasons. And this has nothing to do with the kind of "pluralism" that Mao Tse-tung had in mind while writing *On Contradiction*, his famous book, which Alain Badiou abundantly quotes.[28] In fact, Mao's embrace of dissent is nothing but a polemic subterfuge: he views dissent as a struggle whereby conflict is systematically stirred even if uncalled for, its only reason being to provoke opposition so as to uncover its proponents and take them out.[29]

Badiou correctly upholds the thesis that ethics must stay in touch with the demands of the real world, of particular situations and concerned individuals. He is right to assert that ethics should not become too general a concept, thinly spread over a given set of activities, but that it should remain solidly grounded in what is real, concrete, and distinct.[30] Yet, such a thesis remains itself too general and uncertain so long as it is unclear with what reality it deals specifically. The reality described in Badiou's book is less factual than mythical: it is an imperious and stubborn reality, allegedly shaped by events, class struggles, and conflicts. Process replaces reality, collectives substitute for the subject, faithfulness to events takes over truth, shouting supplants reason, and violence ousts action. If this is the kind of reality to which ethics must be "loyal," then one might as well abandon the search for moral objectivity. It makes no sense to speak of "truth" in this case.

Badiou's analysis of the connection between ethics and goodness shows the same medley of witty perspicacity and abuse of language. He convincingly reminds us that the ethics of truth is closely linked to "the good," only to disconcert us by unexpectedly defining good as an "impossible of possibles" and an object of "vision."[31] But if "good" is indeed a vision of the impossible, then it can be anything and everything. If so, then on what basis could we judge the soundness of the means used to reach it? How are we to assess the goodness of our dominant goals or ends? There is no intrinsic moral value in such a vision of the impossible as there was none to be found in the notion of rebellion discussed earlier. The idea of an impossible world deemed to be better than the one we live in is harmful and irrational. The only valid vision of moral good is the one provided by exercising one's capacity for thought.

Badiou attempts to lock us in a false confrontation between an ethics of conservatism, resignation, and a death wish and his ethics of truth and superhumanity.[32] His conception of ethics, which invokes immortality, calling, and creative events, is closer to incantation than philosophy. It is dramatized by the critique of a subject that is both abstract and hollow. One can nevertheless subscribe, at least in part, to such a critique on the condition of resisting Badiou's false alternative, that is, either renounce entirely the concept of "subject" or adopt the vision of a collective, decentered subject. By leaving behind the false choices between an empty subject and a nonsubject, or between the abdication of reasoning and the prophetic utterances, one can finally glimpse again the essence of the question: what is the difference between ethics and moral reflection? Alain Badiou's book does not tackle this topic. The author offers shrewd criticisms of various trivialized versions of popular ethics and moral standards, but he utterly fails to explain the difference between those versions and moral reflection. Such an explanation remains a pressing demand on ethical discourse. To ignore it while criticizing the misuse of ethics and the efforts to define it is but a fruitless undertaking.

Moral Philosophy and Ethics

The relationship between moral philosophy and ethics appears to have particular relevance to those interested in issues of ethical revival. The 1980s' widespread interest in regulating behavior was centered on ethics, not on morality. Interest in ethics was perceived as new, relatively neutral, and tied to commonly shared values. It connoted lucidity, awareness, and accountability. It seemed modern and profound. Unlike ethics, reflection on morality was seen as neither modern nor secularized but more like a strap-wielding, grumpy old teacher, keen on straightening thoughts and deeds, and eager to invade everyone's privacy for sheer killjoy satisfaction.

Given such dissimilarities, readers might consider my using the terms "ethics" and "morality" synonymously rather unhelpful. I do so because I believe that too sharp a distinction between these terms would show an unwarranted preference for style over substance. There is no doubt, after all, that both terms designate the same field of investigation: they are appropriately used interchangeably in reference to particular thought processes involved in analyzing concepts such as action, good, or justice. Strictly speaking, a much more legitimate distinction could be drawn between morality and ethics on the one hand and "moral philosophy" on the other. Indeed, moral philosophy has very distinctive historical and conceptual characteristics forming an easily identifiable set of hard-core issues and concepts that differentiate it not only from metaphysics but from the other philosophical fields as well. But here again, to overemphasize the distinctiveness of moral philosophy would do more harm than good. Being essentially a discipline of reflection and critical thinking is what secures moral philosophy's place among other disciplines devoted to the study of moral life.

Yet one has to notice a slight, loose, but increasingly marked differentiation in the usage of these terms. The fact that "ethics" has a Greek origin whereas "morality" comes from Latin would not provide a sufficient explanation for such differentiation but, used as a tool for enhancing nuanced thinking and signaling dissimilar perspectives on quasi-identical concepts, the distinction has its merits. Morality points primarily but not exclusively to existing rules and laws, whereas ethics is closely linked to concepts of goodness, virtue, and custom. However, because goodness itself might include an element of obligation while virtue could contain in turn an element of formality, even the distinction between them may prove uncertain and temporary. In any case, difficulties of conceptual differentiation should never be exploited for reducing morality to sets of rules and ethics to mores and social etiquette. Interpretations that drastically oppose morality to ethics have no validity. Just what would such an opposition entail? If we deny the existence of universal obligations, we would have to get rid of the term "morality" in favor of "ethics." Thus, the term "morality of virtue" would be proscribed in favor of "ethics of virtue," while the term "morality of rules" would replace "ethics of rules." These expressions, however, are widely used and perfectly understood, whether proscribed or not. Furthermore, until about twenty years ago, such an opposition did not even exist in the history of moral philosophy or, if it did, it was inconsequential. In fact, references to Aristotle's morality of virtues and to Kant's universal ethics were as common before the 1980s are they are nowadays. Obviously, attempts to impose a dogmatic distinction between morality and ethics are doomed by their own inconsistencies and contradictions, especially when the terms are used in value judgments proclaiming that ethics is okay but morality is not. As for the general use of these terms, people who are fond of using "ethics" indiscriminately would only use "morality" with great reticence, while remaining blissfully unaware of the difference between "moral code" and "ethical behavior"—the only contrasting element that would support such a terminological distinction.[33]

There would be no reason to dwell on the distinction between ethics and morality if it were not artificially dichotomized and often used as a standalone topic in current French philosophy. As the argument goes, because morality merges with the impersonal and emphatic rigidity of the law, then it naturally follows that rigid moralism (i.e., the practice of rigid morality) is out-of-date. One would be tempted to ask what other conclusion could be drawn from such a premise. And if, according to this argument, we have no more moral standards, then what are we left with? As to consequences, the answer varies depending on the temperament of the author. In his essay *Man Made God*, Luc Ferry expects us to seek meaning by reaching beyond morality and to open ourselves to a form of transcendence by rekindling the idea of the Sacred. Gilles Lipovetsky notes that the hard-to-practice idea of moral duty is being replaced by that of "painless ethics," which represents both a way of life and a quest for well-being. Others hail the decline of morality and everything related to it as signaling the forthcoming age of the "sculpture of the self" and of the "accession to the sense of pleasure."[34] These interpretations have all the same flaw: they proceed from the rather dubious premise that morality is only a law and, as such, does not satisfy us anymore and has lost its pertinence. In fact, there are no conceptual or material links between moral standards, rigid laws, and painful duties. Current lamentations on the end, the decline, or the limits of morality are as unconvincing as their rendering of morality itself is implausible. Morality is as little of a credo, a commitment, or a posture as it is a mere form of duty or law.

The present essay consistently links morality and ethics to a process of analytical, critical, and explanatory thinking. This may come as a welcome change, given the profusion of contemporary publications on this subject that avoid discussing the nature of moral reasoning or answering an all-important question: What is involved in grasping, defining, and describing an issue in moral terms? What does it mean to reason, work out, or discuss a topic from a moral perspective? What does it entail to make a moral decision or to morally justify it? Everybody hails, bewails, or rails against the decline of morality, the revival of ethics, the cult of the individual, the vogue of the self, the decline of duty, and the rise of desire, ethical vanity, or serene despair, and all this without anybody ever saying what moral deliberation is.

Yet, going back to the history of moral philosophy, we find that great authors were speaking of little else. Aristotle, Spinoza, and Kant and, more recently, Brentano, Moore, and Scheler never sought to know whether their contemporaries rejected morality or not, whether they were satisfied with their way of life or aiming for a sense of the Sacred. Those philosophers never tried to declare that morality is this and ethics is that. They tried instead to grasp the particularities of practical rationality by discerning its facets and fundamentals. They endeavored to apprehend the ontological nature of moral realities as well as their epistemological underpinnings, and they analyzed extensively the psychological side of morality under headings such as virtue and motivation. Of these core topics of moral philosophy, French publications of the past ten years bear no trace. One finds instead a grandiose performance whereby ethics and morality put in play both heroic and pathetic characters, at times sticking together, at other times fighting bitterly with one another, some being relegated to the backstage of modernity while others look more alluring than ever, all being guided by obvious precepts (ethics demands . . ., morality contests . . .), and all being manipulated by the ruse of reason that leads invariably to modernity. One feels the urge to turn on the lights and ask: Wait a minute, what's going on here? What are ethics and morality? How can one get to them? What reality are they made of? How can they be explained? How can they be used for understanding, thinking, reaching conclusions? Alas, the lights go off, ethics and morality are submerged anew in lamentation and invective, surrounded by inescapable outcomes, by enemies and friends, making one forget that behind all that there are always people who perceive reality, who think about the principles guiding their actions, and who can justify their decisions. If ethics and morality are both products of the mind, why even think of hailing or blaming them? How come that philosophy itself contributes to obscure the question, becomes in turn a source of prejudice and distances itself from common sense? Let us look at a few examples.

Myths of Our Time: Moral Grandstanding

and Ethical Self-Indulgence

In his book *Le Crépuscule du devoir* (The Twilight of Duty) published in 1992, Gilles Lipovetsky claims that morality represents by definition endless duty, sacrifice, pain, and self-denial, whereas ethics embodies the comfortable complacency of good intentions.

The author provides a striking description of the human condition: we are bubbling with "ethical excitement" for "values to be regained" and "new responsibilities to be assumed" at a time when "self-absorbed individualism . . . is prevalent." Morality dwindles while making way for the ethics of well-being and subjective rights—a painless process that "demands no major sacrifices or self-denial."[35] He claims that the dramatic rise of ethics dates precisely from 1950 (?!), that it marks the beginning of "postmoralism" and the abandonment of "formal duty," which had been in turn made possible by the secularization of religion. "The postmoralist society characterizes an epoch in which duty is watered down and weakened, the idea of self-sacrifice has no legitimacy, and moral standards do not demand devotion to ends higher than one's self."[36] He explicitly admits that morality—as he understands it—closely resembles the "religious spirit" from which it inherited "the notion of infinite debt and absolute duty . . ., the imperative character of limitless duty."[37] His views of morality as "infinite or absolute duty," as "a set of supreme obligations concerning what is beyond us"[38] and "a foundation of moral and collective obligations," are presented as self-evident, trivial truths.[39]

Yet, morality was not defined as infinite duty by Aristotle, Descartes, and Spinoza, nor was it defined in such terms by the philosophers of the nineteenth and twentieth centuries, much less by the majority of modern philosophers. In any case, Lipovetsky's tentative definition does not explain what infinite duty and supreme obligation are supposed to mean.

Stripped of bombastic qualifiers, it has not much left to show for itself, other than a rather ordinary attempt to define morality as made of laws and rules, that is, a moral philosophy among many others. Besides, one could rightly ask what exactly is "moral" in a definition whose distinctive feature, "absolute duty," is described as having a "religious form."[40] Similarly biased views can be found in Pascal Bruckner's *La Tentation de l'innocence* (The Temptation of Innocence), which defines morality as merely impersonal, universal, and formal duty.[41] Luc Ferry also considers rules of behavior to be mere formalism, some sort of "utilitarian or Kantian programs" that would "tell us without error what decisions impose themselves in each case," much like "a moral automaton, a robot who, given any hypothesis, does what it should do." Moral philosophy is useful and even necessary, but it remains within the negative order of prohibition. "The truth is not created by human beings; it remains today as yesterday established by the divine law, the universal and objective norm of morality."[42]

However useful to those striving to show that morality is outdated, such definitions only beg the question or improvise ad hoc constructs replete with inconsistencies. It is for precisely this reason that authors like Gilles Lipovetsky, well aware of such flaws, feel obliged to multiply warnings and mitigating factors with regard to their own theses. A case in point is Lipovetsky's warning that, when faced with two contradictory aspects of the same reality—at least one of which could serve as criticism of his thesis—readers should conclude that reality is insidious enough to produce simultaneously a result and its reverse. For instance, his thesis on the "twilight of duty" can be objected to by mentioning the noticeable comeback of moral standards: the modern individual is "utterly indifferent to his kind and to the public good," but he is also thoroughly involved in ethical claims.[43] In his answer, the author dismisses the objection by claiming that morality has been replaced in our time with ethics, which is inherently dissociated, that is, simultaneously permissive and intransigent, tolerant and harsh.[44] In other words, the twilight of duty is simultaneously followed by the abandonment of morality and by its omnipresence. Gilles Lipovetsky comes up with multiple examples of the same kind, whereby being paradoxical and contradicted by evidence becomes a sign of truth. By his lights, the recent boom of voluntary work in France is a result of a neo-individualistic ethos. The disinterested, freely assumed commitment to the well-being of others is but a "new ruse of reason" directly motivated by "ego promotion." As for solidarity and mutual aid, they are only inspired by the desire to make something out of one's life. In short, the twilight of duty "produces moral standards and at the same time ends them"; it juxtaposes disorganization and ethical reorganization;[45] and it equals modern ethics to both morality and its contrary. It would be almost as credible to talk of immoral ethics or unethical morality.

To refute such a thesis, one would only need to ask why should morality and law be identified. What conceptual analysis of the *object* "morality" could possibly persuade us that it only consists of duty? Has there ever been a time when the study of virtue, of deliberate action, of values, of happiness and goodness did not belong to moral philosophy? Such topics have obviously very little to do with obeying rules or an absolute law. When choosing the best course of action among two paths, are we not handling dilemmas and moral conflicts? Do we not qualify a dilemma as "moral" even when it clearly does not involve two opposing *laws* prescribing incompatible outcomes? Many philosophers have sought the source of morality in feelings and emotions, although these do not derive from duty or rules. Truly moral considerations, such as being concerned for personal safety or indebted to a close relative, may lead us to act in ways contrary to strictly defined duty for the simple reason that extreme or simplistic definitions of morality cannot account for the complexity of our moral experience.

Lipovetsky relentlessly invokes a stringent, heroic, sacrificial, even "incandescent" duty, but has such a notion ever existed?[46] We are told that "the duty to devote one's life to one's neighbor is only rarely discharged nowadays," but one can find no fact or argument in support of this claim. We are told that calls to blind devotion have deserted the public arena, but looking as far back in history as we can see makes us doubt that such devotion was ever too common. Besides, who can reasonably prove that modern society is indeed experiencing an unbridled search for personal well-being, as we are tirelessly told? Gilles Lipovetsky seems to admit that our experience is not limited to a "materialistic and libertarian mind-set." Therefore, we are correct in concluding that we are facing two stereotypes that function well together but have no basis in reality. And the author himself seems to acknowledge at times that this is indeed the case.[47]

The question "What is postmoralism?" has yet to be answered. While Lipovetsky, by assimilating ethics to laissez-faire, emphasizes the opposition between the "high duties" of morality and the "subjective rights" of ethics, Luc Ferry looks for an undefined sort of wisdom to materialize after the end of religion and to transcend morality. Even without mentioning again the tendentious definition of morality as law, one might wonder what intellectual content such a wisdom would have, other than the one that has always been the essence of morality, that is, practical reasoning.

Our authors claim that moral standards lack genuine, substantial values, especially love; that if we had love, then we would not need moral codes, imperatives, injunctions, and prohibitions.[48]As with wisdom, one may wonder about the intellectual content of love: what does it mean?

Those who would discard moral standards for love hasten to specify "only if it is true love, of course." But who could verify and confirm the authenticity of love? Could it be the person who is in love? Certainly not: one has only to read Stendhal or Proust in order to shed any illusions on this point. The strongest quality of love is its ambivalence: it has the power of illusion while giving us access to a source of knowledge or truth that remains inaccessible by any other means; it vows a cult to the object of love while striving to possess it, even destroy it. In this context, to speak of a model of "transcendence in immanence" is to talk nonsense.[49] Love is the most precious feeling there is, but it would be unrealistic to believe that it can lead us to self-rule, integrity, and respect for the other, or that it could make us quit narcissism and help us spread happiness in the world. Besides, what does it mean to evaluate the authenticity of love if not to critically analyze it so as to determine its value? In fact, such an assessment is precisely the main objective of moral reflection.

I will not dwell any longer on the links between ethics and morality. Once the source of confusion has been spotted, I doubt that what remains qualifies for philosophical debate. Those who argue in favor of a true semantic difference between ethics and morality must find worthier arguments than stipulatory definitions of morality as duty or of ethics as well-being.[50] The concepts involved are much more important than the words used to designate them. Again, ethics and morality refer to the same intellectual approach, that is, understanding reality, guiding deliberations, and justifying decisions. Refusing to view morality as duty would have no effect on the critical and reflexive process that constitutes moral deliberation. Many of the criticisms formulated in the preceding pages would have been rendered null and void, had the targeted authors asked from the beginning the relevant question: as critical, rational, and introspective reasoning, what does ethics consists of?

Gilles Lipovetsky's book brilliantly illustrates my point. In some of its best passages, he recommends an "intelligent ethics" that would aim at finding "reasonable compromises" and "appropriate measures," well adapted to the circumstances of real human beings; an ethics rising from "negotiation, redistribution, and training."[51] My book is a plea for placing theoretical and practical rationality at the heart of ethics. Therefore, I wholeheartedly support the intellectual ambitions of such a program, but I sincerely doubt that it could be realized without relinquishing the caricaturing and historical dramatizing presently used in France to convey it. Specifically, it is meaningless to regard morality as sacred while ridiculing ethics, and conversely—to glorify ethics while pronouncing moral standards outdated. Morality and ethics share the same intellectual approach based on critical reflection and introspection.

Morals and Religion: The Misconception That Atheism

Is a Prerequisite for Moral Deliberation

Having been viewed with great suspicion, morality and ethics tend to be seen today as a sort of panacea or universal cure for all that ails us. Yet assigning the role of a quasi religion to morality betrays a serious misunderstanding of its nature, of ethical reflection, and of religion. It seems particularly appropriate to underline this danger at a time when many authors attempt to show that ethics is, after the retreat of the divine, the only path leading humanity to freedom from its natural and social conditions. Morality is a source of aid and hope only if seen as an intellectual resource. But—in and of itself—it cannot replace God, nor can it sustain the triumphant atheism of the Moderns without becoming surreptitiously religious in the poorest and most misleading sense of the word.

Most philosophical writings on the modern human condition that have been published during the past few years in France share the underlying premise that the divine and the authority of revelation have withdrawn from the world and that this withdrawal defines the modern condition. We inhabit a universe from which God is absent. There is no divine word that human beings could obey. They have only their reason, their conscience, and their desires to depend on. Religion is only the object of private beliefs. This situation has changed the status of morality, which was previously supported by the word of God and which is left now without any transcendent foundation. We are witnessing a morality whose rules and values are tailored to fit the needs and expectations of its user and, as such, it becomes more often than not a mere disguise of desires and obsessions. This description of the modern condition and its perplexities seems to garner an unwavering consensus. It is, no doubt, the milch cow of popular philosophy today.[52]

Is this portrait of modern humanity realistic? I doubt it. It is not just a description of the modern condition; it also advances two strong theses. The first thesis has a historical content: it claims that in the past morality was dependent on religion. The second has a speculative and normative content: it enjoins morality and ethics—generally understood as the domain of rules, values, and meaning—to do what religion did in the past. In other words, it asks them to substitute themselves for religion. Yet, individual morality has never been entirely absorbed by religion, and today it is far from being entirely detached from religion. The theories that affirm such a neat, irreversible transition from religion to morality rely on shortcuts and biases.

The major Judeo-Christian texts—the Bible, the Gospels, Saint Paul's Epistle to the Romans—carefully examine the place of morality. Starting with the Genesis episode, in which Abraham pleads for the righteous in Sodom and Gomorrah to be saved from God's wrath, the appeal to God's moral persona proves that moral disquiet is central to traditional religion.[53] From Maimonides and Gersonides to Spinoza, most Jewish philosophers consider the Decalogue as the repository of an immutable morality protected by one God, while references to Judaism are nonetheless sufficiently discreet so that its universal reach is preserved.[54] The book of Ezekiel and the book of Job attest to the irreducibility of ethics to religious practice. The theological reflection of neo-Kantian Jewish philosophers has progressively led to the explicit defense of the autonomy of the moral subject and the inalienable rights of conscience as different from the halakha—the religious Jewish laws. Judaism exhibits a fertile tension between religious doctrine, righteous practice, and ethics, as attested in its tradition of the prophets and in its sapiential books.[55]

The place of ethics is even more difficult to define in the Gospels. The Annunciation is the revelation of salvation through God's incarnation in Jesus. Its teaching comes down to the perfect and unconditional love through which human beings can become like their maker.[56] Many times, the promise of salvation is contrasted with "common morality" and Judaic law.[57] Natural morality, which is found even among unbelievers, is one of honesty, loyalty, compassion, personal achievement, and reciprocity.[58] Common morality, present in the human heart, guarantees a form of moral autonomy.[59] He who acts morally acts properly.[60] According to Jesus, natural morality is consistent with human nature and, as such, embodies the moral content of Judaic law in spirit, not in letter.[61] The specific contribution of the Gospels to natural morality was partially developed in the morality of the Stoics.[62] It resides in the idea of love being infinite, of people—even the humblest—being fellows, and of human dignity being conceived in the image of divine dignity, that is, infinite and unconditional: "Truly I tell you, just as you did it to one of the least of these who are members of my family, you did it to me."[63] The Gospel recommendation of renunciation, chastity, poverty, and humility is thus closer to faith than morality. In fact, the morality of the first Christian centuries remains very close to the pagan morality from which it borrows its major topics, that is, the idea of nature, the search for goodness crowned by happiness, and the excellence of virtue. It is also closely related to the idea of the autonomy and self-improvement of the moral subject.

The interiority of the moral principle seen as a form of conscience is abundantly commented on in the Christian tradition. This idea had been introduced by the Greeks and in particular by the Stoics' preaching that the primacy of conscience reveals the primordial orientation of humankind toward goodness.[64] A very similar expression of interiority as moral conscience can be found in the tradition of Judaic prophesies, whereby the law is made in the heart, not in exterior practices or in heteronomy: "I will put my law within them, and I will write it on their hearts"[65] It would be, however, an error to see in the access to one's self through religious revelation a mere form of human submission to an exterior authority. On the contrary, Christians consider conscience to be nourished by the word of God and to belong in the deepest creases of the self. Evoking his conversion, Saint Augustine said: "Too late loved I Thee, O Thou Beauty of ancient days, yet ever new! Too late I loved Thee! And behold Thou wert within, and I abroad, and there I searched for Thee."[66]

It is precisely because this interiority principle is not at all a shadow cast by an exterior authority that the philosophical tradition of rationalism has been so closely associated with religious thought throughout most of its history, and certainly during the Christian era. Those willing to shed their bias about the merciless opposition between reason and religion will find ample proof of their close association in the three scholastics traditions: the Judaic, the Christian, and the Islamic. Since the middle of the nineteenth century, the Christian tradition recognized the historical character of sacred texts written by humans, thus giving a new meaning to Psalm 103: "you mighty ones who do His bidding, obedient to His spoken word." It goes without saying that in Christianity faith does not originate in reason; nevertheless, the task of religious reasoning is to assert the mystery of Christ rationally. To consider the efforts in Christian rationalism throughout history as illusion and superstition, just because they were linked to Revelation, would mean to ignore the scope and power of reason.[67] Natural morality and human rationality are in a relationship of proximity and tension with regard to religion. In this respect, they are similar to the dialectic relationship between the exterior (Revelation) and the interior (awareness of the Revelation) as seen by most authors belonging to the Judeo-Christian tradition.[68]

It is true, as shown by Nietzsche, that the history of Christianity is partly the history of its ambition of becoming a moral Christianity.[69] At the same time, one cannot ignore the Christian reflection on sin, on the human inability to behave morally, on the disarray of the conscience, on the inadequacy of standards and rules, and on the irreducible tension between faith and morality.[70] Many rules and laws, which are either pertinent or justified from the perspective of morality, are neither from the perspective of salvation, and may even oppose the absolute character of faith. Christian thinkers, especially later medieval philosophers, contributed to the ever increasing gap between divine law or charity and natural good.[71] The very idea of a close link between human moral achievement and celestial beatitude, which Thomas Aquinas had so intensely defended, gradually faded behind the concept of an arbitrary recompense by grace, without any direct link to human goodness.[72] Without going so far as to adopt Bergson's idea of distinct sources for morality and religion, most of the Judeo-Christian tradition preserves a tense and uneasy relationship between the two, a relationship that is marked by powerlessness and doubt rather than authority and certitude. Therefore, it would not be plausible to assert—as factual certitude—that premodern and contemporary believers view morality as simply inferred from religion.

One could counter that in well-known recent encyclicals, the Catholic Church has not hesitated to draw a sharp line between good and evil and to prescribe how to live. This is one of the particularities of modern Catholicism, which should remind everyone that Christian tradition defines conscience as the closest standard by which to judge righteous behavior: "Behaving according to one's conscience is to behave well." Moreover, the Ecumenical Council of Vatican II (Rome, 1962–65), which revived moral reflection in contemporary Catholicism, reaffirms, in its Constitution of the Church in Modern Times (*Gaudium et Spe*, 1965), "the legitimate autonomy of terrestrial realities."[73] In moral theology, especially in the Thomist and the Protestant traditions, it is therefore an open question to what extent the Christian faith brings meaning, intentionality, and motivation to moral commitment, and to how it can do so while allowing moral autonomy and rational reflection to define standards that are appropriate to their historical and social context.[74] These questions are the object of a rich exegetic literature.[75] Moral theology traditions appear to be as ignored as the founding texts of the Judeo-Christian religion when our "modern" philosophers persist in viewing religion as a mixture of fanaticism, obscurantism, and superstition, to the exclusion of anything else. Are we still under the influence of the eighteenth-century mind-set? To heedlessly oppose reason to religion is to ape the freethinkers of the eighteenth century, who at least had the merit of not conforming to the received wisdoms of their time. Unbelief and criticism of Christianity during the past two centuries have emancipated us from more archaic forms of religion. Indeed, why should religion be the only belief system to have escaped the development of moral reflection and criticism in our time?[76]

Religion has never made morality into an open book in everybody's reach. Nor has it ever been able to relieve the disquiet induced by human existence and the inevitability of death. The question of the meaning of life does not have an exclusively cognitive sense. It gives rise to a standpoint, a personal perspective, a longing for values. It is doubtful that such a question could be canceled by certitudes such as the one in the existence of God, even if they were set out by faith. Such certitudes could soften the question or make it less acutely felt, but they could never lessen its pertinence.[77] As for the fear of death, one has only to read Tolstoy's religious writings or *The Carmelites* by Georges Bernanos in order to understand what a torment it is, how its anguish is caused by faith itself, and how only faith can help overcome it—as it happens to Bernanos's character, Blanche de la Force—though it remains a torment nevertheless that haunts the believer till death.[78] Those who claim that Christian faith exempts the believer from asking questions about the meaning of life do not realize how deeply religious tradition has meditated on suffering, decay, and death. The force of existential questions was not discovered by the Moderns: these questions were asked as forcefully by the "non-Moderns." Even when they were certain, in the abstract, that an answer must exist, they perceived such an answer with doubt and disquiet rather than certitude. To what extent can it be said that the possibility of immortal life gives more meaning to our lives? If a finite life is meaningless, would an infinite one be even more meaningless? If the certitude in the existence of God enriches and completes the description of our condition, what additional meaning does it hold? Atheists are not the only ones unable to answer such questions.

Scrutinizing prohibitions helps us realize that modern moral conscience is not fully detached from religion. True, our morality is a secular one, but it is still profoundly influenced by religion. Regardless of their claim to either atheism or religiosity, modern moralities rekindle the idea of prohibition, especially in relation with other human beings. As Émile Durkheim used to say, prohibition is the defining feature of religious systems when they take the form of narratives and rites.[79] Narratives and rites have a moral scope because they offer existential models and examples to be followed while helping internalize moral standards. It is precisely through the set of interdictions used by each religion to proscribe certain acts and behaviors that religiousness acquires a normative significance. Religious morality—in the narrow sense of the word—would then relate such interdictions to the revelation of God's word or will. After three millennia of Judeo-Christianity, our modern moralities owe much of their specifics to those old religious interdictions and to the ensuing conception of imperative morality. It is true that today the way in which these interdictions are formulated does not seem to owe much, if anything, to religion. Our understanding of such interdictions and of their justifications is epistemologically detached from any conscious religiosity. A "modern" believer, who shares with most of his contemporaries the convictions that individual dignity must be protected and pain or suffering avoided, would not attempt to justify such convictions as divine revelation or surmise that only a Christian can partake in them. The nonbeliever also considers them to be mandatory. Thus, the belief in God neither justifies moral precepts nor leads one to recognize them as such. Yet, if their conceptual content is not religious, their semantic form comes directly from religion.[80]

Furthermore, religion shapes many of our moral ideas: whether one believes in God or not would not change the conspicuous fact that much of the content of moral reflection stems from religion. Judeo-Christianity refined the concept of an internalized moral principle, which originated with the ancient Greeks. The evangelical equality between human beings has the weight of a universal rational value from which are derived the formal principles of morality in modern rationalism.[81] The dialectics of authority and conviction, which relates to the most ancient search for meaning, and the disquiet caused by the power of human rationality, which leads to the hypertrophy of rationality and to the conviction of its precariousness and amorality, clearly show that modern moralities are marked by religion in often conflicting and tense ways.

Morality cannot replace religious solace and does not have to defend its specificity with regard to religion. Two mind-set changes would have a cathartic effect in this context: the first would come from abandoning the erroneous thesis that, before the modern age, morality had an exclusively religious content; the second would come from ceasing to believe that to-day's morality is entirely detached from religion. The great trends of religious ethics, which view morality as wholly grounded in religion, are as mythical as the view of secular ethics, according to which morality is built on the awareness of God's absence. It is incredibly naive to think that ethics could accomplish today what one assumes religion accomplished in the past. Moreover, it is unfortunate that such thoughts are not presented as philosophers' ideas but as commonly shared opinion or generally accepted truth. For instance, Luc Ferry asserts: "When thinking of the Ancients, or even of the modern believer, we tend to spontaneously place their values among the relics of old traditions. We tell ourselves something like this: they had their religion (or cosmology), we have ethics."[82] But who, precisely, is *we* here? This is a stealthily normative *we*, which tells us what everyone should think. *Pace* Luc Ferry, it would be more appropriate to say: the Ancients had religion and also morality. And it could be that we, the Moderns, have morality and also religion. In our time, one does not need to be a believer in order to be honest, and it was exactly the same in the seventeenth century. Also, when a believer is honest, his reasons for being so are more often than not other than religious.[83]

The world we live in is undeniably different from those of the Middle Ages or the nineteenth century. Religion has today a different place in society, and relationships between morality and religion have evolved. Rules of behavior, political establishments, and institutions are no more subordinated to religious goals. The difficulties encountered when trying to conceptualize these complex changes are partly due to the dogmatic qualities of the categories used to describe them. Consider, for instance, the concept of secularization. We are being told that the last remnants of religion have been secularized. The term "secularization" itself has been invented by our contemporaries in the belief that it would be the magical potion transforming them in born-again atheists. Now, it is often the case that ideas have been separated from their religious source and transplanted in a nonreligious context. However, this is not a sufficient condition for such ideas to become secular. True, the "disenchantment of the world" described by Max Weber or, closer to us, by Marcel Gauchet has reached far beyond institutions.[84] It has touched minds, morality, feelings, and the search for meaning. Yet, the notion of secularization is unable to explain the phenomenon of "reabsorption, overhaul, and reworking" of religious beliefs.[85] More importantly, the problem remains unsolved. If our universal, democratic, and atheistic morality does indeed correspond to the secularization of Judeo-Christianity, then how are we supposed to interpret religious revelation? Should we decide that—because it has been secularized in a way acceptable to us—such revelation has indeed something in common with truth? If so, then religious revelation should be given a prominent place in our society. Or should we decide, on the contrary, that such revelation is a deceitful illusion, an early fallacious manifestation of the secularized truth that became fully visible only at the end of the twentieth century? But then, why is it still necessary to think of our time as a secularized version of this revelation? The matter will surely not be settled by the magical aura of the term "secularization" but by a rational decision on our part. Our problem is the inability even to outline such a decision as long as we think that religion has been wholly discarded from modernity.[86]

The lack of clarity induced by today's most fashionable kinds of analysis also afflicts the term "modernity" when used to fathom the place of religion in our time.[87] If it is taken to mean "the consecration of the individual as free, emancipated, and without religion," then this notion will not help us find the place of religion today, nor will it lead us to properly define religion with regard to morality. Under such a definition, the question of the link between religion and morality is settled in advance. Still, it would be illusory to believe that describing our condition without reference to religion would be enough to erase religion from our world.

Earlier, I reminded readers that ethics is first and foremost a matter of introspection and reflection. Acting morally is acting rightly, fairly, based at least partially on a theoretical understanding of a given situation. This kind of acting is mostly deliberate. It takes effect in a world that is partially contingent and partially necessary, but in which one can explain and justify one's actions. In and of itself, this view of our actions—deeply ingrained in our thoughts, decisions, and moral deeds— is not necessarily religious. It could be a simple recognition of what it owes to the Greek tradition, which defines righteous acts as a manifestation of rational autonomy. The methods, concepts, and arguments that lead to acting are the product of a complex practical rationality. Clearly, the kind of practical rationality that gives legitimacy to our actions owes nothing to religion.

This is also true about moral deliberation and justification of moral decisions—especially the public ones—even when deliberation proceeds from principles such as prohibition, which are generally dependent on religion. It is therefore perplexing to notice that in French philosophical writings published recently and dealing with morality, the authors feel duty bound to state their position on religion right from the beginning. It goes without saying, they repeat, that only a secular viewpoint, entirely detached from religion, would qualify as "modern" in moral matters. Such declarations of atheism sound like an act of faith. The Kantian atheistic humanism proclaimed by some Moderns is often caused by religious disillusion.[88] Others display militant materialism without prejudice.[89] But all of them assign the same task to moral philosophy: to set up morality without reference to religion.

Devising a morality without religious justifications or safeguards is necessary only if intended for further public evaluations and justifications. Founding of an autonomous and agnostic morality is a difficult task that should be carried out by tactfully avoiding ostentatious statements. For, as I tried to show earlier, modern moralities still carry religious traces. These traces do not change our thinking about moral justification, but they should lead us to be more careful when asserting the independence of our moral systems. Most importantly, the idea of acting justly, which is at the heart of moral philosophy, and the sense that rationality is a central part of morality, can be defended without any positive or negative reference to religion. Philosophers who loudly proclaim their atheism do not seem to realize that—because morality is grounded in reason, and reason is the same for the religious and nonreligious (i.e., believers and unbelievers have indiscriminate access to rational contents, principles, and reasoning)—claiming to be a believer or an atheist does not count for much when the philosopher has to reason on morality.[90]

In this context, it would be a glaring mistake to declare that modern morality, being rational, must confront religion. In our supposedly modern world, the enemy of moral reflection is overmoralizing, not religion. It is the enemy of religious reflection as well. Being so blatantly wrong on religious reasoning would lead us to deliberately deprive ourselves of any chance to understand all that is still religious in our world and to grasp the difficulty of trying to explain morality without regard to religion.

As long as the debate is framed so that moral validity can be acquired only through rejection of religion, moral reflection has no chance of reaching a mature stage. Declared atheism is not a precondition for the validity and pertinence of moral deliberation. Morality has its rational believers, and overmoralizing superstition has its atheist representatives. To force a preliminary declaration of what opposes morality to religion is to distort the terms of the debate and to treat matters of reason as matters of faith.

Why should one treat moral philosophy differently than any rationalistic discipline? Would it ever occur to someone to ask a biologist, mathematician, sociologist, historian, or behavior specialist whether they are atheists before evaluating their reasoned arguments? In this, moral philosophy is subjected to the odd habit of suspicion strategies inherited by generations of French philosophers, which conditions them, first, to look for unstated intentions behind any stated thesis ("Is this an attempt to surreptitiously pass a religious message? If it is, who is the beneficiary?") and, second, to attack opinions rather than discuss arguments. In what follows, I attempt to summarize a number of contemporary texts in order to dismantle false ideas concerning the links between religion and morality, and the state of affairs in ethics at the beginning of the new millennium.

Ethics, Meaning, and the Sacred: Unlikely Consolations

Morality cannot be a substitute for religion. Yet this is precisely the aim of current attempts at restoring a dimension of sacredness and transcendence to secular ethics. For instance, the statement: "Without disappearing, the contents of Christian theology no longer come before ethics, to ground it in truth, but come after it—in order to give it meaning attempts to deny that morality is subservient" to religion while continuing to define it in religious terms.[91]

Man Made God: The Meaning of Life, the book first published by Luc Ferry in 1996, is an impressive example of such an attempt, judging by the scope and depth of its arguments. Its model is the modern man, who inhabits a secular world, and lives as a "well-informed atheist or agnostic" in a democratic and disenchanted time. He has freed himself of myths and superstitions, does not obey inherited customs, and rejects a priori the idea of authority. Hardened by certitudes, the modern man remains, however, sensitive to the absence of meaning, to the sorrow of bereavement, the fear of death, and the decline of old age. What could comfort him: "cosmetic surgery or religion,"[92] theology or psychology, new ageism or psychotherapy?[93] The religious solution does not seem to apply any more, and the remaining choices seem pathetic compared to the depth of his disarray. The modern man is therefore confronted with a crisis of meaning that is structural and historical in nature, because it is created by the manner in which the secular and democratic world replaces the "fading world of tradition and of moral theology."[94]

However striking Luc Ferry's depiction, the legitimate question remains whether it bears a genuine likeness to its real-life model, the modern man. From the start, something is amiss in Ferry's dilemmas: religion does not dispel the fear of death, nor does it alleviate the pain of bereavement.

THE CHALLENGE TO MORAL PHILOSOPHY

Psychoanalysis and psychotherapy may indeed help reformulate the question of the meaning of life although they were never meant to abolish it. The alternative is therefore nonexistent. As for the so-called modern solutions of cosmetic surgery and psychological counseling, at best they might increase our resourcefulness in facing the strain of living, but it cannot be said that they were ever intended to abolish it.

Ferry's analysis of the role played by morality in our lives also leaves us under the spell of a false dilemma. He rightly reminds us that the return to morality, which seems to mark the end of the twentieth century, is not a passing fad or the smug posturing of a "moral generation." It is a deep and sincere ethical concern, fully sufficient for refuting the idea of "the twilight of duty."[95] Yet, Luc Ferry adds that modern morality has lost its sacredness to become henceforth "grounded on man," "on a human scale," and to be thus shaped by a few subjective opinions, "a minimum of basic convictions, often influenced by the ideology of human rights." He believes that the weakness of such morality lies in its being solely a morality of duty and law that only teaches respect. This certainly makes it a useful and necessary morality but a limited one nevertheless, because it either prescribes or forbids. For this reason, "a morality without human traits, hence without meaning," is not an adequate one. Something else is called for.[96]

What would that be? Ferry replies: "It would be an ideal higher than life itself."[97] The underlying hope is that a secular spirituality, an idea of the sacred entirely conceived by human beings, would claim the space previously defined and inhabited by religion. Deserted by religion, the field belonging to the meaning of life has not disappeared. "Beyond good and evil," it still needs a transcendence. And it falls upon the secular spirituality "rooted in human beings," which stems from "the order of meaning not law," to fulfill this need by humanizing God while making human beings into Gods.

Ferry defines the relationship between the need for transcendence and modern morality in rather ambiguous terms. Sometimes, the need for transcendent meaning arises from the inability of a morality reduced to duties and prohibitions to exhaust normative experience; this calls for a supplement called "ethical" for lack of a better word. Some other times, the need crops up because moral life in its entirety—ethics included—falls short of expectations. The reader is left to his own devices to figure whether this need of existential meaning arises from an inability inherent to limited morality (duty and laws) or from the inadequacy of normative experience itself (moral and ethical). Also, transcendence is at times defined as ethics beyond morality, and at other times as something that goes beyond both ethics and morality. I have expressed elsewhere my reservations about the strictly legalistic understanding of morality and the forced distinction be-

tween morality and ethics. Here however, my criticism of Ferry's thesis
is based on a conceptual analysis of modern transcendence and secular
spirituality.

First of all, Luc Ferry defines transcendence as a relation of pure exteriority, a relation generated by individuals, a kind of "downstream" transcendence, rather than one that comes from above, from "upstream," as
it were.[98] True, what flows upstream of a given point is as different from
it as anything that flows downstream of it. But getting downstream beyond
a given a point implies to have passed through it. If we suppose that this
point represents a modern human being, then the existence of a "downstream transcendence" is necessarily conditioned by the existence of this
particular point. If this is the meaning of the metaphor, it is a poorly chosen
one, because it suggests a partial transcendence, that is, no transcendence
at all. Besides, the expression "humanization of transcendence" found at
the heart of the argument is itself contradictory.[99] Humanized transcendence cannot function as transcendence in relation to human beings unless
taken in a trivial sense, which would defeat the purpose of the argument.[100]

Ferry adds that such transcendence consists in the exteriority of "others
in relation to me." But if this transcendence means only that the *other* is
distinct and different from *me*, why not call it simply *otherness*? To which
the author replies that what he talks about is more than otherness; it is
rather a requirement according to which "the human existence as such
constitutes an immediate demand on my responsibility," and he adds that
"it is on this specifically modern base which targets *any other*, not only
the one with whom I have a pre-established connection owing to tradition,
that the question of the gift of oneself has to be reformulated."[101]

There is nevertheless a problem with saying that the *other* is not just
somebody else but is the *other in general*. Instead of stating a fact, as is
the case with the indisputable *otherness*, here the philosopher advances
the thesis that, "facing another, I feel directly called upon, and I see in him
any other," a thesis that many Moderns would find doubtful. The specificity of the relation between *me* and the *other* can be explained by many
different hypotheses such as: the *other* is *other than me*, it is a projection
of *me*, it is always found within *me*, that is, in the reflexivity of the self. If
the defining trait of "downstream transcendence" consists in conceiving
the *other* as *any other*, then such transcendence is just one philosophical
hypothesis among many others. Nothing would justify presenting "the
issue of the gift of oneself" as an alternative: either we answer to "the
calling of the *other*," or we act in accordance to the "preestablished connection owing to tradition." When a Roman mother was sacrificing herself
for her child or a father in the seventeenth century was choosing to die in
order to save his son, were they acting in the name of a "relation owing to
tradition"? Fortunately, tragedies, poems, and novels are there to answer

by a resounding no. Conversely, would a modern mother who acts in the same way answer the "calling of *any other*"? Would she sacrifice herself for any human being that she does or does not know as she would for her own children? I very much doubt it. I see nothing around me that would persuade me that, unlike in centuries past, people today sacrifice themselves more willingly for an unknown, faceless *other*. Taken in the most generally accepted and least controversial sense, the *otherness* does not seem to me to warrant any kind of transcendence, be it modern, "downstream," or secular.

As stated by Luc Ferry, transcendental humanism is made necessary by two, seemingly unrelated, reasons.[102] The first originates in a Husserlian, phenomenological interpretation of meaning: the content of consciousness holds more than what I am explicitly aware of; in addition, this content refers to realities that exist outside of me. To cite one well-known example, when I say that I "see" a cube, in fact I only perceive three faces of it. This presupposes that the cube is somehow present in my mind in a fuller form than what I perceive of it. From this idea, the phenomenology infers that the way in which mental contents are present in the consciousness illustrates the transcendence of meaning present in the immanence of life. Yet, how plausible is this analogy? Husserl argues that meaning is inferred from partial perception, but this kind of perception remains entirely "upstream." Moreover, it is not meant to satisfy any need. To identify a transcendence of meaning that is internal and invisible with a supposedly transcendent relation involving *otherness* is just like using synonymously two homonymous terms that mean entirely different things.[103] Were I to provide a phenomenological description of my life's meaning in terms of transcendence in immanence, it would still be mere description, not explanation. What I describe as transcendence could very well be an unwanted product of self-delusion or a result of my familiarity with the absurdity of existence. Describing phenomenological impressions does not allow us to make decisions about reality; it opens a possibility without establishing a presence or demonstrating a necessity.

The second reason would resonate with critics as well as proponents of certain forms of modern Kantian thought. It associates the human need for transcendence with the obligation to free oneself from "the determinism that governs natural phenomena."[104] In the Kantian tradition human beings are by definition "outside nature." The Kantian definition of human freedom, that is, "an unfathomable faculty to oppose oneself to the logic, so implacable for other animals, of natural inclinations," conveys the "mysterious human ability to free oneself from the mechanisms that govern the non-human world."[105]

Of course, there is unfathomable mystery in the heart of the human being, but presuming to decipher it with the concept of "unfathomable faculty" would be like trying to clarify *obscurum per obscurius*, that is, what is obscure by that which is even more so. Quite possibly, philosophy can offer nothing better or more truthful than this darkly grandiose paraphrase. This still leaves unsolved a whole series of issues that I would like to review briefly hereafter.

What does this faculty to oppose "natural inclinations" entail? Unfaltering opposition is obviously no proof of freedom; otherwise, an anorexic would be seen as freer than anyone else. In fact, one could think of instances when giving in to "natural inclinations" would help regain one's freedom of judgment. Thus, when Tolstoy relates the revulsion that overcame him while witnessing a public execution being carried out in Paris, he stresses how this emotional reaction freed his mind from his favorable prejudice about the death penalty.[106] Moreover, we often resist our first impulses because we realize that giving in would harm us later, that it would hurt our next of kin or our community, and because we know that such impulses may contradict commonly accepted principles and values. I doubt very much that all manifestations of such opposition could be explained by a single faculty of "resisting natural inclinations." And if there were such a faculty, it would have no unfathomable or mysterious qualities. An unfathomable faculty is one whose causes and consequences cannot be discerned, and its purpose, even less. Such a faculty could make me do something in spite of my reason, free will, or guiding values. If so, it would be diabolical far more than mysterious.

Fortunately, nothing would force us to choose between this kind of freedom and the complete submission to "natural inclinations." The relentless opposition between freedom and nature can only be detected in the philosophical dogmatism that is unfortunately too easily accepted without questions and uncritically echoed among French philosophers. What should be challenged here are the terms in which the problem is stated: one could reasonably uphold a strong notion of human freedom and define it as normative singularity, without feeling constrained to conceive the power of acting freely in psychologically implausible terms or to see it as a contorted "break from nature." As all human behavior, free action is the product of mental states. This does not mean that mental states necessarily combine according to the "laws of physics." The real choice is different from Ferry's opposition between naturalized spirit and absolute mystery. Human freedom acts through debate, practical rationality, decision, and representation of actions. It is highly probable that this psychological material contains natural elements that an autonomous power to act controls, orients, or even follows, as much as it opposes. Freedom would be a hollow faculty indeed, were it not exercised at each (partially natural) step leading from reason and desire to decision and action. This exercise does not call for a mysterious capacity to elevate oneself "beyond the ontic," into the sacred realm of "reflective existence." The emphatic precondition that practical rationality—which characterizes human intervention and from which morality stems—be detached from our real existence and the reality surrounding it is simply meaningless if not dangerous.

Ferry seems to think that without positing the existence of a mysterious faculty we cannot prove the objective character of morality. In other words, rejecting the existence of the mysterious freedom and of the transcendence it generates[107] would make it impossible to preserve the truthfulness and reality of moral values or ethical precepts. Now, saying that only free human beings are able to choose between good and evil is probably right, whereas asserting that good and evil would not exist if human beings were deprived of free will seems highly doubtful.[108] This assertion would subordinate the existence of good and evil, or of moral realities, to the will to choose between them. Yet, the existence of moral objectivity or the reality of goodness and values is easily conceivable in the absence of a person that is able to choose between them. In order for the existence of a realm of values to be plausible, it is enough to postulate a link between values, human conscience, and the power to act. Otherwise, we would reduce good and evil to an object of our volition.[109]

A further difficulty with this train of thought is that accepting the existence of moral objectivity hardly justifies the presumption of a beyond or of an ideal reality. Objectivity can be achieved by ensuring a partial independence of value from our desires; it can also result from exercising one's critical rationality on these desires or from devising reasons from an impersonal point of view.[110] Norms of behavior are established independently from the variability of human desires, but this does not qualify as transcendence. Values are partially independent from human beings, but not "outside the world," because they are real.[111] What renders the thesis of *Man Made God* self-contradictory is, more than anything else, the insistence that transcendent values are a necessary condition for the objectivity of morals. Modern morality is considered detached from all exterior authority because duty and self-sacrifice are "freely consented to and perceived as an inner necessity."[112] But the first effect of such internal necessity would be to posit the necessity of externality and transcendence. Is this not self-contradictory? The author would no doubt reply that the externality is immanent, the transcendence is internal, and, in any case, all semblance of contradiction is remedied by the idea of "humanized transcendence," which is "free from any argument from authority." Of course, some would think that these answers solve the problem, whereas others may see them as merely restating it.[113]

Confusing the need of transcendence and the sense of the sacred risks making ethics or any quest for meaning into a new kind of religion, a "substitute ideology" that would exhibit theological virtues similar to those attributed to traditional religion.[114] In Ferry's words, "the concern with *Otherness*"—strongly asserted in contemporary philosophy—tends to shape itself as a "religion of the *Other*." Through this concern, the "sense of the sacred" will find its spirituality.[115] If the meaning of humanism is at issue in this debate, there is no reason to have to choose between a spiritualist kind of humanism and an atheistic or reductionistic one. Personally, I reject the idea that the human being is a product of forces far superior to him or that he is mercilessly attached to his material nature. I also reject "transcendental humanism" because it is based on a hollow and muddled definition of the concept of transcendence. Again, such rejection does not imply renouncing moral objectivity nor does it presuppose "to dissolve human beings into their context."[116] But when Luc Ferry attempts to intimidate us by declaring that without the postulate of an unfathomable freedom the human being will be reduced to one of those robots with "dreary looks and clanking voice" portrayed in science fiction movies; or when he is hammering away that the only alternative to crass materialism is the spirituality of mysterious freedom, it seems preferable to reject such alternatives out of hand. We are told that "believers can escape only by positing an absolute subject."[117]Alas, this absolute subject—be it the entire mankind—is pure utopia. The idea that men made gods would bring the reign of Goodness, Reason, and Law on Earth is either wishful thinking or sheer folly. La Rochefoucauld, Rousseau, and Nietzsche knew better: if people became gods, they would still be jealous of each other and fighting one another to death.

The gigantomachy between abstract spiritualism and crass materialism is of only limited relevance to morality. Morality is a matter of rationality, reflection, and deliberation more than it is a product of commitment, a calling from the beyond, something higher than life or external to existence. Ethics and morality do not have to claim a transcendence that is so vague. It would be a dangerous imposture for them to pretend to reign from such absolute heights or try to hide the constant ambivalence, complexity, and fallibility of morality or the precariousness of our moral stances.

The Myth of Modernity

The quest for our historical identity at the beginning of the twenty-first century is a thread present in most French contemporary writings on morality. The answer is unanimous and almost incantatory: we are the Moderns. In the English-speaking world, on the other hand, defining modernity seems to have a less important place in philosophy. Naturally, our present circumstances are radically different from those of past generations. We live in a global world whose Western Hemisphere is democratic.[118] In this part of the world, religion has little influence on morals, education, or political and civic life, and information is easily available to most people. But there is much more: the condition of modernity is a complex phenomenon set up from disparate and ambivalent components. Understanding it requires that we abstain from unreserved praise. When French authors describe modernity as "the advent of a democratic world and its separation from religion," they do not see it only as historic reality but as achievement as well.[119] The normative view of modernity has became commonplace in French essays analyzing the present time. It is supported by a mostly metaphysical definition of modernity, by a fetishism that either glorifies or vilifies the modern individual, by fatalistic rhetoric and theatrical progressivism.

Let us consider the fatalistic rhetoric first: we have to be modern not only because we live in present times but because we are propelled into modernity through the combined effect of forces that are pushing history ahead and bringing the end of religion. In order to show that we are exactly where we were meant to be at this point in time, Gilles Lipovetsky sketches out a brief history of the past three centuries: "Only a long-term view can reveal the true meaning and form of the new historical bent of moral existence."[120] Thus, "ethics completes in radical fashion the epochal twilight of religion," and "postmoralist culture carries on in a new way the modern, unfinished, process of secularizing morality."[121]

This strain of fatalism is imbued with progressivism: We reached modernity after a series of eras whose succession obeys the law of constant betterment. Several recent books tell us how we have progressed morally since antiquity. There was, at first, the aristocratic ethics of "the Greeks" based on principles of hierarchy and excellence, where "nature" determines the aims of humans and "gives them an ethical direction." This is why the Greeks were able to recognize "in the order of things and the reality of the cosmos" an objective basis for morality. After Galileo, the reference to a finite cosmos having become obsolete, we finally reached "abstract humanism, i.e., the humanity of man." Rousseau, Kant, and the "French Republicans" taught us how being free presupposes "tearing oneself from nature." This marks the advent of "modern morality": a morality of duty and merit, based on the "idea of disinterested action and of universality." There is still some lingering doubt as to the nature of a third phase, which brought us the "the ethics of authenticity" in the 1960s: an antimeritocratic ethics demanding that everyone be given the right to be oneself.[122] Gilles Lipovetsky provides the most typical expression of the contemporary consensus that progressivism is the only means for achieving intelligibility. In his view, the first cycle of ethical secularization lasted from 1700 to 1950. At that time, modern secular ethics was reduced to the cult of absolute duty, so important to the French Third Republic.[123] When this cycle ended, "a second cycle" followed, which was "driven by a new logic of moral secularization" marking the dawn of a new "post-duty"age[124] wherein subjective rights and freedoms prevail over categorical obligations as ineluctable dictates of the "historical dynamics of individualistic self-rule."[125]

These stories of deterministic and univocal progress of thought may bring the ghost of a smile on the faces of our readers. "The logic of history" and "the laws of historical future" have always been dubious hypotheses and intellectual cop-outs that mimic scientific necessity without explaining much. Intellectual history—of which the history of moral ideas and ethical thought are an important part—does not look like a long, slow river but like a turbulent one, stirred by clashing undercurrents, moving in impetuous eddies and resurgent swirls. Our "modern" moral vision of the world has many core elements inherited from the moral philosophy of antiquity and Judeo-Christian teachings. And—however paradoxical this may seem to the modern proponents of historical necessity—such elements may still become sources for a renewal of moral reflection. More importantly, interpreting history in terms of phases and periods always leads to exaggerations and approximations. Rousseau's moral reflection has nothing to do with absolute and transcendent duty. The same is true about French Republicanism. The moral philosophy of antiquity has nothing in common with a naturalistic ghost clinging on the cosmos. I will revisit this point further on. Here, I simply emphasize that no history of ideas can aspire to plausibility when its own misreading of intellectual trends and influences makes it despise everything it disagrees with.

What most contemporary French thinkers offer us by way of philosophy is rather a sociological analysis whose legitimacy depends entirely on ideological fluctuations. The least that can be said about such analysis is that it is utterly fallible. There is every reason to believe that in twenty or thirty years from now, there will be no trace left of such analyses, nor of the highly "specialized" tools it devised for its own study. Unless, that is, it backs onto the postulate that all its considerations—in their most particular and contingent form—illustrate a necessary transitional phase or an intrinsic aspect of the evolution of modern human beings. Without the benefit of this postulate, no study of the latest modernistic fads would outlast the phenomena it describes. If only its analysts would be content to speak about themselves or of verifiable facts and objective, commonly agreed upon situations! But no, they chose instead an inclusive rhetoric— "We, Moderns," "Our democratic times," "Our disenchantment with the world"—that includes the reader, the author, and all enlightened spirits in a stealthy manipulation that aims to force their approval.[126] Such rhetoric is meant to eliminate all chances of thinking outside its box, because any differently thinking "I" would be simultaneously neutralized and included in the consensual and soothing "We." These French experts in "modernity" speak of Man in general and of contemporary Culture as realities of which everybody must be aware and cognizant. Yet, in matters related to Man and Culture, descriptions depend on interpretations. For instance, and contrary to Gilles Lipovetsky's beliefs, it is not possible to find uncontested facts proving that "we" have reached "the twilight of duty" and that "we" have embraced laissez-faire.[127] No empirical proof, no conceptual argument could ever show clearly what we, humans, are. Why, then, present such interpretation of modernity as incontrovertible evidence that only visually or intellectually challenged people could miss?

Fortunately, the defenders of "modernity" also admit its relativity. Ferry reminds us that "There is nothing original or modern to be found in the moral values of the Moderns."[128] Lipovetsky recalls that morality always had the same meaning, that is, "a stable core of shared values." There are no "newly invented moral values: they have been essentially the same for centuries and millennia."[129] The sudden surge of common sense goes, however, too far. If indeed ethical values were unchanged, if moral content were the same as always, if reasoning methods and thought processes had remained constant since time immemorial, then what is left to justify this persistent invocation of modernity? For some, the novelty comes from the "modern" meaning assigned to the idea of autonomy: today, age-old morality originates in the self rather than in external authority.[130] For others, the novelty consists in "how we position ourselves with regard to values, that is, in the new social regulation of morality," which "uses eternal humanistic references" to inaugurate "a new ethics."[131] But should one not reply that, at each historical phase, humanity adopted "a new way of positioning itself with respect to values" and that the search for an autonomy rooted in rationality has been at the heart of Western morality since antiquity? Such novelty has no "specifically modern features," unless one gives ad hoc meanings to the terms "rationality," "autonomy," and "values." I therefore reiterate my question: If values are unchanged, if procedures of validation and deliberation are largely the same and reasoning on practical matters is not transformed in any fundamental way, then what justifies proclaiming the advent of "modernity" in such dramatic terms? Faced with the evidence that there is nothing particularly "modern" in at least part of our moral individuality, why would anyone want to rekindle the baseless suspicion that "the postmoralist workings of our societies" ultimately take shape from "the old cloth of morality?"[132] Actually, most "philosophical discourses on modernity" are as questionable as the debates on the "death of man." In Vincent Descombes's very adequate words, "such debates disguise purely conceptual incidents as historical events."[133]

I would like to plead for a different approach to modernity. First, I do not believe that our world is the product of historical necessity or that it corresponds to the neat completion of a transcendent process, much less that it is the univocal result of the emancipation of human beings or of society's secularization. Rather, I believe that we deprive ourselves of opportunities to understand our modernity if we conceive of it as a homogeneous whole that could not have been anything else than what it is. Second, I do not believe that we have just simply reached autonomy or that by now we are far beyond religion, nature, and tradition. Instead, I outline here what I believe to be our present moral situation.

We live in a world that is complex, multifaceted, and, in many ways, contradictory. In it, we find multiple sources of moral value related to universal and impersonal obligations that allow us to examine the consequences of our actions. These sources are relevant to the particular duties we acknowledge toward other human beings, and to the ideal of self-fulfillment. In our world, the presence of morality itself is multifaceted: it can take the form of obligations and interdictions; it can manifest itself either as rightful praise or indignation; and it may materialize in the certitude that there are standards for every action. Attempting to establish an immutable hierarchy of value sources or a typology of standards would seem therefore simplistic and wrong.[134] The uniqueness of our present moral situation has something to do with the heterogeneity of its components. Thus, we are held accountable for our acts and their consequence in many different ways: the respect of persons and of their rights often dominates all others; the idea of human perfection and the intrinsic value of effort and merit often guide many of us. Far from replacing each other chronologically, these heterogeneous components subsist together by either coexisting as discrete elements or clashing as conflicting ones.

The contingency of human history might have led simultaneously to the survival of moral beliefs from different origins and to the disappearance of the conceptions of the world that made each of them dominant at some point.[135] It might also be the case that human beings can only experience morality through its diverse sources and aspects. It is even possible that we can only accede to normative reality in an erratic fashion, to only some of its aspects and only through historical, cultural, or political lenses. Most importantly, it is possible that the categories and terms that shape our thinking about our moral existence are born from the unforgettable experiences of bygone days in the ancient city, or from the tumultuous, painful, if intermittent encounters between a people and its God or between the whole of humanity and God. The particular making of our present is mapped out by past events, yet we may never know whether they were the only possible ones or the best ones. Our moral condition is inescapably

affected by contingency and heterogeneity and, as such, it is both necessary and singular: there were powerful reasons to make it what it is, although its present shape is not an obligatory result of those, nor can our
modernity be seen as having necessarily evolved into what it was supposed
to be. My analysis does not prevent us from recognizing the strong specificity of our time, which strives to create a global humanity. But it does
subject this singularity to relentless questioning rather than treat it as an
undisputed and reassuring premise.

Adopting beforehand an interpretation of modern times that emphasizes
the necessity of progress and global integration drastically limits our intellectual ability to grasp modernity. Reasoning about modernity becomes
identical with examining the process that led to its advent. We are told
that modernity is what happens when human beings achieve emancipation
and secularization. The underlying reasoning is that, by becoming modern, humanity has simply achieved what it was destined to be, that is,
democratic, rational, and emancipated. This flat, self-satisfied, historicist
stand vaguely inspired by Hegel is as unjustified as the views—going back
to Kierkegaard and Nietzsche—that detect barbarism and insanity in modernity, or see in it a close, if paradoxical, association of reason and superstition, of free diversity and constrained uniformity. It is hardly more accurate than opinions that deny or ignore the significance of modern
phenomena.[136] Also, too often modern reality is assessed in accordance
with the part played by philosophy in its creation, because, we are told,
certain philosophical topics turned out to be strong enough to shape our
world, at least in part.[137] It is true that reflection and philosophical specula-
tion devised "criteria" for modernity, by opposing the old, premodern,
world of prejudice, unreason, nature, and religion to the modern world of
reason, autonomy, and self-control. The rise of a "philosophical history"
that whips up the awareness and the will to be modern goes back to the
seventeenth century.[138] But it alone cannot explain the phenomenon of modernity, which it helped engender, because contingency is an irreducible
part of our reality, most aspects of which—not to mention its ambigu-
ities—cannot be explained by means of a homogeneous, historical, or philosophical interpretation.

Modern reality consists of many things: the cult of democracy, admiration for exceptional people, pernickety rationality and superstition, desire
for emancipation and dependence. Proclaiming that "secularization" or
emancipation from authority is the only criterion by which to gauge the
distance from thought to truth is a wish upon which only a very partial
vision of reality could bestow any credibility. Such an assessment of the
present would lead us to erroneously believe that we have reached modernity when, in fact—if there is any such process—it is far from being com-

pleted or could well stop at its present stage and never evolve further. For all we know, this process could well self-destruct, regress to older ways, or take an entirely unexpected path.

Mauled Individualism

Interestingly enough, the same considerations apply to the way our French philosophers interpret modern individualism. For them, the "modern individual" is adorned either with all the world's glories or with all its miseries. In his glorious incarnation, "he finally realizes his potential in a society that respects human rights and autonomy," successfully breaking away from nature, tradition, and authority.[139] In the sad alternative—which is much more common—the individual is defined by "systematically stimulating immediate desires, the passion for the ego, intimate and materialistic happiness, the pursuit of his well-being, and the dynamics of subjective rights." As such, the modern individual, unencumbered by standards and values, is just "a floating space without ties or reference, pure availability"[140] Today it is very fashionable to interpret such self-flagellation as lucid scrutiny of modern pathologies.

Whether grandiloquent or bleak, such descriptions of the modern subject seem highly questionable.[141] First of all, their extremism prevents us from grasping the difficulties inherent in the status of modern individuals. Why is it that any positive definition of modern individuality evokes relentlessly the break with nature, tradition, or kin as a precondition of autonomy? Do we really find our "I" by forcefully detaching ourselves from all that is "non-I"? Why must we preempt the reality of modern man and treat it as a prerequisite for radical self-determination? Why should one consider that the source of every value and meaning is an abstract and hollow autonomy? Why discard as outdated whatever does not fit this model? The "I" is defined more accurately by its interactions with the "non-I," while autonomy is shaped by the constant reworking of our psychological reality. The description of the modern individual as hovering above values, acknowledging only the norms that he likes, and being only concerned with pleasing himself is a ludicrous exaggeration, wholly disjoined from reality. Defending it would condemn us to incoherence and unrealism. Can we really expect to reach a true understanding of contemporary individuality by artificially opposing "subjectivity as awareness of universal principles" to "contemporary individuality as seen in the sixties?"[142] I think not.

The modern individual can certainly be conceived of as an autonomous source of action, but the representations, goals, and values informing his action can hardly be the product of "self-establishment." The atomistic thesis of the individual is ontologically and psychologically untenable.[143] Modern identity, its way of shaping the self, and the ability to act that it engenders have grown throughout a long history, which has always kept alive and integrated the older, Greek and Judeo-Christian, forms of identity. This new identity—a product of the incessant intellectual activity of mankind—is neither riveted to the historical conditions that shaped it nor independent of the kind of society in which human practices and culture evolve around and are tied to the individual. The main aspects of modern identity—that is, liberty, autonomy, self-limitation of the ego, and the quest of well-being—cannot result from a subject's self-positioning or rational self-determination. Rational self-determination is nowadays an essential good, that is, both a real orientation toward morality and a source of practical rationality that is nonexclusively formal and procedural, because it is tightly linked with the reality of the individual that lives in present-day society.

Those who nowadays glorify rational willpower should not ignore that the indeterminacy of human willpower is primordial. If there were a distinctive characteristic of the modern individual, it would be the inability to know what he wants. This is why willpower is both a resource of autonomy and an opportunity for dependency. The infinite mirroring of others' wishes incessantly stimulates the individual's willpower to self-determination even when he cannot give a direction or an object to this power. Being a "modern" individual is a *challenge* more than a product of necessary emancipation, because such an individual is conflicted by heterogeneous aspirations and shapes himself in reference to an external source (social reality, practices, cultural traditions, and loyalties). This challenge is brought about both by the competition of all individuals against each other and by the compulsive need to be recognized as unique.[144] Benjamin Constant, among others, has deftly probed the ambivalence of the modern individual. Rather than glorifying autonomy and condemning the trivial desires of our contemporaries, present-day French philosophers would be better off detecting the multiple aspects of modern identity, including the contradictory ones, as well as its links with the democratic system in which it was born.[145]

In this context, it would not be enough to contend that there is a "structural conflict" between two antinomic logics of individualism (on the one hand, responsible individualism "attached to moral rules, fairness, and future" and, on the other, the irresponsible individualism of "every man for himself" and "après moi le déluge"), for the obvious reason that most people would prefer responsibility to irresponsibility.[146] We should also try to find out why both kinds of individualism are so solidly tied together.

How can we critically analyze the modern individual if we deprive ourselves of the intellectual means necessary to grasp his ambivalence, which goes far beyond the opposition between rule and licentiousness?

In order to better understand modernity we should undertake a serious, normative study of present-day intellectual conditions, including representations and justification procedures. Such an undertaking would require a set of concepts more pertinent, rational, and specific, than the ones criticized in the preceding pages. It would also require an evenhanded description of the various ways of being a human in today's world, a description that would show the current interactions between autonomy and dependence, elitism and populism, rationality and irrationality.[147] The analysis should strive to be realistic and plausible and to faithfully reflect what we are humanly and psychologically.

As stated at the beginning of the present essay, one of my aims has been to show that moral philosophy can play an important role in understanding modernity, and that constructive criticism can only start after glorification and flagellation of human beings have ceased. We would be deluding ourselves were we to deny the heterogeneous and ambivalent character of moral reality or to arbitrarily unify it under the heading of autonomy and emancipation. We would, moreover, betray our duty to understand our situation as completely and adequately as possible. The consequence would be our inability to envision the future beyond what determinism predicts about the human mind, secularization, and emancipation. The fact is that we do *not* know how these elements of modernity might evolve.

Human situations are contingent not only because each of them could have been different but also because—although moral beliefs can claim objectivity and validity—it is impossible to find reasons outside morality that could secure its links to the metaphysical nature of rationality, the universal forms of argumentation, or the necessary processes of modernity. In other words, we are unable to think of morality without starting with morality itself. In his *Nicomachean Ethics*, Aristotle emphasizes that in order to understand moral lessons one must have been raised up to respect morality. At the beginning of his *Fundamental Principles of the Metaphysics of Morals*, Kant reminds us that he is only elaborating on the common idea of morality, which he equals to the concept of duty. At the end of the nineteenth century, Henry Sidgwick, one of the most influential philosophers of the Victorian era and the author of *Methods of Ethics*, assigned to himself what he considered to be the only task possible in moral philosophy, that is, to analyze and present the "methods of ethics" as the rationalization and justification of the moral components of the common conscience of mankind.[148] In order to evolve, moral reflection needs to be able to find its contextual meaning in an already existing morality. Moral deliberation is possible only because we can find our place in the very old, familiar process of growing up morally. Without it, the so-called fundaments of morality—rationality, procedures, or language norms—would be inconceivable.

"All Books Are Open in Front of Me"

In concluding this chapter, I would like to show how my opposition to oversimplifying views of modernity relates to moral philosophy. In the late 1990s, Paul Ricoeur recalled how much his moral reflection was nurtured on the contributions made by other philosophers: "I consider myself to be a sovereign reader."[149] It is necessary to remember this attitude at a time when, for many people, modern moral philosophy can only be rightly understood as a break with the Ancients and as tightly linked with Kantian philosophy. I want to criticize the belief that allegiance to Kantian philosophy is a requirement for all debates on morality.

As I have already indicated, much of the French return to Kant in the 1980s and 1990s, mainly due to the work of Ferry and Renaut, went together with a renewed interest in moral philosophy. But it would be indeed regrettable if all interest for moral philosophy were limited to the return to Kant—first, because it is not at all clear that the need for autonomy in moral philosophy falls within the scope of Kantian philosophy; second, because there are inherent difficulties in interpreting Kantian thought on practical reason and on the categorical and universal imperatives; and, finally, because Kantian philosophy remains silent on many questions that are essential to moral philosophy, such as those concerning human motivation, the role of moral feelings, the existence of moral conflicts, or the justification of moral beliefs. By comparison, one finds considerable resources for reflection and critical thinking on these questions in the philosophy of antiquity and in many other philosophical traditions, such as intuitionism, Hume, and non-Kantian contractualist approaches.[150]

There would be no need to dwell on this topic at such lengths if in much of contemporary French philosophy loyalty to a philosophical doctrine did not imply rejection of all others. Yet morality being a complex and heterogeneous phenomenon, it is quite natural that more than one moral perspective is required for its analysis. The preconceptions mentioned at the beginning of the chapter—all morality is a morality of the law; ethics only deals with happiness; the moral philosophy of antiquity is nonhistorical—are all due to a prior and, I believe, arbitrary loyalty to Kantian philosophy. As for the rejection of ancient philosophers, it can only result from an erroneous interpretation of the evolution of moral philosophy.

Certain characteristics of our moral representation of the world—the sense that to some extent we are historical beings, the universality of obligation, and the all-encompassing idea of mankind—clearly belong to our modern condition. It is likely that the thinkers of antiquity did not have a very strong sense of history and that the idea of a universal moral obligation was not a central one in their notion of ethics. And while it cannot be denied that moral categories are not independent of history, neither can it be said that their only meaning is historical. As stated before, it would be an exaggeration to claim that our experience in its entirety is marked by the distinctive traits of "modernity." Some essential traits of ethical thought in antiquity do belong to the core of our moral reflection. Antiquity's philosophers and playwrights were invoking a plurality of morality sources and their potentially ensuing conflicts. When Greek philosophy and Greek tragedy evoke the pitfalls of moral deliberations, the intractability of moral dilemmas, or the representation of morality as a way of life, we cannot ignore the richness of their moral thoughts and the relevance of the questions they raise, especially because these questions are so similar to our own perplexity when facing heterogeneous aspects of morality. In this, there is much to be learned from Greek philosophy and drama. They have nothing to do with the psychology of solace and wisdom to which it is too often reduced these days in France.

The thinkers of antiquity defined morality as theoretical and practical mastery of action. Thus, Aristotle analyzed the practical dimension of rationality as applied to action, and Plato formulated many ontological and epistemological aspects of the definition of moral objectivity. Practical rationality includes all aspects of prescriptive actions, well beyond morality in the strict sense. And, if the first challenge of any morality is to grasp and define the convergence between intellection of reality, rule definition, and righteousness of desire, then this challenge has rarely been taken up as competently as it has been by the Greek thinkers. Whatever weaknesses and faults the Greek thinkers might have shown, no present-day reflection on morality can forgo references to the Greek definition of practical life.

In fact, most criticism of Greek thought on morality targets a false image of it manufactured by modern philosophy and marketed under the label "Greek thought," often with no valid historical reference. The term "Greek" conveys a sort of misty, naturalistic Aristotelianism, but its usage lacks all reference to the important contributions of Greek thought, particularly to the intellectualist and rationalist approaches. Moreover, the ten-century-long Greek philosophy—from the first pre-Socratics to the last Stoics—so rich in debates, polemics, and breakups, is presented as a homogeneous whole, whereby particular emphasis is placed on antirationalism, antiformalism, and antiuniversalism. This approach may make criticism of the Greek easier to formulate; unfortunately though, it focuses on a dummy target, rather than on historical reality.

The main difference between modern theories of morality and ancient ethics concerns the scope of moral philosophy. For Aristotle, in particular, the depth and adequacy of moral reflection does not reside in procedural and formal elements, nor does it manifest itself in the ability to deal with difficult or singular cases. Yet, those two traits—the ability to find a decision criterion for solving all difficult cases, and the capacity to cut oneself off from concrete, individual, or situational circumstances—are precisely the defining features of modern theories on morality. The difference could not be clearer, although moral reflection in antiquity displays different degrees of systematization, strong in Plato and the Stoics, more moderate in Aristotle. Greek ethics is willing to reflect on normativity in connection with the actor's nature and the ontological weight of the actions. It also focuses on moral life as a whole and preserves a view of rationality that is not exclusively instrumental.[151] True, Greek philosophy did not build a unified theory able to guide decision making, yet its rational vision of morality is of undisputed significance. Moreover, because there is no reason for limiting modern moral philosophy to either Kantian or utilitarian theories, which are the dominant ones in France today, there could be none for imposing such limits on the entire history of morality.[152] The received wisdom, according to which "Greek" thought can have no impact on modern thinking *because* it cannot be reduced to a form of either Kantianism or utilitarianism, stems from a totally erroneous interpretation of the history of morality.

Another oft-repeated criticism claims that Greek moral philosophy is mostly interested in well-being or happiness, producing at best a set of rules on how to live well, rather than a full-blown philosophy of laws, rules, and duties. Therefore, the Greek reflection on morality cannot pretend to represent a true moral philosophy; to call it "moral" is to speak euphemistically. The criticism is begging the question by stating that moral doctrine is by definition a morality of laws, rules, and duties (as I showed earlier).[153] By asserting that Greek reflection is merely a search for happiness—whereby happiness is defined as satisfaction of material interests, detached from any idea of rational autonomy—these critics show their ignorance of history. For those who recognize as valid only modern moral philosophy, Greek thought is not a reflection on the human condition.[154] But this amounts to confusing a particular thesis on happiness with a general interpretation of Greek thought in its entirety. The particular thesis is indeed held by several Greek philosophers, who equate moral wellness to happiness and consider the search for happiness to provide the core of morality. The general interpretation, on the other hand, alleges that the Greeks could not conceive of any source of moral normativity other than the search for happiness or that Greek thought is unable to distinguish morality from self-fulfillment. The Greek obsession with happiness would thus

inhibit all reflection on the specificity of moral reasons, the nature of obligation, and the understanding of someone else's point of view. This general
interpretation is obviously false: yes, happiness is essential to moral reflection in antiquity, but it clearly does not justify, by itself, the normative
goals that the authors of antiquity set for moral reflection. Most Greek
philosophers did conceive of a source of morality other than those framed
by happiness, and of a principle other than the search for Aristotle's *eudaimonia* (happiness), and they were perfectly capable of grasping the prescriptive nature and the impersonality of moral standards. In Plato, for
instance, "goodness," conceived as a perfectly intelligible reality and as a
source of order, is the principle that defines the value of virtue and happiness. This by itself suffices to falsify the criticism that mistakenly equates
Greek morality to the pursuit of happiness.[155]

Yet another unfounded criticism that permeates contemporary thought
claims that the Greek idea of morality is entirely dependent on the Greek
idea of a harmonious cosmos. The flaw of this criticism consists in a faulty
interpretation of the Greek references to the finality of nature. Among the
Greeks, Plato considers the cosmos to be a model for order; Aristotle sees
nature as a paradigm for normativity; and the Stoics believe that the cosmos bears witness to the existence of an organizing principle. Yet, these
philosophies do not claim that the ends of man or the birth of ideas would
be gifts from nature.[156] Aristotle does not define human freedom or political
action in the same terms as free-falling physical objects. Rather, when he
tries to understand the normative character of human action, he uses the
teleology that seems to work for nature and for technical deliberation, as
an instructive and productive model. By this use, he does not dogmatize
the intrinsic value of nature, nor does he assert that human actions con-
form to natural processes.

Some say that there is no loss in discarding the philosophical legacy of
the Greeks because their world involved morally repugnant realities, such
as slavery and infanticide, and also because they ignored the idea of humankind and did not realize that history can shape social and political
ideas. In order to conceive of humanity and history, one must live in a
world in which they are sensed as real. But everybody knows that the ideas
of humankind and history were beyond the grasp of ancient thinkers. Yet
again, where could we find irrefutable proof that the Greeks were incapa-
ble of grasping such concepts? As for the objection concerning repugnant
realities, it is a non sequitur. First of all, the terrible crimes of the twentieth
century should protect us from the temptation of moral self-righteousness.
Second, if certain ancient realities were indeed repugnant, it does not follow that attempts to analyze, understand, or criticize them are also repugnant. Philosophy does not inevitably mirror the world in which it evolves.
Plato's philosophy was radically detached from its worldy circumstances.

Our self-righteous contemporaries, who are indignantly condemning Aristotle for not protesting against slavery, seem not to realize that he was reflecting on a given social reality in order to grasp its legitimacy. One can find his reflection philosophically rewarding without being constrained to judge it based only on the moral acceptability of its conclusions. Those who reduce the intellectual richness of a reflection to the moral correctness of its solutions are sorely mistaken. The criterion of philosophical legitimacy cannot be reduced to the moral criterion.

The critical conception of modernity has many consequences, one of which flows from the relationship between formal rationality and moral contents. It is a platitude to note that present-day democracies experience a de facto moral pluralism: in a democracy individuals may hold radically different views about concepts such as goodness or human perfection. Some philosophers hope that a certain form of universality and objectivity will be attained by submitting personal opinion to mutually critical analysis in a rationally created public forum. Such is, for instance, the stated objective of Jürgen Habermas.[157] His ideas have been abundantly discussed by philosophers. Here, I limit myself to raising two objections. First, the idea that an unlimited activity of inquiry and debate could end in a freely achieved consensus is somewhat utopian, especially if it calls on the participants to determine collectively the defining characteristics of truth itself.[158] Second, the very idea that our normativity should be obtained through rational debate blinds us to some harsh realities of the modern world such as conflicts, dependencies, the inertia of traditions, or the power of archaic arrangements. It would defeat the purpose of reflection to qualify such essential aspects as heteronomy and declare autonomy to be the sole source of debate.[159]

Should moral philosophy be asked simply to explain a variety of moral views so as to facilitate the emergence—by sheer rational power—of a formal core of universal obligations that would only be moral inasmuch as they are detached from beliefs and traditions? The defenders of such moral universalism seem to believe that we could indeed attain the level of rational and universal ethics through public debate, by tearing ourselves from our individuality, our history, our community. Such a requirement elevates the radical distinction between rationality and historical grounding to the status of guiding principle. In France, it inspired the critique of all philosophies, from relativism to deconstructionism, that stood in opposition to the philosophy of the subject.[160]

This being said, it seems to me highly desirable to work out a set of critical reflections on the differences between reason and conviction. The idea that reason can achieve a universal morality would warrant by itself a long and careful analysis. Here, I would express only three reservations on this topic. First, the wish to extract a universal morality from rationality—not only an identity criterion for moral action but a set of obligations that would persuade us and inform our will—has never been fulfilled. Furthermore, nobody has ever been able to say what exactly such morality would involve. Second, I would suggest that it is just as difficult to understand what such a wish really means as it is to reach a consensus on the meaning of rationality. The defenders of such a radical hope rely on a quasi-metaphysical view of rationality. Yet many logicians, mathematicians, and philosophers of mind abandoned such a view. They define rational human behavior by taking into account things like consistency in the way of acting, the context of action, and the way in which action develops. I cannot see why philosophers of morality would be the only ones holding such absolutist views on rationality, especially considering that the first duty of moral philosophy is to be close to reality. Third, citizens of modern democracies are well aware that humans rely heavily on well-established ways of life and, therefore, do not appear to believe in the possibility of extracting norms from human reason. Accordingly, it seems doubtful to me that they would ever accept an abstract exercise of rationality as the only kind of moral reflection available to them. It seems even more doubtful that asking citizens to ruthlessly shed their beliefs would be the most effective way of making those beliefs disappear.

I question the feasibility of a project that purports to extract a universal ethics from an absolutist and abstract vision of rationality. But I also stress the fact that my doubting the capacity of rationality to breed morality does not entail any skepticism with respect to the universality of moral obligations. We do not need to reflect on the foundation of these obligations, but rather on the way they are discovered, defined, and made stable. Contemporary moral reflection does not need to limit itself to examining the formal conditions of common life. It can offer more, without losing its critical capacity and its universalist scope, because moral reflection originates in the individual beliefs that it must examine and criticize. These beliefs stem from individual commitments and represent particular values as well as collective obligations that rule over people's behavior and reach the status of norms, in spite of inevitable violations. And while they do not always perceive every norm as necessary, they nevertheless shape one's awareness of the moral norms. A genuine revival of French moral philosophy requires serious, detailed research on normative behavior, as well as general reflections on practical rationality, autonomy of rational beings, freedom of action, ethical deliberation, and decision. These are also the topics that—as I endeavored to show—have characterized moral philosophy for more than two millennia.

CHAPTER **2**

Goals of Ethical Reflection

To be or not to be ethical, that is the question of the day in France. Everybody wants to buy ethics, talk about ethics, bid on ethics, or govern through ethics, without anybody showing the slightest interest in clarifying the meaning of "ethics" in such contexts. Instead, people seem entrenched behind a prudent silence—and one heavy with innuendos—as if everyone were expected to know what "ethics" means.

Why should we be surprised by this situation? The term "ethics" has gradually lost its meaning through indiscriminate usage, its semantic content being now less important than its utterance. And what does one do by sticking "ethical" to everything in sight and making it into the least determined and most valued qualifier in the French language?[1] One proclaims one's good intentions. One plays up one's rejection of laissez-faire economics and one's willingness to go back to great principles. All of which is praiseworthy, especially because it does not require anyone's commitment. Such a tactic can nevertheless be quite disingenuous when saying "It is ethical!" serves as a subterfuge to exempt oneself from criticism, to hinder the search for valid reasons, to block attempts at understanding conflicting positions, or simply to intimidate opponents.

"We must do something about ethics" is an assertion often heard among journalists, CEOs, scientists, and even among state bureaucrats. At the very least, such a declaration signals an awareness of problems in need of solutions and a willingness to act in this regard. In fact, one can detect the presence of good intentions and desires for efficiency in almost every currently recorded usage of the term "ethics." Good intentions are often necessary for starting a normative or ethical analysis, but they are never sufficient. Being aware of a deficiency and wishing to remedy it does not mean being able to identify it, much less to describe it. Defining a problem often requires great efforts of information gathering and data evaluation. By itself, the quality of one's intentions can only rarely ensure the quality of one's results, especially when those intentions are not passed through the fine comb of critical analysis and through careful deliberation on the means of action, on its consequences and on the constraints that shape decisions. As for the desired efficiency or the "we-must-do-something" factor, it too is a necessary condition for giving ethical reflection a far-reaching scope and ambitious dimensions. But the willingness to act is insufficient if not informed and guided by normative reflection. Only the latter can evaluate the goals to be attained through action, weigh up all options, consider the context in which the action will fit and the instances in which it could fail, and ponder its possibly undesirable consequences and its irreversible effects. Equally important is the way in which ethical reflection legitimizes action by clarifying the reasons that justify it. All along, such reflection remains close to action.

If one is truly involved in ethics, one cannot be content with praiseworthy intentions and a desire "to do something." Talking about ethics while saying nothing may not be embarrassing if one is aware of what one is doing. But problems do arise when a quasi-conspiratorial usage of the term "ethics" obscures the analytical work required for any normative study and exempts the speaker from moral deliberation. The only way to uproot such adulterated usage, whereby the term is bereft of meaning and the thing referred to is deprived of substance, consists in tirelessly repeating the same question: "But what do you mean by 'ethics'?" or "What does that mean to say?" Surely, nobody has a monopoly on ethical reflection, be they philosophers, theologians, scientists, physicians, or law specialists. Any person who is involved in a professional practice, a community, a cooperative endeavor or who has formed a human attachment understands perfectly what is a norm, a rule, a duty, or a commitment. Therefore, my critique of the current French usage of "ethics" does not aim to censure all speech on morality, or to restrict the right of using it to people who know what they are talking about, but it does stubbornly aim to remind everybody that this term presupposes an intellectual process based on accurate knowledge, strict reasoning methods, and consistent procedures for which there are no ready-made solutions. If this prerequisite for reflection is not preserved, then the sense of the word will only amount to a tip of the hat to our sensitivity to the ideas in the air at the present time, or to a sort of airbag for deflecting criticism.

Some might think that it is preferable to talk about ethics than not to, and they would be right. But if nothing is done to stop the hackneyed usage of the term, this preference may turn soon enough into a losing proposition. If the tendency to see in "ethics" a universal solution— as in "It's very simple: be ethical" or "Saying that you are ethical is in most cases enough for being so"—persists or intensifies, then we would have missed an extraordinary opportunity to debate, to deliberate collectively on ethics, and to justify its reasons for being. The opportunity is indeed extraordinary because the need for such deliberation has rarely been so powerfully expressed. Given the obtuseness and tyranny displayed in current ethical discourse, the lack of deliberation would have a worse result than unanswered questions. It would give the wrong answer by letting stand the current prejudices, cop-outs, and dogmatisms.

Detecting a symptom is only a preliminary step toward understanding reality. And the reality behind the tiresome and depleted usage of "ethics" is a complex and forceful one, clearly registered in the publicly expressed need for ethical questions and answers. So, it is well known that ethical deliberation is needed, that it is necessary, but it is less known what it consists of or what it involves. How is this need to be understood? What anxieties does it convey? Why is it perceived as a disquieting solace, a sort of white flag signaling the search for solutions to odds and ends of problems? And is this confidence in the solving power of ethics not resting as much on the valid belief that ethical reflection can indeed inform our action as on a misreading of its nature?

Moral Disquiet

The increased public questioning of the meaning, the scope, and the consequences of human activities is a defining feature of our time—at least in countries with democratic traditions. What is in our power to do? What are the limits of our acts? Can we justify those acts? Do we really know what we are doing? Far from being new, such questions can be traced to the Ancients but seem to have acquired recently new meanings and different aims. I am not sure whether this is because they reflect a "new" morality or an "entirely new ethics."[2]

Western culture shows an impressive unanimity on a set of moral principles that offer a stable frame of reference for answering ethical questions. Generally speaking, these principles include the respect due to human beings, the rejection of attempts to take advantage of somebody else's weakness, and the duty to treat everybody fairly regardless of race, religion, nationality, or sex. One could debate at length how such principles are formulated, what is their nature and justification. Here, though, I am focusing on the fact that these principles are considered by a vast majority of people to be fixed and intangible, even when they go against our interests. This does not mean that everybody and their neighbor respect those principles or act in conformity with their prescriptions. It only means that, even though they are occasionally transgressed, such principles have a normative value that guides our basic moral evaluations and are perceived as practical rules to live by.[3] The forcefulness of these principles must not depend on whether or not they are considered to be "true." In fact, one could doubt or reject the idea of any truth value in morality and still consider such principles as valid and legitimate norms of behavior. I may doubt the existence of truths in morality, but if you asked me why slavery is evil, why must it be prohibited without exception, I would certainly know what to answer. I might use different arguments than you would, or use the same arguments differently, but the working-out of the reasons that justify this prohibition endows it with a certain objectivity and therefore with the same meaning for all of us.[4]

An interesting feature of present-day debates is the expectation that rules and principles be explicitly formulated and justified. Even more interestingly, such expectation does not set apart the elite, or a few *cognoscenti*, but is shared by society as a whole, and is strongly expressed as a requirement not only "to disclose or make public" but also "to make accessible, justifiable, and therefore open to criticism." The guidance offered by ethical reflection does not have the force of an edict or a rule that must be applied strictly. Once made public together with its reasoning, conditions, and context, such advice becomes accessible and therefore open to criticism. Even when it leads to the enactment of regulations that are supposed to remain stable for some time, the moral debate does not cease with the decision to regulate but continues to seek additional considerations for ulterior use if new circumstances warrant it. For each decision, the set of deliberations that have produced it operates as a context for intelligibility and justification and thus allows for later decision making if new circumstances arise. The accessibility of antecedent reasoning and justifications ensures that those who have not participated in previous deliberations have nevertheless the means to examine their content. Otherwise, the very idea of an explicitness requirement or expectation would be only wishful thinking.

The yearning for behavioral regulation bespeaks the present-day realization of the importance of normative questions. People want to witness how rules of good behavior are worked out, how deontology codes are taking shape. In the past few years, in France many professions provided their members with ethics charts, an initiative that required a substantial work of explanation and justification of guiding principles and procedures. It is indeed essential to define rules that ensure the smooth performance of an activity, as well as the respect of the interests of all concerned in a community. At the same time, the interest of our contemporaries in ethical questions should reach beyond the infatuation with statements of principle and charters for good behavior. Beyond the preoccupation with codes and rules lies the hope that it will create favorable conditions for reflection and questioning about the legitimacy of those rules, the good inherent in every activity, and the best ways to instill good practices in social communities. Such hope transcends deontology into morality.

The ethical concerns that characterize present-day society are traceable to current fundamental principles and to the requirement for explanation and justification of rules. Such concerns cannot be met by mere invocation of principles or enactment of rules and norms. The requirement for regulations and for imposition of limits can also be taken as a more general indication of our own disarray. However, it would amount to an abdication from moral reflection if we were satisfied with deontology and rules: they are necessary but not sufficient. We must also seek to understand the nature of the difficulties and conflicts that such rules aim to solve or at least alleviate. And it is in such an undertaking that moral reflection plays an essential role by bringing us closer to understanding our own moral complexity.

We are often confronted with tense situations that involve specific values. Setting up a business in an underdeveloped country creates jobs and wealth. It can also create moral and physical misery if it involves child labor, if the workers in need of a job are resigned to hardships and extended work hours, or if it causes environmental degradation and depletion of natural resources. Business ethics can solve such problems by regulating activities, imposing limits, and establishing operating rules that would reconcile as much as possible the respect due to workers with the goals of maintaining the economic potential of the host country and keeping the business profitable. It is also probable that this type of situation would lead to inevitable conflicts, not in the trivial sense that the enrichment of some means the impoverishment of others, but in the sense that good and bad are inextricably linked together when real needs of work and money are simultaneously fulfilled or when objective values are attained through serving specific, individual interests. One can easily see how important the concern with practical regulations becomes in such a case: it can help putting an end to serious abuses and implementing clear and well-understood rules that could offer guidelines in case of violations. It can also create opportunities to analyze conflicting factors, to grasp the intricacy of advantageous consequences and deteriorating factors, and to compare various needs, expectations, and ways to meet them. The deliberative process reveals its true ethical scope when it is conceived as an exercise in comprehension, analysis, comparison, and evaluation. In this case, deliberation mirrors our moral condition: a heterogeneous mixture, structured around different, even conflicting values, but whose inherited moral traditions stretch from antiquity and Judeo-Christianity to the current culture of multilayered if disparate human rights. Moral deliberation is possible only if it takes into consideration this plurality, which is characteristic of our modern condition.[5]

A New Morality? Reflections on Responsibility

It has often been said that the transformations that define our world compel us to devise new moralities. This is quite natural, given that moral concerns usually arise from relatively recent changes in concrete sets of worldly circumstances. For the most part, such concerns can be traced to new manifestations of human action, which are complex and not easily discernible. For instance, modern technologies expand our ability to act in ways that were hard to imagine fifty years ago. Their consequences are as hard to predict as is the effect of their interaction on our abilities. The propensity to regulate and contain new technical applications can thus be understood as a precautionary attempt to curb their potentially disastrous effects. The unprecedented availability of factual data changes the very nature of current problems and has a threshold effect. To take an example from transportation, the widespread use of private cars to get anywhere very fast can, in certain cases, slow traffic and make it harder for everybody to reach their destination. These kinds of situations quite naturally make us rethink familiar ways of doing things and change our understanding of moral concepts and our perception of good behavior. However, the mere addition of new areas to ethical research is not an indication that the sources of morality have been radically changed or that its central categories have become obsolete.

A case in point is the use of the term "responsibility" in its moral sense as distinct from its sense in the penal code or in civil law. When asking ourselves what does it mean to be "morally responsible," we soon notice that the concept takes its meaning from a set of conditions pertaining to the definition of intentional acts. Strictly speaking, an act is considered intentional only if its agent had the choice not to perform it and realized its full significance, that is, that of the act itself and of its likely consequences. On the other hand, if the act had unexpected consequences or if there was no reason to link any of them to the act, then attributing responsibility becomes more problematic.[6]

The idea of moral responsibility has been abundantly debated in the light of a phenomenology of action that is presently viewed in some circles as either outdated or too restrictive. The classical theory of responsibility draws sharp distinctions between action and omission: I am responsible for what I do but not responsible for not doing something, unless I am knowingly breaking a popular rule by abstaining as, for instance, by not helping a person in danger. The critics of this classical idea claim to belong to the consequentialist school of thought—a philosophy that judges the moral value of actions by their consequences. They want the distinction between action and omission abolished in all cases, with the exception of violations. In their view, by doing something I leave an infinity of things not being done instead. If I pass the evening at the opera, then I do not act as a volunteer for social services, I do not use the amount spent on the ticket to make a donation to an international charity, and so on. In a henceforth unified world, I am also responsible for what I am *not* doing, such as the misfortunes that my involvement could have prevented. In other words, I am concomitantly required not to act wrongly and to contribute to the creation of the best possible world.

Another criticism of the classical theory of responsibility targets its tendency to focus on the immediate and predictable effects of actions to the detriment of the isolated or unpredictable effects. To the extent that the world is a complex system in which distinct causalities constantly combine and interfere with each other, the effects of my action can be far-reaching: by interacting with the causal effects of others' actions, they can even produce results that are contrary to those that I had desired. For instance, I start saving money for later use, and it so happens that everybody else starts saving at the same time; a recession follows, which means that while my savings increase proportionally, their absolute value decreases. Thus my saving more money has the undesired effect that the value of my savings diminishes.[7] Obviously my decision to save has no causal effect on the fact that many others take the same decision at the same time. Nonetheless, according to the critics of the classical theory of responsibility, my decision makes me somehow responsible for the final result (even if they recognize that my action has a noncausal effect on the action of others).[8] Finally, the critics blame the phenomenology of action for ignoring not only the unpredictable consequences but also the disproportionate consequences that can result from an insignificant act, a careless mistake, or a slight negligence. There is nothing in our global village that would ensure our control over the effects of an action or our power to confine them to an isolated part of the world, be it a state, a nation, or a territory. Yet, according to consequentialists, whatever we do—and even whatever we do not do—can be generally seen as an object of global responsibility.[9]

There seems to be general agreement that there are only two solutions to such difficulties. The first solution would expand the scope of "responsibility" to include a very large number of situations, even those to which the strict criteria for defining this concept would not apply (because omission and action would become indistinguishable, unpredicted and disproportionate effects would have the same weight as predicted ones, and interferences with other peoples' actions would be taken into consideration). This would make me responsible for everything in the world. The second solution would restrict "responsibility" to its classical meaning, which is roughly equivalent to the sphere of action of its agent, and would treat unknown or remote effects of our actions not as responsibilities but rather as reparative and compensatory duties. Working out concepts such as "no-fault responsibility" and "unintentional offense" and developing the notion of "civic responsibility" would fit neatly in this frame of thought.[10]

I plead, however, for a third way of solving the aforementioned difficulties that is justified by the need to fulfill the following two requirements. The first one is to restrict the scope of responsibility to the sphere of intentional action, which is the only way to preserve a sense of "imputation"—essential for defining our moral standing in relation to the world. This idea of responsibility is irreplaceable because it alone allows us, moral subjects, to grasp the scope of our actions.[11] Furthermore, adherence to this idea of responsibility does not inhibit one's awareness of its difficulties. We are all aware that contingent or extrinsic factors such as moral fortune, favorable circumstances, or unfavorable turns of events can decide whether the same action remains inconsequential or causes considerable harm.[12] Individuals are inevitably linked to multiple elements that are outside the reach of their intentions. In addition, as subject and observer alike may find themselves unable to access their intentions, we cannot ignore the problematic character of the intentionality criterion. There are situations whereby one cannot ascertain that an action was intentional without risk of being wrong or in bad faith.[13] There are real difficulties at the core of human action, but they should incite us to refine further the idea of responsibility rather than to discard it. Its loss would leave us unable to distinguish our voluntary acts from involuntary ones (whether they were involuntary because we had intended a different outcome or because we had ignored predictable consequences). We are always the cause of our deeds in the sense that full exoneration is impossible, but the kind of moral responsibility that connects us to our involuntary acts is different from the strict or classical interpretation of the term.

The second requirement is to reexamine the idea of responsibility in the light of the relationship that can be established between an individual action and a given state of the world. If we agree to take into consideration the complexity of human action and the variety of connections linking our actions to their results, then we must have the means to differentiate such connections as belonging to different conceptual categories and to define each category properly as a specific concept, distinct from all coordinate concepts and from the concept of strict responsibility. This exercise in nuanced categorization is necessary for multiple reasons. In the classical sense, responsibility comprises one's actions and their consequences but it does not include farfetched consequences, especially those whose enormity had been at the time impossible to imagine. In order to qualify the connection linking my action to its unimaginable consequences, an altogether different concept than responsibility would be appropriate, or at least a different kind of responsibility should be considered. Even when I cannot be held responsible for all the consequences of my acts, I am still responsible for my acts. Yet in certain cases it is impossible to distinguish the act from its consequences. Performing an act may have consequences that are distinct from those of the act itself. Breaking one's promise to a friend makes one forever disloyal in friendship. This is a consequence somehow included in the act itself but not in the consequences of the broken promise (the pain inflicted on the friend, the hardship caused, etc.). If the consequences flowing from the act define the act itself, how can we continue to distinguish clearly between act and consequence? Trying to preserve at any price a single concept of responsibility that would apply to the connection not only between an act and its agent but also between an act and all its consequences (i.e., direct and known ones as well as unknown and farfetched ones) would make it impossible to distinguish between different modalities of human action and would force us to abandon many moral distinctions that are valuable in qualifying such action.

Another way of looking at the relationship between an act and a state of the world is by using the concept of moral *involvement* instead of moral responsibility. For instance, if someone is unintentionally witnessing a situation without being able to intervene, this is clearly a case of moral, if unintentional, involvement. Indeed, in such cases one often regrets having been involved, especially when the consequences are bad. (One harbors regrets for having been unable to intervene, for having known too little beforehand to stop the bad things from happening, and even for having been present there as a powerless witness.) Acknowledging this kind of involvement confirms the possibility of participating somehow in an act without bearing a direct responsibility for its outcome.

General phenomena such as global warming and environmental changes reveal another kind of relationship between an individual action and the ensuing global effect. In such cases, my action has an effect only because similar actions by others have the same effect. The greenhouse effect is produced by mostly intentional, collective actions (X drives a car, Y buys products manufactured by polluting plants and factories) that can be placed somewhere in the causal chain leading to this general state of things. But would it make any sense to assign individual responsibility to each of these countless actions—each with its infinitesimal effect—for the aggregated result? Could we all consider ourselves responsible for the state of the world and its global effects when the question of who did what to create it becomes itself secondary? Instead of using terms such as individual versus collective responsibility, would it be better to state the problem differently? There is a potential state of the world that nobody wishes to see materialized, and that could be avoided only by regulating collective actions. The enactment of such regulations requires enforcing collective rules of behavior not as the result of individual awareness of one's responsibility but because of the need to restrict globally the effects of human actions.

A similar situation occurs in our daily interactions with institutions such as the family or in our performance of collective tasks such as driving a car. What is incumbent upon me to do for having married or for having children is mostly my own responsibility and partly that of institutional commitments beyond the explicit duties that I assume toward my immediate family. The relationship is even clearer as far as driving a car is concerned, because from the moment I start the engine I am involved in a rule-governed activity such that the set of actions in which I participate is substantially larger than the set of actions that I really control. In contexts such as this, one person's "responsible" commitment consists not in claiming one's general responsibility but in making sure to observe the rules. This may not make any concrete difference, but it does make a big difference in the more abstract effort of normative justification. In the framework of classical responsibility, one starts with the action intended by the subject. But in the framework of global effects, the starting point for deliberation is the simulation of an envisioned global state from which one backtracks by questioning what behavioral restrictions could make it avoidable. Individual responsibility is real but limited to consenting to stated rules, considering them legitimate, and applying them dutifully. This is an internalization of regulated behavior, not a strict responsibility or a reparative commitment.

There are many ways of describing the moral scope of the relationship between a human agent and a state of things in the world. I have pleaded here for maintaining clear distinctions between relationships of this kind, for conceptualizing and defining each one of them and, most importantly, for avoiding any confusion between the idea of strict responsibility and other forms that this relationship may take (reparative duty, compensatory commitment, moral involvement, rule enforcement). The danger of casually talking about the need for "extension of responsibility" resides precisely in the tendency of taking it to mean an infinite moral responsibility. I plead for restricting its meaning and for analyzing the different ways in which actions and reality relate to each other, and whether they require reparation, regret, compensation, damages, or regulation. The fact that causalities are usually entangled or that a link is always conceivable between a subject and an action does not justify infinitely expanding the idea of responsibility by isolating it from intentional action, nor does it justify accepting the idea of universal responsibility. The debate is still open on this point, but I consider it essential to emphasize that, even though the current state of affairs in the world and the specifics of resulting human action may very well lead to the adoption of a complex description of human action and of explanatory concepts different from moral responsibility, this does not necessarily render obsolete traditional definitions of fundamental concepts of morality. The criterion of intentional action is central to moral responsibility. It may indeed become necessary to find a better definition for it or to restrict its application further, but there would be no philosophical gain in abandoning it altogether.

Law versus Morality: The Issue of Abortion

Ethical reflection can play a substantive role in efforts to justify public decisions and should not be confused with sociological investigation or legal rulings. The relationship between law and morality has been subject to debate for a very long time. Both are major forms of normative reflection, but their differences are so numerous that one wonders how they can be so often confused. The law is a normative order, a system of rules that regulates human beings' behavior toward one another. It is also an order of constraints, which contains sanctions as well as rights and duties. But the law can have only an indirect effect on moral beliefs or on evaluating procedures used for criticizing or improving such beliefs. More than anything, the legal individual is the fictional locus to which rights and legal obligations are assigned.[14] Law consists of procedures for qualifying actions and situations. It cannot pretend to regroup modes of normativity and structures of meaning under the label of a general imperative. The features that differentiate law from morality have practical consequences. First, although one can distinguish French law from American law, it would be spurious to distinguish "French" ethics from "American" ethics. Whether in France or the United States, the principles underlying ethical deliberation are widely comparable. Any perceived differences relate not to the nature of these principles but to their ordering and respective weight or to their interpretation in light of different cultural traits and sensitivities. Ethics has a claim to a certain form of universality, at least as far as manifestations of collective life are concerned. Next, unlike morality, law is a set of articles and clauses with assorted penalties. An immoral act may cause disapproval, indignation, or disgust; however—at least in the public arena—it is not punishable for being immoral but for contravening specific laws, codes, or internal rules; and punishment for committing such acts is impersonal. One can easily find actions required by law that are morally questionable, loopholes, or legal vacuums in legal resources that allow their use for the protection of acts seen as morally reprehensible by many. Finally, there are acts authorized by law—such as abortion—that pose serious moral problems to some of us.

The Veil law, which was adopted in France on 18 January 1975, decriminalized abortion by medical professionals up to the tenth week of pregnancy.[15] Its intended purpose was to alleviate the burden of a very serious human and social problem. However, legalizing abortion has no bearing whatsoever on the moral implications of the act itself. That abortion can be performed in certain conditions without being punishable by law does not mean that it does not pose ethical questions. Speaking of the "right to abortion" in this context can only increase confusion between law and morality.

The debate that preceded the Veil law was preempted by the will to impose the right to abortion as a fundamental right of women. Yet it is one thing to talk about a "right to abortion" in the sense of a legal recourse for a woman to terminate her pregnancy under certain conditions—because it is unwanted or because she believes it is impossible for her to raise a child—and it is quite another to consider this right a decisive expression of women's autonomy. The first meaning is legal, the second is militant. In the first sense, the right to abortion is justified by considerations of public health, by the availability of safe technical and medical procedures, and by the acknowledgment of a personal sphere of decision and action that includes the control of one's reproduction. The second is quasi-normative, as it makes abortion an issue of women's emancipation, supposed to be adopted unreservedly by all enlightened individuals.

Moral deliberation on this topic has been neutralized as much by the invocation of a woman's right to abortion as an absolute principle as by the claim that abortion should be absolutely forbidden. I hope that the increased acceptance of legal abortions would render obsolete the defensive attitude that treats the faintest reticence concerning abortion as a clear danger to the independence of women. It may also undo the ideological dogmatism that inhibits the debate on the morally problematic aspects of abortion. Clearly, ethical considerations of this controversial issue cannot be used as a basis in law. Conversely, the presence of a law can facilitate moral reflection on this topic rather than frustrate it.[16] Defenders and opponents of abortion might agree that ideally, no woman should ever have to go through it. A stimulating debate on abortion would certainly bring us all closer to this ideal. The free exercise of individual deliberative abilities often makes such outcomes possible. This is not an attempt to blame women or to put ethics into everything but, rather, to make people aware of the seriousness of the act so as to help them avoid a situation whereby abortion becomes the only recourse and, more importantly, to avoid its deliberate use as a regular contraceptive means.

Attempts to discard the moral dimension of the abortion issue whether by invoking a legal device or a biological consideration show only an inability to perceive the moral stakes involved in it. There is no way that a supposedly scientific or ontological thesis on the status of the fetus could dispense with moral reflection (e.g., the thesis that the fetus is a person from conception or the thesis that the fetus becomes a person only at birth). Aside from being impossible to prove, such theses have no moral relevance regarding the decision to abort. Even if the hypothesis of the fetus being a person endowed with human rights were scientifically proved, it would still not follow that abortion should be morally prohibited. One could further imagine an extreme, conflicting situation whereby defending the fundamental rights of the fetus would be detrimental to the

fundamental rights of the mother. She could unreservedly take the stand
that killing an embryo is wrong, that she would not do it in any circumstances other than her present situation, which leaves her no choice. The
inner deliberation whether to have an abortion is of a strictly moral nature.
It cannot be discarded under the false pretense of ontological certitudes or
the pretext of legal circumstances, because, even if the fetus were a person
from the time of conception, the weight of moral decision would still be
the same.[17]

The fact that late-term abortion is sometimes called partial-birth abortion and described as quasi infanticide shows how important it is for moral
reflection to establish time limits in this matter,[18] especially because selecting a limit based on biological or physical criteria is partly conventional
and might involve a concern for the coherence of the judicial system.[19] In
addition to the need for establishing limits, there are other considerations
with strong moral implications. Here are a few: normally the fetus evolves
into a child; it cannot be seen as merely an "intruder" or "part" of a woman's body that she could deal with as she pleases; with the exception of
rape, its presence results from a series of intentional acts on her part; the
relationship between a woman and the child she is bearing is not neutral;
a pregnancy that seemed absolutely imperative to terminate when it was
terminated may become an object of doubts and regrets afterward; and,
above all, the freedom to have a child if and when one wants is guaranteed
to every woman but the decisions and acts that make it so do not have the
same moral status. Thus, the decision to terminate a pregnancy is a very
serious one: much more so than deciding not to become pregnant and
acting accordingly. There are no ready answers for all these considerations,
and each woman would ponder on them differently, but taken together
they may help detect the morally problematic aspects of abortion. And no
legal argument, however perfect, could ever void the gravity of a moral
deliberation on abortion.[20]

These considerations carry no skepticism toward the law and no desire
to set morality up against the law. My main purpose is to dissociate law
and morality while pinpointing the very close connections existing between
them.[21] If this dissociation is not recognized, free moral reflection becomes
impossible. Theoretical hypotheses and counterfactual examples are ad-
missible in ethical reasoning in ways that are entirely different from legal
reasoning. The given or assumed starting point for reasoning has different
essential qualities in law and in morality. Legal systems are not completely
overhauled with each update: their publicly acknowledged principles remain intact. In contrast, moral reflection deals with the very nature of
principles and purports to show the extent to which they are determined
or justified, although philosophers may differ greatly on what exactly vali-
dates such principles (e.g., conceptual analysis vs. empirical confirma-

tion). Jurists build their reasoning on existing legal principles, whereas moral philosophers debate the very existence of ethical principles.

Another basic distinction between law and morality separates factual observation leading to the formulation of norms applicable to all observed facts from reflection on moral norms. However liberal our societies may be, they are still ruled by consensual values. Our daily lives and professional practices are constantly guided by them. The empirical efforts to update these values and the careful analyses of the ways in which individuals interpret them or are inspired by them are all essential to normative reflection. Sociological observation quite naturally begins with the description of social norms, but their existence alone does not prove that they are moral norms as well. Showing that certain people apply the formula "an eye for an eye" as a norm of behavior and acknowledge it as belonging to their system of values does not prove that the practice of revenge itself reflects general ethical values. Such formulas are norms for social interaction, not moral norms. Moreover, the observation, description, and definition of such norms do not automatically allow their critical evaluation or their justification. In order to establish that observed and described norms constitute "an order of the world," one must be able to prove their legitimacy. There are two prerequisites for this. First, one must know whether the identification and evaluation of such norms are purely interpretative. Second, one must discern the conditions allowing justification procedures to be linked to specific norms and values. Moral sociology can complete both tasks only if it has a truly normative commitment.

Description and Dissociation in Ethical Reflection:

The Concept of Person

Pascal wrote that man must seek his human dignity in the ordering of his thought, that thought constitutes man's greatness, and that reason has the right and duty to examine the facts of man's condition.[22] One might add that thinking properly is a basic moral component whose absence makes it impossible to act in a befitting manner. Of course, sound thinking may not be always enough for righteous action, but it is a necessary condition—at least for those who have to justify publicly their choices and moral decisions.

Ethical thinking is reflexive and critical, and it unfolds in stages. Describing the facts that are relevant to a situation and discerning its characteristics are not only prerequisites of ethical reflection but also an integral part of it. Not everybody would expect that to be the case, because describing a state of affairs seems to count among the most noncommittal activities imaginable, thus forgoing any normative commitment. The neutrality of a description may even prove to be a useful fiction, at least until its illusory character becomes apparent. Most descriptions feed on evaluations. One starts describing a situation by using expressions like "to the degree that," as in "Your action—to the degree that it shows your attachment to your parents—presents such and such characteristics." Then, in the course of description, one may take a stand or adopt a particular point of view that would inevitably lead to selecting and emphasizing certain features to the detriment of others. Who would deny that the act of qualifying things or putting them in perspective already entails a normative element? Moreover, when the situation is contextualized and placed in a network of related situations or realities, it begins to be seen in a different light depending on the viewpoint adopted. Which aspect would the description single out, and from what perspective? Which viewpoint would take precedence? Reflection enables us to answer such questions while making us aware that description presupposes a normative commitment that is perfectly legitimate if it is not ignored or used stealthily but identified and assumed as such.

The task of describing reality as rigorously as possible and without any illusions as to one's normative neutrality is indeed a difficult task. The objectivity of moral reflection depends greatly on its success. Being objective is not to be seen here as being either neutral or "just sticking to facts," but as a product of accurate knowledge of observed realities and willful distancing from our own interests, feelings, or biases that we always carry within. Ethics does not consist in mere evaluation, that is, in deciding what is good or bad; rather it requires us to understand what is involved in an action. Thus, it searches for objectivity and forces us to get closer to reality.[23]

Deliberation is the bedrock of ethics. Aristotle compared moral judgment to a perceptual grasp or a vision. There is much to learn from this idea, provided that vision is not taken to mean an act of immediate perception but rather the culmination of an enduring effort of rigorous analysis in search of the best reasons. This undertaking may be achieved with well-tested methods and arguments that many of us spontaneously employ while asking ourselves what we should do in a given situation. As preconditions of a clear vision, one must consider changing the perspectives from which a problem is envisaged (primarily this would entail adopting the viewpoints taken by the people involved in it); one must pinpoint the parameters affected by this contextual change and identify the ones unaffected by it; finally, one could advance multiple counterfactual hypotheses of what might have happened if this or that hypothesis had been modified. Such argument-driven reasoning allows for a firm grasp of all aspects of a situation. It also produces a clearer and more objective vision of it. The first task of ethics is to see the world as it is, and this requires us to exercise realism, to display authenticity of vision and to be fair toward reality. We do not see what we want to see but what is, with the clearly stated caveat that our description of this reality is at least partly underpinned by our normative evaluations. Paradoxically, when such evaluations are acknowledged and submitted to reflection, critical thinking, and rational argumentation, they end up reinforcing our quest for objectivity rather than softening it.

The next question is how to ground normativity in reality. Understanding reality has a normative dimension to the extent that values depend on reality; they are not arbitrarily sprinkled over it. In particular, the idea that identical realities and situations might receive different moral qualifications is counterintuitive. If an action is considered proper and sound based on relevant features, how would it be possible for another action, sharing exactly the same features, to be considered improper or unsound? True, "proper" or "sound" may qualify actions that are very different (return borrowed money, keep one's promise, etc.). But this only means that the relationship of dependence between values and facts is asymmetrical: the same facts cannot carry different values, whereas a value may apply to very dissimilar facts. Most contemporary philosophers acknowledge this asymmetrical relationship, which is generally called "supervenience."[24] This acknowledgment is entirely compatible with many ontological standpoints (in particular, that facts and values may be ontologically similar or dissimilar). I pointed here to the existence of a relationship between facts and values in order to better argue against the idea that values are arbitrary or detached from reality.

The difference between *what is* and *what ought to be* is real, yet facts can be used to justify values. To ignore the need to establish a relation (which is neither strict dependency nor reduction) between the descriptive order and the normative order would only increase the confusion. The concept of person illustrates this difficulty well. Roughly, there are two kinds of definitions of "person." The first kind is philosophical, inspired by Kant and based on the autonomy of a rational being capable of making laws and following them. In the second, one finds a descriptive concept of "person" according to which each exemplar has a specific set of psychological characteristics such as, for instance, the ability to make decisions, to be aware of one's identity, or to make plans. The drawback of the Kantian definition is that it forces us to make metaphysical commitments relating to the status of rationality and the moral purpose of mankind that we cannot reasonably expect to be universally accepted. As to the descriptive kind of definition, it is obviously insufficient: a newborn, a comatose man, or a seriously handicapped individual are certainly "persons" even if they do not exhibit the psychological characteristics mentioned earlier. Clearly then, biological determination does not a person make.[25]

To the extent that there is no unambiguous answer to the question "what is a person?" it is better not to define the concept by means of necessary and sufficient characteristics and to opt instead for a semantic and pragmatic analysis while reflecting on what we are commonly meaning by "person." Indeed, even when we refer to individuals who lack some of the psychological characteristics of adult persons on which is based the definition of this concept, we still know what we are talking about. Different uses of the term share a family resemblance because, after all, the idea of person evokes a set of distinctive attributes that together form a "prototype" of the concept. The individual cases presenting such attributes are "central" (an adult, fully rational) and those without them are "marginal," but the concept "person" applies to them as well as to the others. Acceptance of the concept "person" as a prototype concept throws new light on the relationship between its descriptive and normative aspects. By its nature, the prototype concept can be differently nuanced, the moral effects of its usage variations being thus a particularly apt object of study either from a heuristic perspective or for regulatory purposes.[26] For such an undertaking, we need to consider those psychological features to which the concept of person is never limited but which clearly form its core. Furthermore, when we want to bestow a normative significance on the concept of person by acknowledging the links between biology (growth of the nervous system, birth), psychology, and values, we must clearly state that we approach this concept from a resolutely normative perspective and that we stand by our decision. We cannot, under any circumstances, let the complexity or ambiguity of this concept carry the burden of our moral commitment.

The indeterminacy of the concept "person" is a precious asset in a context of discovery and orientation. But this asset can become a liability when the main task is public justification of the concept's usage rather than the fleshing out of its normative richness. In this case, the reasons we give must be easily understandable and unencumbered by implicit metaphysical commitments or normative decisions. Apart from anything else, a public justification must be neutral in the sense that it must be acceptable even to those who disagree with its clearly stated normative assumptions. This requirement has two consequences in a public justification context: the need to clearly affirm the normative value of certain concepts and the duty to avoid overly nuanced concepts whenever possible. Thus, when the concept of person is needed in such a context, a clear explanation is expected as to whether it is used descriptively (i.e., linked to psychological characteristics) or normatively (i.e., in a stronger but disputable sense). In such contexts, what is being said can be validated only by facts and clearly stated normative commitments. The worst possible case would be to use a seemingly factual concept and allege that it entails a norm. Given the entwining of descriptive and normative aspects of the concept of person, it is clear that facts alone cannot validate its public explanation and that its normative dimension must also be revealed in order for such validation to occur.[27]

Practical Rationality and Moral Decisions

Some of perhaps the most fascinating questions in practical philosophy concern the roles of understanding in acting and of ethical reflection in moral decisions, such as those involved in the transition from cognitive elements—weighted down with normative commitments—to decision and action. Their study touches an essential part of what is known as practical rationality. Aristotle proposed a remarkable system for investigating this field, which is still very much alive in contemporary philosophy.[28]

Moral reflection is dependent on practical reasoning. It draws on the normative qualities inherent to human acts and particularly to those having a defined end; those aiming at certain states of things, realities, and goods; and those with a reason for being and requiring means for achievement. The type of human action that is a prime object of practical philosophy involves one or more agents and is concerned mostly with other persons. Questions such as "Ought I to act in this manner?" "Should I have acted differently?" and "Would it have been better to . . .?" belong to our reflection on human action and help us to understand better who acted, how, and why. They all bear witness to the importance of the normative dimension. The notions of an act's inherent rightness, of its appropriateness and adequacy, are indispensable for reflecting on and defining the normativity of a human act: they allow us to conceive of righteous actions, of appropriate decisions, and of feelings and perceptions that are adequate to a given situation.[29]

At this point, it may be useful to recall a misunderstanding concerning the nature of moral rationality whose specificity comes from the role it plays in action and decision, rather than from a particular kind of reasoning. Yet many authors refer to "moral rationality" as if there were a kind of rationality specific to morals that is separate and distinct from rationality in general.[30] Here is an example.

A number of recent publications influenced by the writings of Jürgen Habermas argue that practical rationality is defined by its requirement that the subject abide by the basic conditions of freedom of thought and expression, that is, that one is accountable for one's statements and should be capable of justifying them. This is indeed a characteristic of rationality, but it cannot be used as a distinctive trait of moral rationality because many other kinds of rational statements are also expected not to violate these basic conditions. A similar argument attempts to show that the specificity of moral rationality resides in the ability to detect a "performance violation" of these basic conditions wherein the utterance of a statement is incompatible with its content (e.g., "I was on that ship when it sank and there were no survivors"). In this case, the "I" uttering the statement cannot also be the "I" denoting the object of the same statement. It could be argued that such incompatibility differs from logical contradiction and therefore does not pertain to demonstrative rationality; it would be a specific case of moral rationality. Yet common rationality obviously follows the same rule: the "performance violation" in question entails no logical contradiction, or, better still, no contradiction of any kind, only an incompatibility between the statement's material conditions (i.e., that there must be a survivor) and its conceptual substance (that there are no survivors). Therefore such an argument cannot prove the singular character of moral rationality. While practical reasoning is obviously different from demonstrative rationality, it is neither the reasoning method nor the access to certain kinds of truths that distinguish practical rationality from theoretical rationality; only the kind of conclusions reached and the role of reflection in taking action or making decisions could be used to that end. Rationality covers the same thought processes in both practical and theoretical thought, and there is no reason to assume that they would use radically different notions of identity or contradiction.

The assumption that normativity is inherent to human acts has definite consequences for the status of moral reflection and decision. To begin with, questions about the nature of goals, the adequacy of means, or the acceptability of results acquire a legitimacy that makes them appropriate tools for evaluating the rightness of an action. Certain actions, given their stated ends, could not be completed by such and such means because of a perceived incommensurability between ends and means. Other actions cannot be undertaken at all either because they lack objective or normative reasons that would justify them or because they go against the "impossibility clause" of actions, such as the interdiction to inflict pain gratuitously. Again, these aspects concern only the legitimacy of actions, not their logical or physical possibility. If actions are nevertheless carried out against all such considerations—and let there be no doubt that people can inflict considerable suffering or use loathsome means in order to reach appalling ends—then such actions are seen as extraneous to normativity, morals, and, more importantly, practical reason.

In this category are included prohibitions and deeds that make us burst out: "It's beyond me!" or "I could never do such a thing." Absolutely forbidden acts are being so not only because they would infringe a formal rule of a more general application than any particular act, but also because of the kind of acts they are. The study of such prohibitions requires an analysis of the human will, for, typically, one is unwilling to perform this kind of forbidden acts and yet this unwillingness does not originate in subjective will.[31] It also requires an inquiry into the nature of human rationality. A hotly debated philosophical question asks whether certain ends or goals are rational. In order to answer it, goal rationality can be weighted, and prohibitions can be justified by means of minimal prerequisites for rationality, such as the duty to treat similar cases similarly or the interdiction to inflict unnecessary pain. A decisive role in such justifications is played by reasons relating to the nature of human cooperation and to the impossibility of survival in a community where no acts are consensually proscribed. Such reasons impart a form of objectivity to prohibitions and strengthen the justification of moral decisions.[32]

The Normative Character of Human Acts and Practices

Absent the assumption that human acts have a normative dimension, it would be senseless to ask moral questions about human actions. By itself, normativity is clearly not a deliberate human product (it is not because I wish to act in a certain way that my action will be properly performed); neither does it rise to the status of logical necessity (it is not logically impossible to perform an action in an absurd manner; it is sometimes physically possible to do that). Normativity must be defined in relation to the human abilities of understanding, acquiring knowledge, reasoning, and acting; in relation to the world and the manner in which it can be acted upon; and in relation to the persons involved not as individuals or because of their connection to the issue, but in light of the circumstances in which the action in question affects them. Analyzed according to such criteria, the normativity of action closely links morality to intellectual activity or, as some prefer to call it loosely, theoretical activity. Morality requires an understanding of the distinctive traits of a situation and its particular cognitive, motivational, and affective needs. The appropriateness of an action depends on the adequacy of its comprehension and the rightness of its motivations and emotions.[33]

I illustrate my point by a few examples. In my encounters with educators, physicians, and business people, I am often being asked to define ethical reflection. Philosophers usually have ready-made answers to questions such as "Where does ethics comes from?" They say that ethics originates in the Judeo-Christian tradition, in our respect of human rights, in our familiarity with virtues, in our certainty that well-meant interests always end up in agreement for the common good. There is undoubtedly some truth in all these answers: the universal character of rules of human behavior, the consideration of particular interests, the reference to virtues, and other similar considerations help advance moral deliberation. Nevertheless, these answers miss the distinctive features of human activity. The moral compass of human action is best grasped through the search for its ends, for the good it envisions, for the norms that it follows. I often say to my interlocutors: "Are you wondering which type of ethics would be best fitted for your own practices? Stop wondering and ask yourself about the reasons for your activity, its ends, the rules it should abide by, and the values it fosters." This is the foundation of ethical reflection about all human endeavors. The analysis of the distinctive features of a given activity leads to its definition in terms of norms and values, which in turn makes ethical reflection relevant. I cannot think of a single human activity deserving of ethical reflection that is not linked to a particular set of goods or that lacks an intrinsic normative quality.

If we ask ourselves what conditions a sound medical ethics must meet, particularly with respect to the doctor-patient relationship, then our first priority is to understand the nature of this relationship (including its theoretical aspects) rather than trying to establish a list of rules that apply to medical ethics. The doctor-patient relationship is a form of action on one's fellow creatures, and an asymmetrical one at that, because the patient is by definition vulnerable, anguished, and often in pain. The doctor's action takes the form of diagnosis and care and cannot be separated from a sense of uncertainty and an awareness of human finitude. The ethical principles of such a relation can only be found and evaluated based on the conceptualization of the human connection underlying the relation between doctor and patient. This process involves compassion, respect for the patient, and a duty to do good while caring for the patient's individuality, values, and commitment to life. The aim of ethical reflection in medicine is to articulate accurately all these components, beginning with the specificity of caregiving.

Many other activities share medicine's grounding of ethics in practice: the field of economic production is an obvious example because it is also goods-oriented (creating riches, stabilizing exchanges, balancing society's supplies and demands). Defining the aims of corporate ethics would require, in my view, taking into consideration the reality of many modern enterprises that see themselves less and less as mere physical units of production and more and more as hubs of exchanges with the world. It would also require revising the description of the internal structure of the enterprise, because its network structure is closely linked with the economy as a whole. Finally, no ethical norms can be defined in the absence of a prior definition of "business" in itself and in its social role. Only by fulfilling these conditions would a business ethics transcend its present threshold of maximizing profits while ensuring transparent internal relations and solving conflicts.

The anecdotal usage of ethics mentioned earlier in this chapter misunderstands the nature of ethical reflection, which is grounded in a clear vision, an effort to understand, and a normative study of what constitutes human practice. Such usage would mislead us into believing that ethics has obscure and blurred origins; that we can care about or ignore it depending on circumstances; or, worse, that we can sprinkle it as seasoning on whatever we fancy or whenever we feel like it. In fact, ethics is not arbitrary precisely because, far from becoming whatever or wherever we want it to be, its core remains solidly anchored to practices and realities with strong normative qualities. Ethics is certainly much more, but, absent this mainstay, it would be meaningless to discuss ethical norms in human practices.

Pluralism and Objectivity: The Debate on Human Cloning

Moral reflection entails a multilayered effort of reasoning and justification. Describing a situation or grasping its pertinent traits in view of moral evaluation already involves associating a neutral act (enumerating traits) and a discerning activity, because description presupposes a prior distinction between pertinent traits and nonpertinent ones, as well as a choice of perspective from which to proceed. A minimally complex description already requires a normative commitment. The intellectual requirement to represent reality in its richest and most interesting aspects also has a normative value. To the extent that we can find—among the multiple traits of a situation—those which are conducive to deliberation and will justify making a decision, we will be able to keep less relevant traits in the background only if we make a conscious effort in this respect while realizing that the deliberation and decision process will end up retaining only a few of them. The same requirement to describe reality in the most nuanced manner possible leads to willfully maintaining a pluralism as rich as possible. Finally, the concern for knowledge that sustains the will to describe the reality surrounding human action in the most complete fashion possible materializes in the determination to show how the normativity of action relates to reality. This requires not only grasping the situation as seen by the agent but also anticipating the plausible consequences of his action and their possible effect on the actual definition of his action, and on his cognitive, motivational, and affective states after carrying out that action. The ability to grasp the multiple aspects of reality is an important factor in understanding the normativity of action and justifying it. The last point on which normativity links intellectual activity to morality is the requirement that any action being carried out by a given agent, toward certain persons, and in a determined context must provide its reasons and justifications. Justification consists in finding reasons for an act. Without it, the rationality of human action or its objectivity would be inconceivable.[34]

Normative analysis often reveals complex and finely nuanced realities that present multiple, heterogeneous, and sometimes conflicting dimensions. In life and literature, the perception of a problem's multiple moral components, or of their opposing each other in dilemmas, is a common occurrence. The contentions and conflicts discussed here are indicative not only of the usual uncertainty about what must be done but also of the real heterogeneity that marks duties and sources of morality alike. Not all philosophers readily acknowledge the existence of such dilemmas. Some object that moral conflicts are only apparently so and that by formulating conflicting imperatives in a more precise manner, it becomes possible to find a common dimension (for instance, by judging these imperatives by their conformity to moral law or by their consequences). Yet, negating the existence of moral conflicts goes against our experience of life situations in which we are asking ourselves what could be done. The phenomenon described as "value fragmentation" takes us back to the heterogeneity of our moral experience and its various components: universal and impersonal duties, consequences to be assumed, special consideration to be given to those closest to us, and values of personal fulfillment. Attempts at organizing such value sources into a fixed hierarchy are doomed to failure.

In this context, it is fitting to emphasize not only the importance of moral dilemmas and to recognize the plurality of moral dimensions, whether conflicting or not, but also the need for such plurality to last beyond the decision point.[35] When after serious consideration a particular moral dimension becomes the prevalent one, this does not mean that the others would simply disappear; they usually continue to reflect real aspects of a moral situation, although those are temporarily inactivated during the final stage of deliberation. What proves their lasting quality, however, is the fact that even when such dimensions are not considered before a decision is taken, one can still justifiably regret to find oneself in a situation that made their consideration impossible. Besides, their temporary inactivation can be partial, so that they continue to make their presence felt by putting up a certain resistance: the defense of freedom may come in conflict with the search for justice, but the legitimacy of aspiring to justice does not devalue the defense of freedom. Moreover, it is not always easy to find a dominant consideration. Situational analysis involves secondary principles or considerations that may block deliberation for a short while, either by prevailing over others or by silencing them. In such a case, conflicting status is neutralized without being suppressed. Therefore, the interests, perceptions, knowledge, concerns, requirements, and principles that are gradually revealed during situational analysis cannot be said to form a closed system. Rather, their system presents a variable geometry that allows for its distortion and reshaping as understanding progresses.

Emphasizing the importance of pluralistic values does not mean embracing relativism or putting all values on equal footing. The strength of a pluralistic point of view resides in its affirmation of the objectivity of values and duties. Individual tastes and preferences do not lead to a definition of values. Values are not shaped by individuals; they impose themselves on individuals. The fact that changing viewpoints do not necessarily soften such conflicts creates a biconditional demand: one must acknowledge the conflicting values as a basis for deliberation and justification; at the same time, one has to identify the values in play, knowing that, when weighting is impossible, a moral decision inspired by dominant values will have to settle the conflict.

When the cloning of the sheep Dolly was announced in February 1997, the public debate in response to the news gave rise to a search for a decisive moral argument against reproductive human cloning. Official declarations and recommendations published at the time were adamant: reproductive human cloning must be permanently banned because it demeans human dignity. Nevertheless, a few authors objected by suggesting that cloning could fill a real need in exceptional or tragic situations, such as when both members of a couple are afflicted by sterility or a terminally ill child could be saved only by a bone marrow transplant from his own clone. They stressed that—considering the serious and exceptional character of such cases—reproductive cloning should not only be allowed but justified by important moral aspirations such as the desire to start a family or to save the life of a dying child.

In this type of situation, there is a widespread public discomfort that a possibly justified demand comes in conflict with the instinctive response that recourse to cloning is morally problematic even in exceptional cases. Such a discomfort, however, is not decisive because it enables reflection and encourages attempts to identify those values that would be eroded by such practice. In my view, respect for human dignity is not the value that would be most endangered by reproductive cloning in exceptional cases. For the time being, lawyers and philosophers do not seem to have shown precisely in what way cloning practiced in such cases would radically undermine human dignity. Clearly, a person's dignity is not determined by the manner in which one was conceived (whether by impregnation, artificial insemination, or somatic cell nuclear transfer). It is hard to see how the fact of having been conceived via somatic cell nuclear transfer technology instead of the old-fashioned way would deprive a person of his or her humanity, when every human being has rights for being born human and a dignity deserving of respect. It is also difficult to understand how one's moral status would be affected by having been cloned. Therefore, reproductive cloning does not put at risk values such as the dignity of the human species or the integrity of mankind's genetic inheritance, at least not in a direct or obvious manner.

Nevertheless, there is in our moral culture a fundamental value that would be directly affected by the practice of reproductive cloning. This value relates to our defense of negative freedom and concerns the necessity to protect a person from another's meddling. In order to clone a human being, a nucleus must be chosen for transfer, and with it, a genome is selected for reproduction. If we assume that one's genome, that is, genetic identity, is an intrinsic determination of one's personality, the clone would be right to consider that at least one aspect of his individuality is the product of somebody else's deliberation, because that somebody has decided what the clone's individuality will be. The decision is both negative and positive. Somebody else has decided not only whether an individual will exist (as is the case with classical birth) but also what exactly a cloned individual's genetic identity will be. In this case, the value we assign to negative freedom as rejection of another person's interference will certainly be infringed upon by reproductive cloning. The clone could legitimately object to being denied the right to an open future by having a positive determination of his personality imposed upon him by someone else. It does not matter whether the imposed personality is perfection incarnate, or whether he was cloned from Einstein or Marilyn Monroe. What matters is that at least to a certain extent, the cloned individual has been the object of someone else's deliberation.[36] We are witnessing here a conflict between expectations or requirements that may have true moral significance and values concerning the respect and integrity of individual persons. Thus formulated, the conflict of values cannot have a favorable outcome for negative freedom. No requirement, however morally justified, can ever transgress the value of negative freedom. Far from being a matter of personal self-regard, this concerns the objective resistance of such a value—one that no relativism or perspectivism could ever configure differently.

Justification and Moral Theories

At first sight, it may seem contradictory to delve into the plurality of justifying reasons while arguing for the objectivity of best justifications, because the search for objectivity often occurs in tandem with that for a unique justification, rather than multiple best ones. Arguably, the view I attempt to promote here might lead to a "competitive" concept of objectivity based on the selection of best reasons. True, epistemological questions are being debated frequently in moral philosophy, but they tend to justify moral beliefs rather than seek their truth value (after all, some well-justified beliefs may lack truth value). Should we justify new beliefs by grounding them in more basic beliefs having axiomatic status such that ulterior moral judgments derive their own truth value from those preceding them, or should we opt instead for a consistency-driven model, whereby the truth value of a given belief hinges on that of all others so long as the resulting whole remains contradiction-free. This would ensure that the truthfulness or objectivity of a moral belief could never be determined in isolation. The either-or debate pitting proponents of the precedent-based justification model against advocates of the consistency-driven one is much prized in philosophical circles. Regrettably, though, such debates also tend to take on a life of their own, thus obscuring the very problem they were intended to solve.

I am pleading here for a nimbler approach to justification. The possible reformulations of the precedent-based approach have already been duly investigated and could be summarized thusly: basic beliefs are refutable, the precedent-based model is fallible, and justifications may be grounded not only in beliefs but also in justified feelings, emotional experiences, and the like. For instance, it is not unreasonable to agree that the fitting quality of the loathing I feel in the face of an intrinsically evil reality may help justify my moral beliefs. The consistency-driven approach could also bear substantial revision. But why should we remain confined to either one of these options instead of resorting to all available means of justification when attempting to account realistically for a complex situation that involves multiple sources of morality, principles, and values? A widely framed interpretation of moral beliefs that includes the refutability of justifications could very well allow for axiomatic beliefs and strong affective states to articulate justifications. Consistency-driven components could also blend in this mix. In addition, situational grounding and moral reflection could play their part in the search for best reasons and moral justification. In any case, accounting for heterogeneity and confliction is often a prerequisite of moral objectivity. A dynamic, nondoctrinal approach to justification should be able to structure and advance the arguments and reasons in its favor, most of which may have been strengthened by answers to objections previously leveled at them. It is on this condition that decisions and ethical enjoinders will be predicated, not on dogmas, abstract principles, or authoritarian say-so, but on robust deliberation and open-mode justification.

There is nothing new in this kind of association between vision and reasoning. Plato and Aristotle were already discussing it, and it is still well represented in contemporary philosophy. It clearly opposes a simplistic view of moral theory. The fact that we use a theoretical frame in moral deliberation does not necessarily make us inflexible, blind, or insensitive to the particular problems, moral conflicts, or complexities of moral existence. It is also true that moral objectivity can be achieved without acknowledged inspiration from an "official" moral theory such as Kantianism, consequentialism, ethics of virtue, and the like. Theories in themselves often present less problems than the rigid use to which they are put. Theories are not always set collections of proven assertions derived from a unique and infallible principle. A theory may be the product of harmonized beliefs, some of those resulting from reflection on principles and some others from emotional responses. Moral theories are not necessarily doctrinal, based on a unique principle or likely to undergo irrefutable justification. Quite to the contrary, they could be used as a critical resource against attempts to elevate customs or casual circumstances to the status of an indisputable foundation of morality. I support an approach that opposes the caricatured use of moral theory and resists the temptation to mistake the casual or the customary for unique sources of legitimacy. The return to a familiar world is beneficial if it helps open a pathway to reality and if it remains an option among others. However, if it pretends to represent the ultimate philosophical approach, it should be ranked among the doctrines that prevent the thoughtful search for best reasons, as it would stymie the efforts to explain and elucidate reality and would drain the resources of critical thought.

Ethical Reflection and Freethinking

The relevance of a critical evaluation mind-set as a prerequisite for ethical reflection cannot be emphasized enough. Only such a mind-set can ensure the clarity of vision, the search for reasons, and the ability to grasp plurality and to pursue objectivity that are all so much needed in ethical reflection. This mind-set is shaped by the ability to distance oneself from the object of reflection while paying attention to a plurality of viewpoints. Being able to build up a strong and productive critical mind-set is a highly regarded intellectual virtue. The critical mind-set is vital for gauging rough data before analysis can begin and for pinpointing unjustified arguments as well as views of the group-think variety. Critical thinking requires the ability to discern reality from its look-alikes, the strength to resist dogmas or self-proclaimed "authorities," and the mental fortitude to adopt another view or a different stance and to change one's outlook or perspective of investigation. Being able to perceive the multiple elements of a given reality greatly facilitates every step of a critical thought process. The critical mind-set also includes an element of self-criticism for one's own thinking: not self-denigration but permanent awareness of the possibility of having to rectify one's own judgments, decisions, and reasons. In order for this possibility to be available, the multiple elements of a situation must not only be perceived but be ready for use.

Another basic prerequisite of ethics is to strive for a complete independence of mind when considering a given situation. In the initial stage of reasoning, all hypotheses should be envisaged and all possible counterscenarios imagined. Farfetched hypotheses can often improve intelligibility, especially when it comes to pinpointing the most pertinent moral traits of a case. This stage of moral reasoning calls for imagination and creativity. Therefore, reflection must not be inhibited by concerns for propriety. It is, of course, to be wished that these preliminary stages of reflection remain private: making them public could prove harmful because it might blur the line between deliberative rationality, on the one hand, and decision or action, on the other. Moreover, the common response to excessive or counterfactual hypotheses is to promptly resort to guilt by association through analogies to catastrophic events, so as to show that—intentionally or not—such ideas can serve only nefarious ends. Independence of mind is thus denied: the holders of such ideas are berated for having accepted beforehand what they are supposed to debate; also, the value of laborious reasoning and justifying is dismissed in spite of it alone being able to distinguish good reasons from bad ones.[37] Reflection in moral philosophy must be protected from two constant threats: witch-hunts conducted by accusations of malevolent premeditation and hasty, baseless analogies whose deterrent effect is eagerly anticipated.[38]

So much philosophy, one may think, for simply attempting to define an activity—moral reflection or deliberation—that human beings carry out in almost every aspect of their lives and that plays a crucial part in all things allowing us to recognize and empathize with representations of human acts in real life, literature, and cinema. The kind of philosophy that I defend is grounded in rationality and argumentation. Moral justification is unattainable without constant rationalizing. Moral rationalism grants an essential role to intellectual efforts that produce a vision of reality by seeking the best reasons and allowing for the critical evaluation of personal and cultural factors (one's interests and soft spots, strong beliefs, stereotypes, and polemic stances) that might befog reality.

This is not at all meant to lessen the importance of emotions and dispositions. For, what would be the meaning of morality in a world such as the one envisioned by Ridley Scott in the movie *Blade Runner*, inhabited by beings displaying all our mental capacities but lacking our emotional characteristics? It may seem strange to associate emotion and objectivity, but this is perfectly justified when trying to find out the role of emotion in moral cognition—one of the most widely debated topics in contemporary philosophy. The idea that emotions invariably disrupt an otherwise objective ethical understanding of reality is simply a philosophical archaism. A much more likely idea would be to accept that certain emotions pave the way for objective understanding, that they help enhance particular traits of the situation under consideration and contribute to a better grasp of their interconnections. Nothing could facilitate comprehension more than the feeling of indignation or injustice that overwhelms us in certain situations. Our evaluation of such a situation will be unaffected by our feelings, nor will it be validated by our emotions. Nonetheless, these emotions enable our understanding of it by showing it in an ethically interesting light. The intellectual effort put in moral reflection also requires questioning whether the feeling is appropriate or justified. In most cases a critical evaluation of emotions is warranted, but denying the role of emotions in our ethical orientation toward the world would be tantamount to depriving ourselves of an essential ethical resource.[39]

Confusing Ethics and Democracy

The demand for ethics is always firmly asserted, although it sometimes lacks clarity of purpose. In France, it is publicly voiced by ethics committees and human-rights bodies whose members are either co-opted or designated. This selection process is not entirely adequate, but what would be the alternative? Elections would certainly not do, because the representativeness of interests and beliefs makes little sense in ethics. As for drawing lots, the very idea is absurd. Normally the selection process seeks a certain kind of competence that, in the case of ethics committees, is not clearly outlined but nevertheless seems to implicitly guide their selection of new members. Regardless of the reasons that govern this process, it is strikingly obvious that, in France's ethics committees, most members have no particular interests to protect or lobbying priorities to advance, and they do not promote their privately held moral opinions. Rather, they feel duty-bound to issue recommendations based on careful evaluation of data pertaining to the problem at hand and a clear understanding of its possible consequences. Committee-issued views are only marginally influenced by abstract, theoretical considerations or affirmations of principle, whereas in-committee deliberations focus on case analysis, question-specificity tracking, perspective outlining, and assessment of counterfactual hypotheses. To the extent that these French committees contribute to ethical reflection, it is necessary to grant them the time, funds, and information needed for their operation and, above all, ensure their impartiality and independence.

Is there a contradiction in terms between the fact that ethical reflection is carried out in ethical committees and the often-stated demand that moral deliberation be carried out democratically? Increasingly, democratic debate is called upon to solve ethical problems, while expert advice is relegated to research interests or viewed as factual, nonnormative opinion. It is often said that final decisions must rest with political entities and that, ideally, they should be inspired and supported by publicly held democratic debate. A few comments spring to mind on this topic. First, the ideal requirement of public debate is hard to translate into concrete reality. Beyond the obvious organizational difficulties, it is clear that public debate cannot be achieved without delegation and representation or without safeguards for true pluralism, that is, one that is not confined to doctrines and interests but extends to the diversity created by a plurality of moral sources and values. Moreover, if moral deliberation must be carried out in public, then ideally it should be distinguishable from two other forms of decision making: bargaining and negotiation. In an ideal public debate, one knowingly assumes a perspective allowing for the revision, transformation, and improvement of one's beliefs and convictions. This does not give one leave to impose a particular belief over all others, or to use it as a blocking subterfuge. Rather, it requires a sincere commitment to seek the best reasons and justifications of one's decision. Without such a commitment, public ethical deliberation is impossible.

Public debate on ethical topics is an ideal whose inherent complications cannot be ignored. For instance, it must fulfill seemingly contradictory requirements: on the one hand, it must flesh out the best reasons; on the other, it must stay close to public opinion sensitivities. Yet the latter forces the recourse to procedures such as reflexive balance and building consensus from heterogeneous convictions, both of which do not always coincide with the normal practice of ethical reflection. Another complication comes from the fact that more often than not the conclusion of critical examination is an acknowledgment of disagreement, whereas public debate seeking to reach political decisions strongly recommends consensus-based conclusions. Lastly, concepts and arguments used for seeking reasons in discovery-driven deliberations cannot be used always in justification-oriented ones. Specifically, moral evaluation of issues requires factual information, scientific data, and real expertise, whereas a public debate aspiring to solve a problem democratically tends to discard such requirements rather arbitrarily as an interference of science in democracy. These comments make one wonder if there is not something terribly wrong with the arbitrary distinction between expertise and ethical public debate, or at least something in stark contrast with my attempts in this essay. In my view, it is necessary that elements of scientific evaluation give substance to democratic debate. Without their real if limited value, such debate will fast sink into obscurantism. For this reason, the link between democratic debate and moral reflection should be treated as a challenge, not as a given. More to the point, democracy should not serve as an excuse for the absence of moral reflection. Difficult ethical questions should not be abandoned to the clash of opinions and interests, which is the realm of democracy.

Two conclusions can be drawn from these remarks. The first underlines the necessary role that intermediate instances play in a democracy: they make possible a public debate that integrates elements of real expertise while constantly leaning back against moral reflection. The second concerns the obligation—when the debate cannot be conducted entirely in the public eye—to make its issues and reasons known. In this respect, the members of French ethical committees have a very clear duty: whenever possible, they must conduct an open debate and justify their recommendations; their work must never appear to be inspired by an alleged moral expertise that is used as proof of authority, but must be always accompanied by public justifications and qualified conclusions. In other words, their recommendations must be the product of ethical reflection. In turn, ethical reflection shows its utility for public debate to the degree that it provides explanations and justifications on committee recommendations, thus enabling citizens to evaluate them in an informed and precise manner. True democratic oversight rejects the insidious moral paternalism that claims to know what is good for people better than they know themselves.

Let us not make this use of ethics into yet another expression of the yearning for solace. Rather, let us make it into a resource for reflection and action. Nobody needs another ethics-seasoned sprinkling of self-righteous humanism in order to understand the moral issues of our time. What we need is reflection, deliberation, and well-justified recommendations, not hasty regulations; it is democratic involvement, not peremptory announcements or pledges inspired by ideological commitment. It seems to me that, faced with such a wave of interest for ethics, those who profess to provide an adequate response should try to transcend the immediate need of regulations and codes of behavior by encouraging reflection on their sometimes entwined, and even conflicting, values. A major question remains unanswered: how can ethical reflection live on in a civil society? The answer would take into account factors such as the recognized value of public debate, the acknowledgment of a diversified world, and the chance for citizens to shape, criticize, and evaluate their understanding of goodness. Ethical reflection can certainly play an important role in creating a public space if it is undertaken by the citizenry.

Ethics without Solace

I would rather see the term "ethics" being used carefully than complacently. There is much to gain in replacing the simple expression of good intentions with a complex reflection on morality. In the absence of a clear vision or critical understanding of a situation, naive optimism and good-will—the idea that, if one wants to do something, it would be a good thing in any case—can very well have the worst consequences. In such a situation, one may be tempted to ignore the fact that bad things often accompany a good outcome and that unexpected consequences may cause a good outcome to later generate a few bad results. What is doubtful on a deeper plane is the idea that one can realize things that could be described uniformly and indisputably as good. Attentiveness toward the plurality of moral dimensions begets cautious consideration of the risks to attain outcomes that are different or even contrary to the ones expected, if seemingly lesser factors had been ignored that afterward proved their relevance. Working out reasons and justifications for actions requires many detours through what is seen as different from good or as downright bad.

My preceding remarks show some of the pitfalls to be avoided. First to avoid is hollow language—declaring to be involved in ethics while abstaining from doing anything about it, taking all meaning out of terms such as "good," "bad," and especially "ethics." Next to be avoided is misreading the specificity of moral reflection, which albeit not juridical, scientific, or sociologic, does integrate contributions from science, law, and social studies. Also to be avoided is arrogance—making statements supposed to reflect one's ethical expertise without explaining the nature and duties of such expertise. After that, one must avoid ethical bigotry—proclaiming values without providing explanations or justifications on their account, without questioning the true nature of the situations under consideration, yet loudly criticizing everything else. Finally to be avoided is the fetishism of particular norms—multiplying the rules and constraints of action without considering the ethical reflection from which they proceed. We have no other term than "ethics" to justify "norms." It should not be used abusively lest the norms would lose their meaning. Careless usage of the term "ethics" and peremptory say-so in ethical matters can only invite skepticism. Both ignore the fact that ethics is not a gimmick or an incantatory formula and that almost anyone can carry out ethical reflection.[40]

Can we still take ethics seriously? Is it still possible to defend the seriousness, the importance, and the consistency of moral reflection? The reason I criticize the trite use of "ethics" is that it comes down as a conclusion in the debate on moral reflection rather than as an opening statement for such a debate. It is for the same reason that I criticize ethical grandstanding and rule fetishism. There are just a few fundamental moral principles, but a serious commitment is expected from those who abide by them. True, rules are a necessary part of moral reflection. But the act of issuing a rule has never replaced such reflection. Rather, it incites to further the search for normativity; to develop a form of moral orientation whereby beliefs, emotions, and motives for action play a valid role; and, above all, to strengthen intellectual and critical approaches to ethics that ensure its beneficial influence. This is not a minimalist stance on ethical matters. It is a maximalist standing in matters concerning criticism, reflection, and cautious application of principles; it is a blend of realism toward values and their fallibility, strong moral rationality, practical reasoning, and a critically minded search for justifications.

Thought is our main resource for practicing ethics. We should never forget that at times it acquires a tragic dimension. But how can we presume that we can shape our morals without risks or losses? Modern Western morality is mostly inherited from ancient Greece and Judeo-Christian thought. The Greeks persuaded us of the omnipotence of virtue, of the possibility to attain moral autonomy through reasoning and learning. The Judeo-Christian tradition subjects the human being to God's law and places the individual in a world of fellow human beings. Coming from such a tradition, how could moral philosophy be free from tensions and conflicts?

Ethics is not for solace. Nor is it a seasoning sprinkled on the reality of our institutions, practices, and ways of life to make them more palatable to us. There are many things with which ethics has nothing to do, but there also are some others in relation to which speaking about ethics must be followed by action. The worst slight to morality is to speak about ethics without critical reflection. It usually starts with highbrow moralizing about others and benevolent complacency about one's own certitudes. Nietzsche's *The Gay Science* defines very well the challenge we face. Are we capable of a morality that is not a matter of doctrine, law, or propriety? The intellectual resources that will allow us to face the future depend in part on the seriousness of our response to it.

CHAPTER 3

French Moral Philosophy and
Its Past Misfortunes

THE STATUS of moral philosophy in France was affected to a certain extent by its twentieth-century history, more specifically, by the period of neglect it went through from the 1950s to the 1980s and the incomplete, controversial revival it witnessed in the 1990s. The present—and rather superficial—infatuation with ethics has the same cause as its previous disregard: the lack of interest for serious moral reflection. The study of recent developments in French moral philosophy shows that long-winded moralizing can not only thrive in the absence of any kind of moral philosophy but also arouse public suspicions against philosophy. For this reason, the study of moral philosophy's recent past in France is quite instructive.

What made it possible for this discipline to have been almost totally wiped out from the French intellectual landscape? Before analyzing this phenomenon, and in order to better understand how strange it seems today, let us briefly review the status of moral philosophy in France at the turn of the twentieth century, fifty years before its quasi extinction. Between the end of the nineteenth century and the First World War, moral reflection in France developed into a rich and diversified field of research that played a decisive role in the birth and growth of the French philosophical community and its institutions.

A Philosophical Revival: French Moral

Philosophy in the Early 1900s

The widely held belief that philosophy developed continuously and without major changes from the end of the eighteenth century to World War I is inaccurate. The fact is that between 1880 and 1895, prosperous national philosophical communities sprang into existence in both Europe and the United States. Furthermore, by the end of the 1890s a strong philosophical community was built at the international level, which has no parallel today in spite of the contemporary advances in communications. This assertion may seem excessive, but the facts support it.

Between 1885 and 1895, the main institutions for the expression of philosophical ideas were put in place in France: societies and clubs, on the one hand; journals, periodicals, and information bulletins, on the other. In a few years, philosophical studies were created in French universities, thus confirming philosophy as a professional activity. This is not to say that until that moment, there had been no published articles on philosophy, or that philosophers had not known each other or communicated among themselves. The movement of ideas cannot be contested: scholars had been corresponding with Descartes from all over Europe; Leibniz had been on the road most of his life, and French philosophy had been influenced by English and Scottish thinkers before it discovered German philosophy. Yet until the end of the nineteenth century, philosophical contributions had not been published in specialized journals but in critical reviews and cultural publications.[1] Also, meetings and exchanges among philosophers had been informal, not institutionalized.

The year 1893 was a watershed in international philosophy: most of the great philosophical reviews were founded within a few months from each other, including *La Revue de métaphysique et de morale* (*RMM*), which soon became the voice of French philosophical revival and an open international forum.[2]

The young founders of the *RMM*, Xavier Léon and Élie Halévy, were motivated by the desire to "bring to public attention the general theories of thought and action, which—under the label 'metaphysics'—are the only source of rational beliefs."[3] They feared that "philosophy has lost its standing and its influence in France when the eclecticism of Victor Cousin became the philosophy of the State." They deemed it necessary "to throw the light of reason on the middle-road between fact-limited positivism and superstition-prone mysticism." Their formulation had an immediate international resonance. They reminded the readership that "being tired of hearing constant praises of the inexhaustible productivity of German thinkers, the delightful British wit and the originality of American philosophers, the founders the *RMM* wanted to encourage the development of philosophical thought in France, hoping to make it obvious that French thought is second to none."[4]

RMM's regular contributors were the stars of French philosophy of the time, Henri Bergson,[5] Léon Brunschvicg, Louis Couturat, Henri Poincaré, Élie Halévy, Victor Delbos, Gabriel Tarde, Louis Weber, George Sorel,[6] Alfred Fouillée, and Émile Durkheim,[7] as well as important foreign thinkers, MacTaggart, Bertrand Russell, and Frege.[8] The *RMM* also published well-argued reviews, some of which were strongly critical.[9] Lively debates on much-disputed viewpoints were published in successive issues.[10] Obituaries published in the *RMM* were almost never simply respectful toward the deceased; instead, their influence was assessed with the kind of clear-headedness that comes from the conviction that one witnesses the beginnings of a new philosophical age and therefore can discern outdated contributions from what will really matter in the philosophy of the future.[11] Another item of interest in each issue was the column dedicated to the teaching of philosophy at university, which—in the editors' words—"is the best way of informing the public on the movement of ideas in our country."[12]

At about the same time, similar trends of philosophical revival and institutionalization became discernible in several European countries and the United States. In Great Britain, the journal *Mind* adopted a new format in 1892, which is still in circulation. The Mind Association and the Aristotelian Society were established shortly afterward and were followed by the first philosophical clubs. From then on, general-interest reviews such as the *Contemporary Review* and the *Fortnightly Review* all but ceased publication of philosophical articles. This trend was strengthened by the reform of English universities at the end of the nineteenth century.[13] Much like the *RMM*, the *Mind* regularly offered summaries of all important articles published in foreign periodicals, which confirms the impressive diversity of philosophical orientations displayed by its editors.[14]

In Germany, philosophical publications had had a head start over the rest of Europe. The *Zeitschrift für Philosophie und philosophische Kritik*, founded by Fichte, was competing with *Kantstudien*, founded in 1896, and even more with *Archiv für Geschichte der Philosophie*, founded in 1895, as well as *Archiv der Systematische Philosophie*, where Frege was to publish his first articles on logic. The *Jahrbuch für phänomenologische Forschung* published its first issue in 1913. In Italy, the *Rivista italiana di filosofia* was also founded at the end of the nineteenth century. But the most striking example is provided by the United States. With the creation of the *Journal of Speculative Philosophy* in 1867, its editors wished to help establish a philosophical community that would be truly American.[15] Their wish was fulfilled in 1893 with the creation of the *Philosophical Review*, whose first issue comprised works by John Dewey, William James, and Frederick Schiller and which proclaimed its fervent hope for a glorious future.[16] In 1890 Paul Carus founded *The Monist*, which was followed three years later by the *International Journal of Ethics* (shortened to *Ethics* in 1938.)

French philosophical journals, starting with the *RMM*, were unusually well informed about philosophical developments outside of France. Each issue abounded in synoptic articles on the main philosophical currents in Europe.[17] The teaching of philosophy in the United Kingdom and Germany was regularly described.[18] The influence of German thought, in particular of Schopenhauer and neo-Kantianism, was very strong on French moral philosophy, but so was the interest for English thinking, including

English idealism, empiricism, and utilitarianism.[19] French philosophers paid attention to the divergent interpretations of Kantianism, neo-Kantianism, and Hegelianism that divided English and German philosophers. They noticed with great perspicacity that English moral philosophy, influenced since 1870 by Kant and Hegel, experienced at the end of the nineteenth century a return to empiricism that heralded the later analytical philosophy.[20] They also described various controversies fueled by the development of psychology and by German psychologism.[21] Another burning issue was the interpretation of the aims of social sciences in Germany and France.[22] The participation of Russell, Poincaré, and Couturat in the debate on the philosophy of science attracted considerable attention. At the time, one could find at the heart of philosophy questions about social issues, socialism, and women's access to higher education that today belong to the "societal" category. The editors of the *RMM* were eagerly seeking and publicizing philosophical novelties, but they had no qualms about criticizing some of them.[23]

In most cases, the development of philosophical communities was accompanied by the search of a national philosophical identity. But while many late nineteenth-century thinkers believed that national cultural traits help shape a philosophical identity illustrated by a few great names, they also knew that the philosophical milieu is partly shaped by "second-tier authors" who often express most strikingly the dominant ideas of a national tradition. Yet the "philosophical nationalism" displayed at the turn of the century was not overwhelming, as the countries claiming a national identity were themselves going through some form of philosophical birth or revival. Such was the case for France and the United States. Also, it bears mentioning that national distinctions seemed much more clear-cut in sociology and psychology than in philosophy: there was a "German sociology," a "German psychology," a "French psychology," and an "American psychology," whereas in philosophy, national tradition was more often than not a matter for retrospective definition.

The International Congress in Philosophy, August 1900

The International Congress in Philosophy held in Paris from 1–5 August 1900, was the first in a long series of international philosophical meetings that still take place every four years.[24] In his opening remarks on 1 August 1900, Émile Boutroux gave voice to the hopes that French moral philosophy nursed at the time.[25] He contended that the need for a vibrant international philosophical community was brought about by an internal transformation of philosophy that started in the 1860s, when philosophy drew closer to science while continuing to assert its autonomy. Before that, "the debates that the bold dialectic constructs of Schelling and Hegel had stirred up in philosophy and science caused dissension between these orders of knowledge." Nobody, he added, was able to find a middle way "between a philosophy excluded from science and a philosophy fully dependent on it." In the practice of their profession, some philosophers believed that they possessed "in their individual consciences, all necessary conditions for philosophical research" (thus rendering superfluous any encounter among philosophers); some others believed in a kind of philosophy that subjects itself to science, and for which it becomes necessary to bring together "professional scientists, not pure philosophers."

Boutroux observed that philosophical studies must increasingly share the fate of natural sciences and seek a truth that is "universal to human beings, not relative to an individual spirit." Philosophy needs "to collect, compare, control, and evaluate from all angles as many facts as possible, and as much knowledge as possible." To a certain extent, philosophy must contribute to "the law of scientific development," which is "progress through division of labor and convergence of efforts through organized research. The impressive advances in communication achieved in our century make possible a much more sophisticated intertwining of minds than was ever conceivable in the past."

The minutes of the debates conducted during the first congress show that international cooperation among philosophers was a high desideratum.[26] This is confirmed by the resolve to take into consideration the contributions of minor authors in addition to those of great philosophers. The first volume of the proceedings published in the *RMM* contains an article stating: "Philosophy constantly aspires to unity. At least from time to time, it is to be hoped that such aspiration will find as much satisfaction from the systems created by the despotic genius of individual thinkers, as from the collective creations of workers that have agreed to unite their efforts, thus smoothing out their divergences."[27] The need for cooperative philosophical work also explains the creation in France of a Société de philosophie with the explicit goal to "find a solution for the dispersal of philosophical works by establishing a communication and information center" to facilitate "exchanges among thinkers in order to clarify problems and outline possible solutions."[28] In Louis Couturat's words, "We are hereby witnessing the realization of a dream that Leibniz nursed for a long time: the creation of an international association of academies."[29]

What are the consequences of this philosophical renewal for the social standing of moral philosophy? Compared to usual practices in moral philosophy at the beginning of the twentieth century, the International Congress was different in three ways: it encouraged open debate, it emphasized commonly shared philosophical issues, and it took a problem-solving approach to philosophical conflicts. The school of thought to which a philosopher belonged did not dispense his critics from taking seriously his arguments. All participants shared the conviction that there were common philosophical problems awaiting solutions. Notwithstanding participants' positions on specific moral philosophy issues, no one doubted the actual existence of such issues or the possibility of agreeing, at least to a certain extent, on unified definitions for them. An energizing "can do" attitude prevailed; thus, during the first session, Bergson interrupted the speakers time after time, to help them realize their agreement on essential points.[30] The recognition of the primacy of philosophical issues over personal stances helped to establish a sense of unity.

In this new atmosphere, French philosophers seemed less intent to confine themselves to their own philosophical traditions and more interested in taking a stance with regard to topical philosophical issues in theoretical and applied research. For instance, philosophical reflection applied to moral issues could draw as much from Durkheim's writings on social philosophy as from moral philosophy writings. Moreover, societal problems received as much attention from philosophers as did various political issues of the period. New issues were tackled, such as the taxation system and the education of women. Toward the end of the congress, after a presentation by Gaston Mach on world peace, a draft resolution was submitted to participants in support of maintaining peace and reducing weapons. The move was defeated, but the participants declared their resolve to serve peace "by working together to bring about an age of reason and . . . and to develop intellectual and personal relations among participants from various countries that ensure their mutual respect and friendship." The congress of 1900 and those that followed were seen less as attempts to stop wars than as signals that wars would not be allowed to happen.

During the next decades, the challenge issued by the young founders of the *RMM* was taken up, and French philosophy witnessed a rationalist revival that marked one of the brightest periods of its history. On this, it can be favorably compared with English, American, and German philosophy of that period. By the end of the 1950s though, a state of affairs that the first congress wanted to put an end to in 1900 came back with a vengeance. A mixture of positivism and mysticism, of platitudes and grandstanding became again the menace to open and stable rationalism that has been haunting time and again French philosophical culture.

French Moral Philosophy in the First Half of the
Twentieth Century: A Dwindling Discipline

Let us now switch to France in the mid-1960s, when, in French universities at least, moral philosophy was represented by only a few outstanding figures. Their writings were noteworthy but failed to incite the kind of philosophical cooperation sought by the philosophers of the 1900s. By then, other countries had witnessed massive changes and a complete renewal of moral philosophy, while in France moral philosophy entered a period of slow decay rarely seen before. The discipline was still acknowledged to exist but only as a second-tier one, or as an application of a general philosophical orientation such as phenomenology or existentialism. Studies on the specificity of moral philosophy had all but disappeared. With rare exceptions, French works had no influence on the advance of moral philosophy. In the intellectually ebullient France of the 1900s, nothing presaged such an outcome.

Why? What happened in the meantime? What exactly had France missed? The answer requires a brief detour through the history of moral philosophy during the first decades of the twentieth century, before dealing with the radical transformation that moral philosophy underwent forty years ago.

Many people agree that G. E. Moore's *Principia Ethica* (1903) radically changed moral philosophy.[31] Moore defended the idea that ethics is an autonomous branch of philosophy, whose object is the study of terms such as "goodness" and "fairness" and predicates such as "good" and "just." According to him, the properties designated by such terms are specific and distinct from either natural or supernatural properties. The requirement that morality be considered in and of itself is therefore based on the specificity of moral predicates. To the extent that moral properties form a specific order of reality, morality could never be likened to science, the study of nature, the analysis of desires, or metaphysics. Moore's ideas on the autonomy of morality are not entirely without precedent.[32] He gave, however, new meaning to those ideas by emphasizing the singularity of moral language. For the first time in the history of modern philosophy, the study of ethics was set free from the tutelage of a global conception of philosophy and assigned its own field of investigation.

The effort to analyze the language of morals has shaped the whole history of moral philosophy in the twentieth century. Before attempting to deal with content-related questions of morality, moral philosophy had to examine the definition and usage of the basic concepts in its field. G. E. Moore defined his method as "trying to get really clear as to what on earth a given philosopher meant by something which he said, and . . . discovering what really satisfactory reasons there are for supposing that what he meant was true, or alternatively, was false."[33] The study of the logical and linguistic conditions of morals has been appropriately designated by the term "meta-ethics." In the United Kingdom, it attracted important thinkers like Alfred Ayer, whose emotive theory of ethics was inspired by logical positivism, and Richard Hare, the defender of a prescriptive approach to the language of morals.[34] In Austria, the dominant approach to meta-ethics during the first decades of the twentieth century was linked to the Vienna Circle, as shown by Moritz Schlick in his *Problems of Ethics*.[35] In the United States, Charles Stevenson's *Ethics and Language* was hailed as the manifesto of emotivism.[36] Meta-ethics was far from being an exclusively British project and—judging by its effect on philosophical traditions in other countries—its weak resonance in France is quite perplexing.

These developments had a considerable influence on the history of moral philosophy in Germany during the first half of the twentieth century. First and foremost, the theories of the Vienna Circle and of logical positivism—postulating that moral judgments, being nonanalytical and unempirical, cannot aspire to truthfulness or objectivity—greatly influenced developments in meta-ethics. Moore's own *Principia Ethica* owes much to the Austro-German philosophy of values known as "axiology" and in particular to Franz von Brentano, a forerunner of phenomenology.[37]

Brentano defined the proof criteria for the internal perception of goodness, which he distinguished from conviction, and rejected both Kantian formalism and Humean relativism. Edmund Husserl, the founder of phenomenology, outlined in *Logical Investigations* (1900) the first guidelines for a universal criticism of the axiological approach.[38] On the practical level, phenomenology attempts to describe ethics and deal directly with objects and proofs.[39] Husserl thought that phenomenological ethics must provide an immanent description of the intentional background of moral consciousness and axiological meaning.[40] Because it deals with rationality in terms of intentionality, values, and action, this approach leads to a phenomenology of the will.[41] His student Max Scheler built bridges between axiology and phenomenology. Adopting an intuitionist phenomenology that is critical of Kantian formalism, Scheler gave precedence to values as experienced by individuals. He viewed ethics as based on a system of a priori laws that is not formal but "material" and existential, defined by intentional feels and preferences and by an objective hierarchy of values.[42]

It is sometimes difficult to dissociate existential philosophies from phenomenology. Jaspers reminds us that "existence," in the Kierkegaardian sense, is another name for reality. What is essentially real for me is so only because I am who I am. I am not here only as a mere fact but am entrusted with my life and my body in order to fulfill my original liberty. Without being simply a moral or practical approach to philosophy, existential philosophy includes the analysis of the moral being and the thirst for the absolute. In Jaspers's view, existence does not belong to the world of facts but to the realm of liberty. To shed light on existence is to stir liberty toward an authentic realization that cannot be reduced to a morality of desire or of norms. Heidegger's thinking can also be considered as existential philosophy because his "existential analytics" is part of the wider project of a basic ontology linking being to temporality.[43] Heidegger, as well as Husserl, criticized the neo-Kantian philosophy of values. In addition, they make a substantial effort to integrate Aristotle's practical philosophy by way of a new concept: "facticity." For Heidegger, Husserl, and all phenomenologists, however, moral philosophy is just a small part of a much larger effort to elucidate reality.

With the exception of the theorists of values and possibly Max Scheler, most thinkers associated with phenomenology strove to describe a reality that includes moral experience rather than one that analyzes moral language or builds normative systems. In this sense, contributions from phenomenology and existential philosophies remain extraneous to the development of moral philosophy in the first half of the century, which asserted its autonomy and the specificity of its language. At the beginning of the 1960s, when this premise faced rising criticism, phenomenology started to exercise a stronger influence on moral philosophy, to the effect that today it is considered an integral part of it. Thus, the phenomenological concept of signification can help us define meaning and intentionality as applied to practical philosophy.

France was not very receptive to the eventful history of moral philosophy unfolding on the other side of the Atlantic, across the Channel, and in Germany. Moore's theories and those of his successors passed unnoticed, and, to my knowledge, very few French thinkers even alluded to the ongoing debates on meta-ethics. True, certain philosophers, particularly in England, had gradually reduced moral philosophy to a formal analysis of moral judgments while all but ignoring their content. They had drawn a sharp distinction between meta-ethics and normative ethics, which they viewed somewhat condescendingly as a form of moralizing. The unexpected result was that interest for meta-ethics led to the neglect of moral conceptions. The beginning of Richard Hare's book *The Language of Morals* expresses well this attitude: "The language of morals is one sort of prescriptive language. . . . The study of imperatives is by far the best introduction to the study of ethics."[44]

The analysis of the moral language made the autonomy of ethics possible and was the source of vigorous philosophical developments. For the next fifty years, the history of a newly autonomous moral philosophy evolved in parallel with that of analytical philosophy. It is clear, however, that modern moral philosophy is not necessarily identical with the analytical view of meaning and that it cannot be limited to meta-ethics. Even the thesis according to which moral predicates are absolutely irreducible to other kinds of predicates finds itself under a cloud of doubts. Indeed, most contemporary philosophers do realize that the study of morality is not limited to the analysis of moral predicates and that important moral issues belong rightfully to moral philosophy.

It is nevertheless difficult to believe that French philosophers neglected meta-ethics because they were aware of its shortcomings. While moral

philosophy was not entirely absent in France in the first half of the twentieth century, French philosophers largely ignored analytical moral philosophy. True, French philosophy tried to integrate phenomenology and existentialism in a moral and practical perspective, as exemplified by the work
of Gabriel Marcel[45] and Jean-Paul Sartre. The latter, however, never wrote
the moral philosophy that he first announced in 1943 at the end of his
Being and Nothingness.[46] Three years later, he published *Existentialism
and Humanism*, a mere outline of the moral philosophy that he repeatedly
promised without ever achieving.

Sartre's reflections on moral philosophy from 1947 to 1948 were posthu-
mously published in 1983 as *Notebooks for an Ethics*, which give us a
glimpse on his envisioning a mainly Sartrean moral philosophy rather than
a phenomenological or existential one.[47] They show the rather large extent
to which Sartrean thought is influenced by phenomenology and especially
French existentialism.[48] Sartre interpreted Heidegger's concept of "facticity" as the absurd and futile aspect of existence, such as experienced in
nausea. According to Sartre, "facticity" has a moral dimension, given that
the subject is fully responsible for his situation in the world (yet not responsible for the fully contingent aspects of his existence). The individual
can deny his responsibility either by pretending that there are "values"
that preexist his freedom and thus guide him or by avoiding responsibility
and adopting what Sartre calls "bad faith." The only authentic solution for
the individual is a permanent conversion to freedom. "This is humanism
because we remind man that there is no legislator but himself. That he
himself, thus abandoned, must decide for himself; it is always by seeking,
beyond himself, an aim which is one of liberation or of some particular
realization, that man can realize himself as truly human."[49] Morality depends on the reconciliation between individual authenticity and the recognition of other people's freedom, or, in other words, on bringing together
the pure apprehension of the self and the interdependence between the
active self and the world. However deep such reflections may be—and
even if the best and worst of Sartre's thought were essentially what foreign
philosophers took to be French moral philosophy at the time—it is striking
to see the extent to which he ignored both the historical tradition of moral
philosophy and its main debates at the time.

When one peruses recent works on the history of moral philosophy in
the twentieth century written in English, German, or Italian, one can see
that the common perception of French moral philosophy is not entirely
limited to Sartre's thought. This perception includes the neo-Thomist philosophy of Étienne Gilson and Jacques Maritain. In *Freedom of the Modern
World*, *Integral Humanism*, and *The Rights of Man and Natural Law*, Maritain attempted to ground democracy and human rights in an unwritten
natural law and to treat it in relation to the evolution of moral conscious-

ness.[50] The task of including the social nature of human beings in a pluralistic perspective depends on the will to promote the common good in a temporal order. Maritain's intellectual objective was to review Thomism in the light of freedom and democracy. His work provided the inspiration for Christian-Democratic movements in Europe after World War II.

The history of moral philosophy in France should include other important philosophers. Alain, for instance, focused his highly original writings on the primacy of practical reason and human will as manifested in knowledge and in action. His work abounds in brilliant insights about the status of active and powerful virtues, and about an idea of happiness that is predicated on determination and courage. The spiritualist tradition includes Jules Lachelier, Jean Nabert, René Le Senne, and Louis Lavelle who, as disciples of Henri Bergson and Léon Brunschvicg, promoted a form of reflective neo-Kantianism inspired by the theory of values. Jean Wahl and Wladimir Jankélévitch were also influenced by Bergson as well as by the Christian philosophy of Maurice Blondel and Gabriel Marcel. Emmanuel Mounier developed the concept of person, understood as transcending the given, and as a movement of internalization and externalization. In his treatise *The Character of Man*, Mounier defends a phenomenology of moral behavior based on the concepts of presence and person.[51]

Paul Ricoeur and Emmanuel Levinas are equally important. Paul Ricoeur has gradually worked out a philosophy that connects existential phenomenology with hermeneutics. Initially based on a simple description of the eidetic structures of the voluntary and the involuntary similar to Alexander Pfänder's,[52] his philosophy acknowledges the centrality of the concern for "corporeal existence" and links it to a strong vision of limited freedom or consent. His reflection on this topic amounts to an anthropology of fallibility. In order to explain the transition from fallibility to guilt, Ricoeur takes the long and difficult road of the hermeneutics of symbols and myths.[53] As for Emmanuel Levinas, his rejection of Heidegger's existential analytics takes the form of the *humanism of the other*. Because Levinas's ethics emphasizes the dimension of proximity and vulnerability, freedom loses its status as a primary ethical concept and becomes, in Levinas's view, one's responsibility by answering to the freedom of *the other*.

These major contributions might seem to undermine my thesis that moral philosophy gradually dwindled in France during the twentieth century, becoming quasi-extinct from the 1960s on. In fact, to acknowledge the successes of French moral philosophy during the first half of the twentieth century does not contradict the fact that, at the beginning of the sixties, morality and ethics had ceased to be an important field in French philosophy.

During the first half of the century, French philosophers worked in isolation from each other. A dialogue between authors of different allegiances was hardly conceivable: they either ignored each other or clashed point-lessly. Debates on the autonomy of moral philosophy as well as moral philosophy elsewhere in the world were largely ignored.[54] The very conditions that had shaped the vibrant character of philosophy at the beginning of the twentieth century were totally extinct by the end of the 1950s.

The 1960s: Moral Philosophy's Rebirth in Great Britain, Germany, and the United States

In the second half of the twentieth century, moral philosophy underwent considerable change under the influence of the social and political movements of the 1960s. These movements were active on many fronts, fighting against colonialism, for democracy, and for civil rights. The inhabitants of former colonies were aspiring to affirm their independence from the metropolis after years of bloody fights, while, in developed countries, in particular in the United States, popular movements were fighting for minority rights. In communist countries, serious attempts to reform communist regimes were recorded. At the same time, the Western world was experiencing a dramatic change in the way authority was exercised, primarily in intergenerational and intergender relations and, to a lesser degree, in the workplace and in higher education.

These massive changes played a role in the redirection of moral philosophy. The emancipation witnessed in private life and the increased freedom experienced in social life contributed to increased expectations in the justification of moral principles. It is also plausible that—finding behavior rules less stringent and conformism less valued and less comforting—people were feeling more intensely the need to justify their decisions and choices. They were searching for principles on which to base their decisions; trying to better understand the effects of their decisions on themselves and on others; they also began to demand public justifications for measures affecting the life of every individual. In addition, they were showing an increasing interest for questions relating to political justice. Moral philosophers felt directly concerned by questions such as how to formulate principles for rightful action that would be publicly justifiable and deserving of wide support, how to account for the widespread plurality of values in contemporary society, and how to define the rules of conduct that should govern public life. Being dedicated exclusively to the formal analysis of the language of morals, meta-ethics was ill-equipped to answer such questions. Moral philosophy's inability to address such issues or help settle at least some of them, called its own usefulness into question and caused the comeback of normative (or substantial) ethics, which deals precisely with moral contents and principles.

From then on, normative theories prospered based on people's need for guiding moral principles, criteria for right action, and procedures for decision validation and justification. This resurgence of normative thought has been equally propitious to deontological views inspired by Kantianism and hinged on fundamental principles (duty, moral obligation, right action), as it has been to consequentialist views providing rules for evaluating the moral value of human actions based entirely on their beneficial consequences. Both deontology and consequentialism define themselves in terms of universal duties. They are both universalistic, imperative moral theories, even though consequentialism defends a teleological stance aiming to achieve some good state of affairs, whereas deontology follows Kantianism in placing the absolute moral value of certain duties above and before any consideration of goodness or desirability.

John Rawls's *A Theory of Justice*, a manifesto of antiutilitarian and deontological ethics, played a pioneering role in that context.[55] The main reasons for the book's success were, first, that it advanced a substantial, nonformal conception of social justice; second, that it added the theory of rational choice and game theory to the panoply of tools available to moral philosophers; and, third, that it rehabilitated common institutions, shared moral principles of justice, and carefully weighted convictions in ethical reflection. But, above all, Rawls brought forth a new conception of moral theory. In his view, the validation of a statement with respect to a theory cannot consist exclusively of that statement's reduction to general principles or experimental evidence; it must also evaluate the extent to which the statement backs up the consistency of a preexisting set of already validated statements. Likewise, moral reasoning begins with firm beliefs that may be contrary or resistant to principles of justice, but it develops as an adjustment procedure for achieving a well-thought-out equilibrium between principles and convictions. It can therefore be said that a moral theory is similar to the evaluation of experimental evidence in scientific theories. For instance, Rawls's view of justice as fairness should be able to reject slavery in order to preserve the balance between shared ethical convictions and the fundamental norms that structure our moral representation of the world.

In the early 1960s, Jürgen Habermas published his first book, *The Structural Transformation of the Public Sphere*, in which he outlines a theory that would later become his discourse ethics. Reasserting the basic insight of the Frankfurt School that reason is situated in language, he quoted Horkheimer's correspondence with Adorno in 1941: "Language intends, quite independently of the psychological intentions of the speaker, the universality that has been ascribed to reason alone. Interpreting this universality necessarily leads to the idea of a correct society."[56] According to Habermas, the idea of public sphere must be understood in terms of both the actual infrastructures that support it and the norms and practices of public use and rational deliberation. Arguing that individual communicative competence follows the rules that structure communication and act as a quasi-transcendental limitation, he often likens speech acts to claims for validity that can be justified rationally and are therefore "cognitively verifiable."[57] This is the rational basis of Habermas's theories and ideas about society, modernity, and morality. His social theory defines the validity criteria for norms of action in the public sphere as those criteria on which all affected by such norms engage in practical discourse evaluating their validity. His moral philosophy is clearly linked to deontological ethics because it defines the legitimacy conditions intersubjectively as ideal communicative conditions. It is also linked to cognitivism because it acknowledges that moral statements are likely to possess truth value, thus being a form of knowledge, and that their objective character is based on the common requisites of general argumentation. Habermas's universalism is procedural in the sense that he considers the norms of morality to emerge from a discussion that follows a given procedure. The importance that Habermas attaches to communication and to the rules shaping moral statements' claim to validity shows the palpable influence of meta-ethics also present in the works of Karl Otto Apel.

Another characteristic of the 1960s was the renewed interest for the utilitarian and consequentialist conceptions of morality, which were equally claiming the status of critical theories of ethics, adept at steering moral deliberations and at justifying their decisions. The primary effect of this interest was a theoretical remake of utilitarianism into an *indirect* utilitarianism in which defining right action requires consideration not only of the consequences of individual acts but also of the rules followed by such acts. This was obviously intended to bring the theory in compliance with common moral intuitions. At the same time, utilitarian thinkers engaged in an impressive effort to answer the objections they regularly came up against. One such objection concerned the likelihood of interpersonal comparisons regarding an individual's utility, which—according to utilitarian orthodoxy—should be measurable by a public procedure. Thus, when evaluating the goodness of certain consequences, consequentialists began to consider—in addition to utility— certain impersonal values such as beauty or to gauge consequences in a probabilistic manner, that is, according to the spirit of consequentialism rather than its letter. The new utilitarianism spread well beyond the English-speaking countries and was particularly well received in Germany, Italy, and Spain.[58]

It would be wrong to think that the only effect of the criticism leveled at meta-ethics was to rehabilitate deontology and consequentialism. The discredit afflicting meta-ethics at that time had ensued from the rebuttal of its central thesis—the distinctiveness of the language of morals and the singularity of moral predicates—which was opposed by the British philosophers Elisabeth Anscombe, Peter Geach, and Philippa Foot.[59] They argued that moral predicates such as "courageous" and "good," whose judicious use requires knowledge of what they are applied to, have an evaluative moral sense that is very close to their factual descriptive sense. Any attempt to define the objectivity requirements of their use would be therefore perfectly justified. More generally, those same philosophers were opposed to an exclusively formal validation of moral principles and to viewing moral terms as necessarily prescriptive. Saying that something is good does not force one to choose it; at best, it gives one more reasons to do so. Such objections challenged the thesis that the language of morals has a specific purpose and that ethics is radically autonomous. Consequently, the declaration of principle that ethical naturalism is false seems largely unjustified. The influence of Wittgenstein and his disciples played a decisive role in this debate by destroying the prejudices that meta-ethics had erected as prerequisites to the study of morals. In addition to this radical challenge to linguistic philosophy as applied to morality, many other stances in moral philosophy were freed from the constraints of the anticognitivist bent of meta-ethics, which rejected the idea that moral judgments could be considered as knowledge-based judgments. If values exist independently of our choices and behavior, then they must be grounded in reality. The possibility of defining knowable moral properties gave rise to many philosophical works that were pleading for the reality of moral properties and the possibility of assigning truth values to moral judgments; their authors belonged to what was called from then on moral realism or moral cognitivism.

Soon after, deontologism and utilitarianism became the favorite targets of critics that were opposed to reducing the definition of morality to a universalistic, imperative conception. Indeed, both theories can also be viewed as dogmas, and, to this day, it has not yet been proved that they offer an exhaustive reflection on morality. Viewing morality as an impersonal universal set of rules that apply to individuals from the outside and are indifferent to what these individuals are, could very well lead to a misinterpretation of the nature of moral life. The predispositions toward right action or virtues, the consideration of needs, psychological abilities, and other forms of human accomplishment are all essential for the definition of right action. They are all closely tied to motivation and offer an image of moral reality that is both realistic and psychologically plausible. It is such thinking that made possible the modern success of both neo-Aristotelianism and the ethics of virtue. Another consequence of the criticism of meta-ethics was the rehabilitation of practical rationality. The most spectacular rebirth of practical philosophy occurred in Germany, where it was as clearly distinguished from meta-ethics as it was open to hermeneutics.[60] The singularity of moral judgment is also strongly endorsed in Paul Ricoeur's work. Works by Charles Taylor, Alasdair MacIntyre, and Bernard Williams cannot be aligned unreservedly with the ethics of virtue or with practical philosophy, but they also have been conceived during the philosophical revival of the 1960s, when meta-ethics was being abandoned and new theories of normativity were being developed and criticized.

The 1960s: French Moral Philosophy, Stranded

between Suspicion and Neglect

By the end of the 1970s, when I started to study philosophy at the university, no other discipline seemed more doomed than moral philosophy. French philosophy appeared to be oblivious of the intellectual movements that—from the beginning of the sixties on—had transformed not only the philosophical interpretation of moral content but also society's perspective on moral philosophy. More tellingly still, nobody in France felt any need to explain this utter disregard for everything related to moral philosophy outside of France or thought it appropriate to keep debating the central issues of that discipline. Looking back, one can detect many warning signs that, by that time, French moral philosophy had already fallen into disgrace—where it would remain for more than thirty years.

The lack of interest for the issues that had been the constant focus of philosophical tradition was the first, and quite distressing, sign that in France the end was near for questioning and reflection in moral philosophy. In those years, a few remarkable studies were still being produced on the moral philosophy of various authors, ancient and modern. Rarely, though, were such studies even mentioning the great figures in the history of moral philosophy such as Aristotle and Kant. The previously hot topics of moral deliberation, prudence, human goodness, and free will and the debates on the moral indifference of desire or the existence of moral laws could not find any interested takers beyond what transpired in studies on their formulation by other authors. Until 1980 one had to turn to the United Kingdom, the United States, or Germany in order to acquaint oneself with the ongoing debates on moral knowledge and the status of virtues, to ascertain which interpretations of the concept of *akrasia* were in competition with each other, or to learn how to reconcile determinism and free will. French writings dealing with those questions were few and far between at the time. There were nevertheless no indications that such questions had been answered or that they were not going to be asked any more: in fact, they have concerned philosophers for twenty centuries and continue to greatly concern them today.

It would not do to invoke the essentially historical training of French philosophers as an excuse for their lack of interest in the very issues that they were studying in other philosophers' writings. I readily admit that the historical definition of an issue is essential for its understanding and analysis. But I cannot see how it could prevent one from studying that issue for oneself, nor can I see why it would render such a study superfluous. Most of the issues dealt with by Aristotle, Hume, or Kant are still topical. Recognizing them as such would be but a new way of paying tribute to these great authors. The fact that French philosophers have given up studying the issues bequeathed to us by the history of philosophy leads us to a rather paradoxical conclusion. Contrary to the preconception opposing analytical philosophy to the French interest in the history and tradition of philosophy, in the 1960s traditional moral questions were tackled only by philosophers trained in the analytical tradition, and entirely neglected by French philosophers, their essentially historical training notwithstanding.

The manifest indifference toward the theoretical and empirical research in sociology, psychology, and economy was another sign that moral philosophy had lost its early twentieth-century drive to keep its eyes open on other disciplines that had an interest in normative issues. As a consequence, moral psychology incurred a similar disfavor in France.

Finally, the absence of international exchanges involving French philosophers was the third clear sign of near extinction of moral philosophy. Now, at the dawn of the third millennium, when it has become a commonplace to criticize French philosophers from before the 1980s for their lack of curiosity about foreign philosophical traditions, it is worth reminding our readers that this was not at all the case at the beginning of the twentieth century. True, especially during the 1960s, the French philosophical community did display a general tendency to think that one can philosophize only in French or, if need be, in French as translated from German, and that the only explanation for some authors and issues not being mentioned in French philosophy was their lack of worth. This tendency was particularly disruptive in moral philosophy, where the discipline's research field was relatively less well defined. If a set of fundamental questions and research topics had been established—as was the case at the same period in philosophy of science and political philosophy—one can imagine that French moral philosophers would have been better informed about what was being accomplished by their discipline in other countries and that they would have seen the interest of non-French contributions.

I have already mentioned the fact that France had ignored most of the research done during the twentieth century in English-speaking countries.

However, what distinguishes the French philosophy of the 1960s is that this ignorance was not limited to the twentieth century but included the work of David Hume, one of the greatest authors in moral philosophy, Thomas Hobbes, John Stuart Mill, Henry Sidgwick, T. H. Green, and Francis Bradley. France had to wait until the 1970s for its philosophers to begin studying Hobbes and Hume. And while Mill's writings have been recently translated, those of Sidgwick, Green, or Bradley are still largely unknown in France. Philosophical exchanges were extremely productive between France and Great Britain until the turn of the twentieth century, but they were brutally severed after World War I—at least in part—for political and cultural reasons. British pragmatism and political progressivism from before and after the war were a far cry from French intellectuals' ideas of revolution, "big night out," and radical political upheaval that had so profoundly marked their mind-set in the 1960s. They did not care for British common sense and rejected what they viewed as scientistic approaches to philosophy; they had a vaguely unsettling feeling that they were ill-prepared for the argumentative jousting common among philosophers trained in the British philosophical tradition. Were it not for this communication breakdown between the two countries, there is every reason to think that French moral philosophy would have been very different from what it was at the time under consideration.[61]

In clear contrast, philosophical relations between France and Germany were much warmer in the twentieth century—as attested by the influence of phenomenology and existentialism in France. Beginning with the reflexive philosophy of Jules Lagneau, Jules Lachelier, and Jean Nabert, and until the revival of Kantianism in the 1980s, the little moral philosophy that was done in France was mainly influenced by German philosophy and in particular by Kant. Hegelian thought was also avidly read by French political philosophers, but it never became the focus of debate in French moral philosophy, as it had been for nineteenth-century British idealists or U.S. and German contemporary philosophers (who still consider it a major reference for communitarian trends in both countries).[62] As for Nietzsche's critique of morality, its influence on French thought consisted mainly in neutralizing moral reflection instead of challenging it, as was the case in other countries. When all is said and done, the fact remains that, with the exception of trends tied to Jürgen Habermas's discourse ethics, whatever good fortune German moral philosophy might have had in France during the past two centuries is still largely ignored today by the French intelligentsia.

During the 1960s, while French research on moral philosophy was dwindling, philosophical and intellectual activity was flourishing as never before. Jacques Lacan's *Writings* (1966), Michel Foucault's *Order of Things* (1966), Louis Althusser's *How to Read Marx's Capital* (1965), Jacques Derrida's *Of Grammatology* (1966), Gilles Deleuze's *Difference and Repe-*

tition (1969), and *Anti-Oedipus* (with Félix Guattari, 1972) had an immediate and resounding success in France and abroad. The contrast between
the success of the French philosophy of the 1960s and the quasi extinction
of moral philosophy could not be greater. How was this possible? How
could a remarkable philosophical development, which helped make
French philosophy known outside of France, toll the bell of an entire research field in which French philosophy had been toiling for so long?
Studying this phenomenon should be as interesting from a structural perspective—showing how hegemony manifests itself in intellectual life—as
from a philosophical perspective. It constitutes a textbook case for understanding how a mixed collection of philosophical theses, beliefs, and
shared intellectual achievements can nullify a whole way of thinking or
strip it of all pertinence. In what follows I focus on dominant works of the
period to the exclusion of less authoritative ones, even though some of the
latter outlived the former. The reason of my choice is that—during the
period under consideration here—none of these less noticed works managed to prevent the general disaffection with moral philosophy in France.[63]

In the 1960s most of the towering figures of the French philosophical
scene believed—with varying degrees of intensity—that philosophical reflection on morality was futile or unwarranted. That was the main reason
for the extinction of moral philosophy. Whatever their ideological or stylistic divergences, they all stigmatized as illusory the idea that human beings
are subjects accountable for their actions and at least partially aware of
their motives or capable of seeing themselves as members of a historical
community. In his writings, Michel Foucault had grandiosely developed
such themes. He claimed that man had been ignored by classical thinking,
had been briefly discovered by modern thought, and would soon pass: "As
the archeology of our thought easily shows, man is an invention of recent
date. And one perhaps, nearing its end."[64] At least, Foucault saw clearly
that the consequences of such theses on morality went far beyond the
mechanization of man: "Superficially, one might say that knowledge of
man, unlike the sciences of nature, is always linked, even in its vaguest
form, to ethics or politics; more fundamentally, modern thought is advancing towards that region where man's Other must become the Same as himself." Put more bluntly: "For modern thought no morality is possible."[65]

What Caused These Developments?

It has become a commonplace to qualify French thought of that time as
antihumanist. This label applies to the thinkers of the 1960s because their
objective was to criticize the modern metaphysics of subjectivity, in other
words, the conception that defines reality as that which is known and mas-

tered by the human subject. The criticism became popular because in the 1960s it was widely believed that social, psychological, and historical reality may sometimes shape the human subject regardless of his will. Subjects, the story went, are not transparent to themselves, and they cannot know how and why they influence the world. The theme of the opaqueness of the subject—forming the background of Nietzsche's and Heidegger's writings—was tied to the criticism of "presence to the self" that establishes the individual as a subject of his own representations and discourse and as the source of actions for which he will be held accountable. Expressed in the then fashionable style of Marxian structuralism and Freudian psychology, the conclusion of such thinking was that the individual is just an illusory product of social and psychological forces. Pushed to the extreme, such views define the subject as a surface effect, as a familiar yet artificial means for achieving self-consistency. It should suffice to recall on that point the notorious first-chapter pages of *Anti-Oedipus*, where actions are "mechanical acts" performed by "desiring machines" similar to the subject. "[S]omething on the order of the *subject* can be discerned on the recording surface. It is a strange subject, however, with no fixed identity, wandering about over the body without organs, but always remaining peripheral to the desiring-machines, being defined by the share of the product it takes for itself, garnering here, there, and everywhere a reward in the form of a becoming or an avatar, being born of the states that it consumes and being reborn with each new state."[66]

The idea of the death of the subject is actually not an incongruous one among possible philosophical conceptions. After many decades of discussions on this topic, one should be able—with the benefit of hindsight—to outline its main aspects. The first approach to the topic of the death of the subject is metaphysical: its best expressions can be found in Heidegger's writings, in certain existentialist trends, and in the works of contemporary French philosophers.[67] The human being is but a place, a site where the being deposits itself, a location inhabited by existence, a spot whereto various configurations of meanings and events are converging and materializing. The materialist version of this interpretation asserts that if the world is conceived as strictly natural, then my identity, *me*, is only a place among others on a web of phenomena. Yet another version of the same topic is sociological: *I* am defined by a set of social realities—be they superstructures and determinations out of my control, or social roles defined by the requirements of the situation in which I find myself. Not only is *I* a mere product of those elements, but its *unity* is nominal. Lastly, the psychoanalytical approach to the death of the subject considers all constitutive elements of *I* (my beliefs and desires, all my mental and physical states, etc.) to be in perpetual change. Uttering *I* is therefore a simple turn of phrase destined to help designate an *individual* reality, regardless of its ceaseless mobility.

Moral philosophy is primarily focused on the study of human action. In Aristotle's view, this type of reflection concerns the *prakta* or "things to do." Who does them? How does one act? Why do we act? What rules are to be followed, what deliberations embarked upon, what motives or emotions invoked? The minimal requirement of moral philosophy is that at least some of these questions should be meaningful and that the human subject should have at least a partially justified access to his own beliefs and desires that explain his actions. Without this requirement, moral reflection is annihilated and many of the problems that are essential to human action risk being dodged or conjured away.

Do arguments in favor of the death of the subject call into question moral philosophy? Even if on a metaphysical level *I* am only a product of a complex causal system, the fact remains that in such a system *I* am myself a cause, a reality through which things happen. Therefore, the metaphysical argument that asserts the absence of the subject cannot refute the plausible hypothesis that there are human agents out there, who possess psychological faculties and complex mental states, beliefs, and desires, and who rely on a variety of motivations. In addition, to use an Aristotelian turn of phrase, those agents are self-moving and self-organizing entities, which is more than enough for justifying a philosophical reflection on human action and its norms. Furthermore, even if my identity were reduced to a more or less coherent set of social roles, it would still be true that *I* am this set of rules and that the manner in which my *I* is structured cannot cancel its reality. Further still, even if *I* were entirely determined by economical forces or by subconscious impulses, this could never mean that *I* do not exist, or that *I* would be unable to interpret myself independently from what supposedly determines me. Lastly, personal identity is not even the only criterion for proving the existence of the subject, because one can very well conceive of more complex forms of identity wherein continuity and connection would be as important as numerical unity. Consequently, none of the previously mentioned arguments can be said to demonstrate the death of the subject (at least not in the minimal sense of "subject" required in moral philosophy). It is quite strange that it was enough that some philosophers assert the death of the subject for moral philosophy to be more or less abandoned in France at that time.

But perhaps the antihumanist creed alone cannot explain so radical a detachment from moral philosophy. After all, the French antihumanists promoted a kind of genealogical critique that superficially resembles Nietzsche's assertion that the genealogy "is pushing the *partie honteuse* of our inner world to the foreground, and looking for what is really effective, guiding and decisive for our development, where men's intellectual pride would least wish to find it."[68] In his view, "British psychologists" had carried out this task rather imperfectly, while Pascal, Stendhal, and the French moralists—especially La Rochefoucauld—had "denied that the moral motives which men claim have inspired their actions, really have done so" and had emphasized the importance of selfishness and pride for human action. In fact, Nietzschean genealogy goes even farther by rejecting the idea that moral judgments are based on truth[69] and by attempting instead to show how the illusion of freedom and the misrepresentation of norms of action take shape in the human mind. It does not amount to mere suspicion but describes the various forces at work in morality and establishes a hierarchy that distinguishes morality's low origins from its noble ones.[70] Nietzsche's moral philosophy owes a great deal to Kant's reflections on the possibility of practical philosophy, as presented in the *Critique of Practical Reason* (1788). But Nietzsche does not conceive of rationality as determining the will by reference to a purely formal moral law. In both *On the Genealogy of Morality* and *Daybreak*, he emphasized the conflict between freedom (defined as the expression of dynamic, creative forces) and the morality of morals as well as reason's inability to free the power to act: "To be moral is to act in accordance with custom, to be ethical means to practice obedience toward a law or tradition established from old."[71] It is in relation to this critique of morality that Nietzsche's moral philosophy finds its meaning. Nietzsche refers to an assertive morality that is "beyond good and evil," destined to shape a "man with his own, independent, durable will, who has the right to make a promise—and has a proud consciousness."[72] The depth of his critical analysis, and his intellectual vigor in defining the aspirations of any morality, made Nietzsche a vital contributor to moral reflection. In contrast, Nietzsche-inspired French authors made his genealogy of morality into a discourse of denunciation and, in the process, watered down the antidemocratic and antiliberal aspects of his work. These authors inherited his suspicion toward moral philosophy without answering his call to transcend morality in order to discover a new kind of moral life.[73] Thus, their critique of the traditional forms of moral reflection led them to assert the futility of seeking or devising new ones.

It would be very difficult to challenge the vaguely stated theory that the individual could be partially determined by something else, beside his desires and beliefs. As is, it still leaves open a window of opportunity allowing research and debate to continue in moral philosophy. The problem was not with the antihumanist theories that I am criticizing: while they made life difficult for moral philosophy, they did not annihilate it. Rather, the quasi extinction of moral philosophy in France during the 1960s and 1970s is due to the fact that antihumanist theories were being presented as *factual* truths. Whoever dared contest them was accused of being blind to his own self, therefore confirming the irrefutable truthfulness of what he was denying. In the eyes of those who were denying the existence of a subject whose will can be rationally determined, moral philosophy was guilty of ignoring the obvious existence of conflicting desires and social forces lurking behind "rational" motives. The subject that considers himself free and accountable for his actions is in fact deluding himself, they claimed; he should know that he is a mere product of determinations well beyond his control. Seen retrospectively, the intellectual poverty of twenty years of criticism, systematic suspicion, and bullying questioning poured on any defender of a pertinent theory on human action is striking. Their only achievement is a long series of loud programmatic statements supported by little argumentation. Anybody wanting to speak about human beings and their action in the world was told that, after all, psychoanalysts and critics of dominant ideologies were better placed to do it, because they would know how to flush out what was hiding behind philosophical debates on morality.[74]

The incessant referral to psychoanalytical wisdom had a disastrous effect in those years. The talking cure seemed to illustrate the belief that whatever one says is voiced by an inner other. The stubborn belief persisted that the most rational and best-argued speech can only put the resources of rationality in the service of mind's subconscious forces. This belief created a false impression of psychoanalysis, which is in fact one of the most fascinating intellectual adventures of the twentieth century and, as a technique and practice, it remains a remarkable resource for alleviating mental and physical suffering. Its main object is to study the makeup of an individual personality starting with the deepest mental processes rooted in the singularity of the human being. What counts in psychoanalysis is not the set of instinctual components that make a person but how they are taking shape in that particular person. By definition, psychoanalysts are masters in rediscovering the fragments of the self, but they do not treat a case with ready-made formulas and do not expect to draw universal lessons from it. Unlike them, philosophers look especially for the general psychological and normative characteristics of human beings, their decisions, theirs choices, their reasons and motives. Psychoanalysis reveals the subconscious life, which is made of obsessions, repetitions, and hidden vital forces: those are the factors that psychoanalysts must evaluate in order to formulate their claims. But proving their existence cannot invalidate what moral philosophy has to say about the philosophical aspects of human action and human existence.

Psychoanalytical knowledge can be said only to challenge moral philosophy, not to provide supposedly tough answers to its questions. Many contemporary philosophers acknowledge the subconscious even if, unlike

Freud, they define it as a set of "mechanisms" that carry no meaning. They are actually studying a great variety of topics on the subject's self-opaqueness, such as self-deception and the failure of deliberation.[75] Had their work, which had nothing to do with the antihumanist dogmas of that time, been known to the defenders of those dogmas, it could have helped their own cause or at least shown that handling such topics is not harmful to moral philosophy.[76] It would be a misuse of language to call psychoanalysis a "homogeneous" field of research or a "theory" disconnected from clinical practice, and it would be wrong to expect that it produce a global reflection on the norms of human action.

During the period under consideration, grasping human reality presupposed adherence to the slogan "Everything is political!" where "political" usually denoted a Marxist view of reality. The Marxist sympathies displayed by many French philosophers between 1950 and 1980 were deemed sufficient to put moral philosophy in doubt. The reasons that made this possible were, first, that the historical determinism of Marxist rhetoric does not leave any place for human initiative and accountability and, second, that according to the Marxist genealogy of moral principles: "Law, morality, religion . . . are so many bourgeois prejudices, behind which lurk in ambush just as many bourgeois interests."[77] In other words, shared moral principles and ethical beliefs that incorporate roughly the values of humanist culture are but another proof of how alienated we all are. Such assertions—which should have been taken with a grain of salt—have nevertheless fed the disdain of French Marxists intellectuals for moral philosophy. After all, only an ideological condemnation can legitimately settle ethical disagreements!

Yet, considered objectively, Marxism does not necessarily lead to a negation of moral philosophy. In fact, a different interpretation of Marxism could lead to opposite conclusions. Many philosophers have been interested in Marx's moral philosophy, and analytical Marxism still represents a strong current in contemporary moral and political philosophy.[78] It is not surprising that moral criticism takes a larger place in political currents advocating radical reforms than it does in conservative movements. It is, for instance, the case of anarchism, where moral reflection plays an important role.[79] Moreover, Marxists distrust morality only when they mistakenly assimilate it to a version of dominant ideology with universalistic ambitions. But such a view deliberately ignores the reflexive and critical aspects of moral philosophy. In addition, the contempt shown by this generation of French Marxist-leaning intellectuals for morality is only partly due to Marxism itself: it is mostly due to the particular version of Marxism that exercised its dominance as an antihumanist orthodoxy radically opposed to the humanist and ethical traditions of French socialism.

In hindsight, it was the morality of commitment—the only political morality accepted by French intellectuals since the Dreyfus affair—that most effectively impaired their ability to see morality as a reflexive and critical discipline. This is clearly apparent in the work of Sartre, whose writings, especially *Situations*, never failed to condemn the behavior and character of his contemporaries. His name-calling and invectives (bastard, SOB), and even some of his analytical categories (bad faith, alienation, etc.), suggest a psychic determinism strangely akin to the object of Freudian analysis. In spite of the admiration that his talent and prolific writings command, one could hardly ignore his: "An anti-Communist is a rat. I couldn't see any way out of that one and I never will."[80] There is no doubt that the pervasiveness of Sartre's implacable moral verdicts has contributed in no small measure to the diminishing credibility of moral philosophy among the younger generations.[81]

Interestingly enough, the years that marked the disappearance of moral philosophy in France were also those when its intellectuals prized moral stances more than ever. Obviously, they did not take "moral" to mean compliance with existing values or general reflection on human action; rather they meant personal morals based on individual commitment. The interest in commitment survived long after existentialism lost its influence.[82] I mentioned earlier how the Sartrean opposition between heroes and bastards served to produce easy moral judgments and denunciations. Morality of commitment naturally encourages condemnation: if the values-creating act is that of adhering to a cause, nonadherents are by definition wrong and calling somebody an SOB or a bastard is thus largely excused by the value of the cause to which the name-caller adheres. Adherence justifies any acts aiming either to clear the obstacles to the cause or to heap opprobrium on its adversaries. Clearly, reflection and critical analysis would have undermined the very foundation of both such commitment and denunciation, thus considerably diminishing the chances of the Sartrean prophecy that morality will be revolutionary socialist or it will perish.[83]

These reasons explain why the reflection on morality became an object of suspicion and reproach. The height of absurdity was that such reproach was itself sharply moralizing. A philosophy that denies that human action is wholly determined by hidden forces is proclaimed *guilty* of believing in freedom and accountability. The intellectuals of the 1960s—who have artfully mastered this moralizing rhetoric—have also decreed that the critical approach to moral philosophy was a thing of the past. The intellectual climate of the sixties was marred by the certitude that morality belonged to ideology, by the obsessive argumentation to the effect that, in the last analysis (as it was fashionable to say), political verdicts coupled with cut-and-dried moral judgments would succeed in proving one day the conceit of morality. Its distinctive tone was one of grandstanding and condemnation, rushed judgments, final verdicts, and an intimidating conviction that whatever was said here was decided elsewhere—a place difficult to locate but easy to invoke. Its numerous victims were not only those philosophers whose recent recognition should not let us forget the ostracism that they were subjected to but also entire fields of research, including moral philosophy.

The First Signs of Moral Philosophy's Revival in the 1980s

The slow transformation that started in the mid-1980s is the last component of my brief history of French moral philosophy in the twentieth century. It was heralded by the decline of rhetorical grandstanding, the disrepute of dogmatic psychoanalysis and Marxism, an increasing impatience with moralizing, and a rising awareness of the world's complexities, coupled with the discovery of the horrors of communism.

Other factors, more specific to philosophy, had also contributed to these developments. For instance, the incantation "Everything is political" was replaced by a properly philosophical reflection on politics. The dynamism of French political philosophy became a force of renewal in moral philosophy through the critical reflection movements inspired by Tocqueville and Raymond Aron. Many other groups and movements also benefited from this new environment: some were inspired by Kant, some others were reconsidering the conceptions of natural law or the principles of functioning democracies as expounded by Claude Lefort and Cornelius Castoriadis, while a few were yet again promoting the rebirth of Marxist studies. There was increased interest in the works of Anglo-American philosophers (John Rawls, Robert Nozick, Charles Taylor) and German authors such as Jürgen Habermas. The high-quality historical research under way in political philosophy and the diversity of its orientations and currents, as well as the mutual tolerance manifested by participants in the exchange of ideas, were all proving that the discipline was becoming again a true field of study.

Moral philosophy's reawakening was taking longer. The comeback of Kantianism greatly contributed to it through the work that was accomplished at the Collège de philosophie under the direction of Luc Ferry and Alain Renaut. Concepts such as those of goodwill and universal moral obligations—which had been practically erased from philosophy's conceptual panoply—regained their pertinence and legitimacy. Another contributing factor was the return to the procedural ethics of discourse, which considers that argumentation in practical discussions must lead to universal interests, and helps define the modern universals of morality as pragmatic universals.[84] The newly regained legitimacy of moral philosophy was

also due to the interest generated by Paul Ricoeur's work on selfhood. In
Oneself as Another he defines moral philosophy as including both practical
reason and the understanding of normative action, thus pushing the philosophical debate beyond a merely procedural or formal understanding of
morality.[85] Individual action applies universal criteria produced by willful
self-regulation, but it is also inspired by convictions and beliefs that form
the substance of moral attitudes. This double allegiance explains why some
convictions may clash with certain moral stances. At the same time, new
topics enriched the research in moral philosophy. Aristotle, Epicurus,
Montaigne, and Spinoza provided a basis for a variety of reflections: the
ethic of joy, bliss, and happiness, based on Spinoza, and on the goodness
of desires and their realization in human happiness, based on Epicurus
and Montaigne.[86]

This brief overview of the 1980s is based on an article I wrote in 1992
for the influential French quarterly *Le Débat*. In it, I evoked the perspectives of ethical reflection and outlined some of its possible future developments. In the same spirit, I edited a series of classical and modern basic
texts in moral philosophy published by Presses Universitaires de France.
I thought that the promotion of German and English moral philosophy
was the surest way to help the rebirth of normative thought in France.
Some of those works thus made available in French deal with meta-ethics
and analytical moral philosophy, which were partially eclipsed in the 1970s
by the renewal of moral philosophy. But it would be wrong to conclude
that, seeing that many English and American thinkers consider meta-ethics to be outdated, it is worthless and, consequently, that French philosophers would better dispense with research on the meaning of ethical predicates or the status of moral judgments. Quite to the contrary, I strongly
believe that the study of analytical moral philosophy and meta-ethics remains not only important but necessary. One can understand why the British heirs of the sixty years' reign of meta-ethics rose against it, but one
should not forget that they were challenging only the supremacy of meta-
ethics, not the relevance of all issues it raised. Moreover, one cannot deny
the role played by meta-ethics in consolidating the critical spirit of English
moral reflection. Lastly, contemporary philosophers are better-suited to
tackle the legacy of meta-ethics. They have already criticized its most out-
landish claims and feel no need to maintain a rigorous distinction between
meta-ethics and pure moral research.

If the roads thus paved lead in the next decades to a shared pool of
research topics, if French debates on different views do not preclude dis-
cursive compatibility, and if moral philosophy regains a global vision of
its own field and redefines its relation to history, traditions, specific topics,
and research styles, then it could be said with greater confidence that
French moral philosophy has been reborn indeed. The historical knowl-

edge possessed by French philosophers might become an asset if it helps them avoid the verbal jousting carried on in English much in the style of medieval *disputationes*.

If it continues on this path, French moral reflection would be very different from what it was at the dawn of the twentieth century but will still display recognizable traits: it will still be issue-oriented, informed by recent theoretical and empirical contributions on specific topics, concerned with clarity and intelligibility, and never backing from efforts aiming to clarify issues and solve problems. One can certainly wonder whether such an ideal suits all philosophical research regardless of philosophical tendencies, or whether it is perceived as an undue extension of rational philosophy's habits of thoughts. Even if that were the case, the fact remains that it is an ideal shared by the French philosophical tradition (at least until the 1950s) and by the philosophical tradition of English-speaking countries.

PART TWO

Human Life

For J. S.

What the philosophers say about reality is often as deceptive as
when you see a sign in a second-hand store that reads: *Pressing
Done Here*. If you went in with your clothes to have them pressed,
you would be fooled; the sign is for sale.
—Søren Kierkegaard, *Either/Or*[1]

"HERE, you will learn how to live well"; "Here, you will know what
wisdom is." Are philosophers deceiving us when they claim to reveal the
meaning of the good life, the need for transcendence, or the virtues of the
Moderns? Are they talking as expert moralists and critics of human behavior or as philosophers? This essay aims to show that they have nothing to
say to us about the wisdom of the Moderns or contemporary forms of
happiness—at least nothing of a purely philosophical nature. At the same
time, they would have much to say about human life and its condition—
a prodigious intellectual task that, sadly, contemporary philosophers have
barely touched.

The philosophers of antiquity considered the study of human life to be
the first object of philosophy. Only marginally and half-willingly had they
let themselves be talked into explaining how life should be lived. Plato
never ceased to ridicule various proposals for models of virtue or wisdom,
but he was very interested in the inner order and the presence of the good
in the human soul. In his treatises on ethics, Aristotle studied mainly the
formal structure of virtues and, only in passing, the acts inspired by it.
The Hellenistic philosophers, especially the Stoics but also the Epicureans,
sought to define a way of life. Reading their works without reducing their
thinking to folksy remedies for existential discomforts reveals that their
philosophy is not at all a prescription for a better or happier life. Rather,
they argue for a way of life that is entirely shaped by philosophy. Like
their contemporaries, these philosophers were wise enough to know that
an ideal of righteous or well-rounded life could never be a one-size-fits-all
solution. The philosophy of antiquity, much like contemporary philosophy,
was not expected to tell people how to live better, easier, or happier lives.

What is expected from present-day philosophy is a careful—if laborious
and tentative—reflection on human life, not soothing descriptions and
self-indulgent criticism of our morals, not denunciations and dire prophe-
cies as those heaped on us by contemporary philosophers, certainly not
their praise, and even less their derision.[2] If philosophy's true aspiration
is to acquire knowledge, should its first priority not be to analyze what

we are, what the human condition amounts to? If philosophy had any connection to reality, should it not explain to us our existential condition and how we could achieve a certain kind of goodness in our lives?

The great thinkers of antiquity, as well as Montaigne, Spinoza, Hume, and many others, have all emphasized philosophy's strong connection with life. Socrates said that the unexamined life is not worth living (Plato, *Apology*). Modern philosophers seem to have forgotten the greatest concern of their predecessors for many centuries. Analytical philosophers, for instance, are mainly interested in defining strict conditions for the meaning and truth of statements and consider—almost without exception—that the questions on human life and human condition largely exceed the object of philosophy. As for many French philosophers, who feel the need to answer such questions because their own intellectual training is grounded in history and philosophy, they prefer to do so by focusing their description on contemporary life-styles, thoughts, and beliefs, thus contributing to the reflection on what it means to be a modern human being. However, much like the reflection of the existentialist philosophers who preceded them, this contribution does not even begin to answer the questions of ancient philosophers: What is the inner order of human life? How is one's life shaped by reflection, by analysis, or by the search for explanations? Is there a link between the finite character of human life and the actions that occur within it? Those are truly philosophical questions that remain as pressing today as they were in ancient times.

The general indifference for existential analysis has not made the topic any easier to explain. How is it conceivable that a philosophical question seen for a long time as the most fundamental and legitimate could gradually become meaningless and obsolete? Is it because philosophical reflection went through a radical transformation? Is it because our contemporaries are living, perceiving, and reflecting on human life in different ways than the Ancients were? If so, then at what moment has the continuity been broken and how serious is the break? There seems to be a general consensus that only writers and psychoanalysts are qualified to talk about human life. True, literary fiction and reflection can often be deeper, truer, and more beneficial than philosophical advice. Literary accounts, testimonials, and case studies can bring us close to all sorts of life stories, from the most humble to the most spectacular. But is this enough for truly understanding life? Should we conclude that philosophers have nothing of interest to say about the human condition? I would like to focus my rebuttal on this hypothetical conclusion. Trying to make sense of human actions and to seek the basic components of human life or the basic scenarios that structure it are not pointless efforts. In what follows I attempt to examine the way in which human beings reflect on their life from their own perspective, based on who they are, on what happens to them, on what is waiting to happen before they die, and on what is the weight of their own past.

It would be misleading to mention wisdom in this context. Ancient philosophers only used this term to designate the absolute primacy of thought over life. For them, wisdom was neither a body of knowledge nor a set of rules, not a prescription of the good life or an outlook on life but a quest for the kind of reflection that endows one's existence with a set of formal constraints and that structures one's desires and emotions. The presence of wisdom in one's life was directly tied to one's comprehension of the goodness that is characteristic to human life, and to one's desire of molding one's soul on this specific goodness, of making it the guiding light of one's actions. Such goodness was seen as order, equilibrium, harmony, and measure, and also as the most complex, most refined, and most stable result of rationality.

This ancient interpretation suggests a careful usage of the term "wisdom," especially now that its initial meaning—namely, the strong hierarchical organization of human activities and the absolute primacy of intellectual activity—has almost disappeared. On the other hand, if the current meaning of wisdom is trivialized to the degree that the term only designates the ability to go through life with equanimity and in good spirits, then it can be said that there is no more of *such* wisdom to the Moderns than there was to the Ancients. Indeed, nobody has ever presented a theory of the talent for living a happy life. And if philosophy did present such a theory, it would be much like the sign on sale in Kierkegaard's story. As Chamfort said, "Happiness is not easily won; it is hard to find it in ourselves and impossible to find it elsewhere." If, however, we go back to the original meaning of wisdom, it is clear that certain men and women, in both ancient and modern times, did and do aspire to be guided in their lives by rational thought and philosophy. This aspiration shapes their outlook of the world, influences their cognitive abilities, and modifies the scope of their actions. It defines the good they seek in life; it frames their desires, emotions, and imagination.

Does the drive to attain a kind of goodness that could be internalized in human life still have any meaning for us? The very idea of a good specific to human life could make some people smile, muttering to themselves, "wishful thinking." Freethinkers would claim that good in itself does not exist, good being always relative to one's self or one's culture. They would tell us that goodness is always defined by particular societies, situations, and individuals; that the good is not the same to all; and that, because there is no good in life, there is no meaning to life—life being often an absurd experience that must be overcome. And, yet, if disenchanted people doubt the existence of goodness and of the meaning of life, this does not necessarily mean that such notions have become irrelevant.

Their pertinence for the Ancients and their quasi disappearance from contemporary reflection on human life should, on the contrary, incite us to examine them anew.

Reflecting on our own life or on the life of other people leads us to formulate requirements of meanings and expectations of intelligibility that are often attuned to our own point of view, to the weight of our past, and the contingency of events. Explanations and justifications provided to fulfill such requirements cannot ignore the fact that a human life belongs to a subject to whom things happen, who lives in time and who will die. I define the conditions that determine our requirements for meaning and our expectations of intelligible responses by using the concepts of living subject, event, and plan or project. I also intend to show that reflection on human life is governed by constraints relating, on the one hand, to the general traits of life evoked earlier and, on the other, to the goods and values that shape our motivations. It makes perfect sense to try to find out whether there is a specific goodness to human life—not the substantial goodness derived from having a good thing or being in a good mental state but a goodness defined by essentially formal constraints, that is, the very conditions that give reflection on human life its specificity.

Human life is not a topic forever relegated to the dust of past philosophies. Therefore, it is neither outdated nor postmodern to find out under what conditions one can talk about the meaning of life, that is, a meaning that is unrelated to transcendence or to any substitute for sacredness but deeply rooted in the reflection on human life. On that topic, we would very likely find more important issues to think about than the deification of human beings or the heroic model of Sisyphus. To quote Schopenhauer: "Life is an unpleasant business; I have resolved to spend it reflecting upon it."[3] A life of reflection is already less sad or, at least, it is sad in a different way.

CHAPTER 4

The Absurd and the Meaning of Life

The Meaning of Life: A Meaningless Question?

The solution of the philosophical problem of life is seen in the
vanishing of this problem. (Is it not the reason why men to whom
after long doubting the sense of life became clear could not then
say wherein this sense consisted?)

—WITTGENSTEIN, *Tractatus Logico-Philosophicus*[1]

WITTGENSTEIN acknowledged that "the object of philosophy is the logical clarification of thoughts."[2] Such ambition is not devoid of ethical purpose because existential questions can be answered thus: "We feel that even if *all possible* scientific questions be answered, the problems of life have still not been touched at all. Of course there is then no question left, and just this is the answer."[3] Philosophical reflection contributes to moral understanding if it leads to the realization that it is intrinsically impossible to give a theoretical answer to questions such as the one on the meaning of life. At the same time, Wittgenstein reminds us that every speaker wishes "to go beyond" intelligible language, to use words and phrases in ways that transcend the bounds of the constraints delimiting their signification.[4] The question of the meaning of life—as, by the way, all ethical questions— manifests a linguistic desire that would be frustrated if one would attempt to state a clear answer, explaining, for instance, what precisely is the meaning of life.

In fact, the question has no answer because it makes no sense. Once one understands that the problem is not the difficulty to answer but the nature of the question itself, one would abstain from asking any question of this kind. We would thus stop wondering about the meaning of life, unless we were bent on pouring out nonsense.[5]

Thus, philosophers would play the role of a public park keeper on the watch for the slightest impropriety, the main intellectual impropriety being to trespass into the murky grounds of metaphysics.[6] Put differently, the philosopher would become a therapist convinced that the only raison d'être of philosophy is to dispel everybody's metaphysical doubts, including those of professional philosophers, about the existence of reality, the source of human reason, the meaning of life, and the like.[7] The therapy consists in making the patients speak, showing empathy, evaluating together the manifestation of their affliction, and suggesting a complete description of it. The therapy ends when the diagnostic is achieved and agreed upon. Once the symptoms are completely described, the various levels of meaning restored, and the illusion unveiled, the patients will see the inanity of their question and stop asking it. The deception resides in expecting any moral and cognitive result: "This method would be unsatisfying to the other—He would not have the feeling that we were teaching him philosophy—but it could be the only strictly correct method."[8]

But is this indeed the case? Let's say that it is nonsensical to ask what the meaning of life is, and that the therapist-philosopher has neatly disposed of all possible answers to this question, such as living according to God's designs, defying the world, acknowledging the human condition with lucid despair, and so on. Supposing that the condescension of such critical empathy does not bother us in the least and that we are focusing on preventing the surreptitious comeback of metaphysics; would that be enough to make us aware of our delusion when inquiring about the meaning of life? For some, it may well be the case; others might be impressed with such philosophical prowess, while others still might remain unconvinced. But all those people would probably consider a philosophical critique that finds such a question to be only an abuse of language as being—to put it mildly—quite inadequate.

In fact, this critique concerns itself only with the means by which the question about the meaning of life is asked, that is, by words normally used to request explanations or facts. Very probably this is precisely our dogged way of seeking the meaning of life. As Dostoevsky imagined, that was how Dmitry Karamazov had asked his questions in his dreams: "he felt that although he was asking these questions wildly, without rhyme or reason, he could not prevent himself asking them in just that form, and that that was the form in which they must be asked."[9] Philosophical criticism aims at exactly the same target: the particular ways in which a request for meaning is expressed, not the reasons that would explain or justify it.

When we are asking ourselves whether our lives have meaning—and, if so, to what degree such meaning can be unified or generalized—our reasons for asking such questions remain off target for philosophical criticism. The "therapy" offered by philosophy cannot stop them from being asked, nor can it make us abandon our ways of narrating or representing human life. It is the search for meaning or for a multiplicity of meanings that guides and structures our biographical narratives. We may see a major episode in our life as illuminating a whole series of preceding ones; we talk about the subsequently revealed meaning of a series of events; we often say that an encounter, a decision, or a particular event has given a new meaning to our lives. More generally, our answers to our questions on life are usually multiple, insufficient, incomplete, and not mutually exclusive; but they all help us better understand and make sense of our life; they have a real impact on our awareness of our own actions. Would this be at all possible if our questioning about the meaning of life were nonsensical?

Karl Jaspers said: "When the question of ultimate meaning and value arises, life no doubt gains seriousness through the possibility of an *Existenz* that can now be grasped."[10] If philosophy were indeed unable to provide any answers beyond a critical elucidation of our question, then that would be reason enough to be disappointed in philosophy, if not definitely worried about it. Philosophy would claim to solve a puzzle, which many would consider to be a serious one, by neglecting precisely what most of us believe to be the essence of the problem. The question of the meaning of life is one of the most interesting that could be presented to philosophy. It marks the starting point of the philosophical reflection on human life.

This question is more than a modern interrogation produced by the sickly conscience of our time, supposedly unable to reach the happy harmony with the world attained by ancient Greeks. The truth is that Greek lyrical poetry and tragedy had fully grasped the discrepancy between the grandeur of human aspirations and the vulnerability of their fate exposed to hostile forces. The belief that the realization of the absurdity of life has occurred only in our time comes from the myth of Ancients' health and of Moderns' sickness.

Philosophers' Answer to the Existential Question

Leo Tolstoy describes in memorable terms the intense self-questioning that disturbs the familiar course of our daily existence:

> At first, I went through short times when I did not know what to do, or when I had the feeling that I did not know how to live. The times will come and go at first and then I will go on living. Then they started to happen more and more often. Each time they came with the same question about anything I was doing at the time. Why are you doing this? What does it lead to? At first, I thought these were easy questions, and if I should ever take the time, I could find the answers with little trouble. But I told myself that I did not have the time to find the answers just then. . . . These questions were like the little pains that a person feels before learning that he or she has a sickness that no doctor or medicine can fix: what starts as a little thing, in time leads to their death.

And I could find absolutely no reply. . . . My life came to a stop. I could not help but breathe, eat, drink and sleep because I could not stop doing those things; but there was no real life in me, because there was nothing I wanted strongly enough to do it.[11]

Tolstoy's autobiographical account conveys the emotional intensity of existential questions, and although emotion has no direct link with the conceptual content of the question, it often makes its presence felt in the rhetorical context in which the question is formulated. After all, it is perfectly conceivable that one might ask such questions with serenity. More generally, there is no indication whatsoever that an existential question was either the cause or the effect of the powerful emotive state that often accompanies it.[12] Freud said that simply starting to ask questions about the meaning or the value of life is in itself the sign of deep psychological troubles. This may indeed be the case, but until strong empirical proof is provided to that effect, it remains essential not to confuse the conceptual content of the question with the accompanying emotive state, and not to consider that studying its symptoms is enough to understand the existential question. The question must first be analyzed for its intellectual content, and it must not be reduced to the pathology of the individual who asks it.

Philosophy is on familiar ground when dealing with the logical and linguistic difficulties inherent to the question on the meaning of life. There are a few analytical philosophers who tried to make it easier to understand.[13] When asking what the meaning of life is, one knows already that the question has no evident meaning, and that the interrogation might often be a rhetorical device. Besides, the concept of "life" does not represent here a set of characteristics common to all living beings. In fact, nobody feels the need to explain what one means by "life" before questioning its meaning in order to justify the question. One would rather know whether the question refers to a particular life or to life in general. The two concepts cannot be mistaken for one another. For an *individual life* to have meaning or value, it is not a necessary precondition or consequence for *life in general* to have a meaning. There need not be one thing that forms the purpose of every life. Evaluating an individual life necessarily involves particular circumstances, while evaluating life in general requires leaving them aside.

The ambiguity of the question on the meaning of life permeates the expectations about its answer. Speaking of the "sense" made by one's behavior refers to its discernible intentions. Making sense equals having a purpose, as for instance, when we decide to attain what we believe to be a desirable goal in a given situation. Yet we are clearly unable to determine whether such a goal exists for every life. Even if it were possible to show that the facts and events of a particular life seem to be structured so as to attain a specific goal, it would still not be enough to prove that this particular life leads quasi-intentionally to that specific kind of goal, much less that life in general leads to it. Explaining behavior and describing facts or events that apply to one's life would never fully explain how such behavior, facts, and events are contributing to fulfill its purpose. And this conclusion remains valid regardless whether the retained explanation is teleological or mechanistic in nature.[14] Explanations are limited to linking realities (states of affairs, events, acts) to facts presented as causes or ends but, however general these explanations may be, they never guarantee that one of these facts would truly be the dominant purpose of life.

It follows that the answer to the question on the meaning of life can be neither factual nor descriptive. Indeed, there is an obvious qualitative difference between the search for explanations and justifications during one's life, on one hand, and the idea of a final explanation, on the other. No description or explanation—be it teleological or not—could ever provide an answer to the question whether life has a general goal.[15] The only available answer to the existential question consists in a broader description of the scope of the question, thus, in a certain way, repeating it. Speaking about the meaning or the purpose of life will always consist in a more complete description of the fact that we live. Such a description can never reach a level where specific facts can be predicted. And even if nobody would ever mistake a redescription for an answer, repetition could still bring us a measure of comfort once we realize that there is no answer to be had.

The Impossibility of a Final Justification

Camus maintains that our certainty of life's absurdity comes from our failure to "reduce the world to a rational and reasonable principle."[16] In reality, the idea that the absence of a final justification renders our lives meaningless or that a global justification would give meaning to human life, does enjoy widespread support. The demand for seeking this sort of justification increases in proportion to the place that this search takes in our lives. This is, perhaps, the most common form of reflection that allows us to talk about our own life. It would seem that this demand should apply to all human life. But if it turns out that a final or global justification is impossible, would this not reduce to nothing all reflexive activity, thus rendering meaningless precisely the human feature that makes us masters of our own lives, that is, reflection? If there is no justification for life, then there is none in living it and the existential question will thus remain unanswered.

Such a conclusion seems utterly dubious to me. It presupposes that the justifications of our actions render them meaningful only if they are linked to a global justification of life: nothing would make sense in our lives if our lives were devoid of a final purpose. This presupposition stands on a flawed definition of "justification." The concept relates to a project or an action whose explanatory reasons are sufficient to justify them. Also, a justification that leads to the justified action constitutes a good justification and does not need to be tied up to a broader and exhaustive justification.[17] To our minds, many of our actions are perfectly justified upon being performed and need no ulterior, or broader, justification. Moreover, in certain cases, it would make no sense to look for ulterior reasons. When I see a child in danger, my only justification in rushing to his help comes from his being in danger. I can certainly explain my intervention, and—if pressed—I could also explain what is wrong when a child is endangered. But these explanations are not needed to justify the act itself of coming to somebody's help. There is no reason to think that such justification is not a good one, and even less reason to believe that—unless I provide a justification for justifying my coming to a child's help—I could not justify my action.[18]

Some would counter that there are very broad justifications that apply naturally to a whole class of phenomena; so why doubt the existence of a global justification of our life as a whole? At this juncture, it may be appropriate to specify what constitutes an accessible reason or justification in one's life. According to the American philosopher Thomas Nagel, an existential justification is one that gives meaning to our acts.[19] Based on this definition what would be the sense of a justification covering the totality of our life? I may believe that my whole existence is justified by the good that I am able to do for others. But if I am seeking a final justification, I cannot stop there: I must learn what justifies the larger whole formed by my entire life and those of all the people involved in my good deeds. Thus, all that an alleged broader justification could do would only move the justification question one notch up.

Nor is there any reason to think that the absence of a global justification diminishes either the value of the justifications we use in our everyday life or our confidence in them. On the contrary, there is every indication that only the likelihood of a global justification could deprive our ordinary justifications of meaning. Their pertinence, which resides precisely in their particularity and their connection to individual acts, would be undermined by the hypothesis of a final justification that would absorb the ordinary ones so that they could finally reach completion. Saying that life has no meaning because there is no dominant end that would represent its final justification is therefore a non sequitur.

Immortality and the Vanity of Human Life

The prolific literature devoted to lamenting the mortality inherent to the human condition often suggests that only immortality would give meaning to life, that our lives would acquire full meaning only if we were immortal. Death will unravel the tangle of goals, pursuits, desires, and ideals that shape our lives; nothing will be left from what drives us to continually reinterpret and take on our own life, that is, our complex and sophisticated web of thoughts and desires, as well as our refined maze of explanations, justifications, forced rationalizations, and commonsense reasons. At best, what would be left of our life will be a narrative—a series of events, actions, and thoughts that others will remember or talk about—as viewed by a third person, not by the subject, because death irrevocably abolishes the subject's limited point of view and all its justifications.

However striking this train of thought may seem, it remains essentially slanted. As it has already been shown, even if immortality were to pass for life's final justification, the absence of such justification would not constitute proof that life is meaningless. Furthermore, the certainty of one's death is not incompatible with the search for justifications during one's life. Rather, it could be said that our mortality is precisely what confers relevance to our life's justifications. As Sartre liked to emphasize, the meaning of one's life is on hold until death takes over. Being "on hold" is an incentive to search for life's meaning. Many of our justifications owe their gravity and their extraordinary importance—in our eyes—to our awareness of our own mortality. Kierkegaard thought that a truly human life never ceases to react to death. As for Sartre, he argued aggressively that human finitude is related less to human mortality than to our constant need to choose and decide. And he concluded that even an immortal life would still be—as a sequence of choices—caught in finitude.[20] I would add that our finitude is also present in the search for the justifications that give meaning and cohesiveness to the act of choosing. The mortality of human beings is certainly not a sufficient condition for meaningfulness, but it might be a necessary condition for it because it forces us—precisely by virtue of our choosing—to justify our choices in our own minds over and over as long as we live.

Wittgenstein said only half-jokingly that eternal life is as much of a riddle as actual life. We may wonder what would become of the search for meaning and justifications of life if we knew that we were not going to die. Immortal life would not be threatened by death but by repetition and boredom, which are as destructive of meaning as death itself—unless, that is, a person's character underwent massive changes during its unending life. In this case, however, could one still speak of the immortality of the *same* person? In order to avoid the sensation of repetition and boredom that would undoubtedly spoil immortal life, we would have to assume that immortality provides more than an ordinary human life, that is, a quasi-divine, heavenly life, free from desires, deceptions, and weariness. It would not be the simple immortality of our regular life but an ideal, superhuman life never experienced before.[21] If our conception of human life does not change, and the definition of justification remains the same, then there is no apparent reason to believe that immortal life would have more meaning that mortal life.

Another much lamented shortcoming of human mortality has to do with time. The complaint consists in noticing that after a short period of time on the cosmic scale, such as say, two centuries, our lives would not represent anything to anybody anymore, thus inescapably loosing all meaning. If death does indeed annihilate life and all meaning that it carries, then after our death, nothing that we had done or considered important would matter in the least. This would lead some to infer that whatever we are doing is worthless.

Such a conclusion seems to me over-reaching. Very probably, my life would have no relevance two centuries after my death. In which case, its worth in two hundred years should have no relevance for me today and have therefore no effect on what gives meaning to my life now. Conversely, if I had good reasons to believe that my present deeds would be relevant in two centuries, would this give meaning to my present life? Should we not suppose, in addition, that my present life, such as it is, already has meaning? Otherwise, if I were to consider my present life meaningless, the certainty that it will be meaningful in two hundred years could not change my belief in its present absurdity.[22] Only if I considered my deeds to be meaningful today and also in the future would my hope that they will be relevant in two centuries make me think that they have additional value today. That my life would have no worth attached to it in two hundred years does not imply that it has none now: no alleged certitude about the future could justify an inference about the present. The same slippery reasoning is found in the complaint that our life amounts to naught in cosmic terms. Again, we may wonder, what would justify the conclusion that the infinitesimal length of our life deprives it of meaning? If human life were to last as long as the cosmos itself, how would that make it more meaningful? In my view, even if our lives were as vast as the universe, this would still not preclude them from being meaningless.

Does the meaning of life depend on transcendent factors, such as the existence of God or of larger realities that infuse meaning in human projects (a cause to fight for, a political movement, the will to become useful to mankind or to remain famous after death)? Let us consider the simple case of an individual who would find a meaning to his life only in a reality that goes beyond him, for example, all his past and future interactions with other people—already dead, still living, or yet to be born—whose lives have been or would be improved by his actions. Let us say that he intends to bequeath his considerable fortune to all these people or that he volunteers to undergo an experimental medical procedure whose outcome would save many sick people. All those who are benefiting from his gift are also giving meaning to his life, but what meaning have the lives of those who are benefiting from his good deeds? And if the latter were irrelevant, then why should the former matter to the individual in question? The same reasoning would apply to the views that deny any meaning to individual existence but acknowledge it for future generations or for the whole history of mankind. Why should those broader sets of human lives be exempted from questions about their own meaning? The same goes for high causes and ideals said to transcend human existence. The higher status of an ideal should not exempt us from inquiring about its meaning.

In the last pages of *My Confession*, Tolstoy acknowledges that the only way to make life bearable is to choose to believe in a benevolent and all powerful God that transcends the material and natural universe. Much of the existentialist tradition is inspired by religious meditation on the vanity of human life and by the human beings' aspiration to put themselves in the hands of a higher power whose reason of being escapes us. For many believers, God's existence may be the answer to the existential question, but the conceptual content of such an answer remains very likely unclear. Also, it is by no means certain that the belief in God suffices to give a definite meaning to human life, or at least an adequate meaning to the expectation of intelligibility entailed in the existential question.[23] As for unbelievers, they will probably remain indifferent to this option. They will likely ask on what is based the certainty of a divine intention concerning human beings, or they will counter that if indeed the answer to the existential question is so easy to find in God, why could we not find it in human beings, period. The faith in the existence of God may defer the question on the meaning of life but cannot answer it properly. Surely, faith makes it easier to accept the mismatch between human designs and an incomprehensible world, but it is unable to suppress it or to justify it completely. In Tolstoy's words, "I knew that I could find nothing in the way of rational knowledge except a denial of life; and in faith, I could find nothing except a denial of reason, and this was even more impossible than a denial of life."[24] This is not to say that faith is unreasonable, only that rationality generates demands for meaning to which faith cannot provide a definite conceptual content.

What conclusion can be drawn from this critical analysis? First and foremost, our own mortality, the fact that each human being is doomed to extinction, the uncertainty about God, and the human inability to grasp the divine are not sufficient for establishing that human life is devoid of meaning. Moreover, pessimistic and nihilistic arguments claiming that life has no meaning unless we secure a transcendent justification have little value. For his part, Nietzsche saw in this search for final meaning an unfortunate outcome of grammar: "The nihilistic question 'for what?' is rooted in the old habit of supposing that the goal must be put up, given, demanded from the outside—by some superhuman authority." But this does not preclude "the search for an immanent spirit and a goal within."[25]

The Meaning of Life in a Naturalistic World

Human life is the life of a being defined by a set of physical and psychological abilities and experiencing mental states—such as hope, fear, and desire—that are fully natural. In addition, human life is made of events, choices, outcomes, and other realities whose ontological status is not clear, but which could be plausibly viewed as natural. Lastly, human life evolves in a natural world and is in itself a natural phenomenon. Should this fact alone not render the search for the meaning of life pointless? Could one hope to discover more meaning in human life than there is in the physical universe? At best, such a search could reveal some form of coherence merely based on a chain of events linked by contiguity or causality. Should one not conclude that the lack of meaning in human life is but a consequence of a similar deficit in the natural world?

It is true that from the nineteenth century onward, science offered a representation of the natural world in which the human being, his body and mental states, is but a product of complex causal phenomena. This representation replaced the older view of the universe organized by spiritual values and final causes. That such a "scientific representation" describes human life as devoid of meaning should come as no surprise, because in the traditional and sometimes quasi-ideological definition of science, scientific explanations have no access to meaning.

Such skepticism is all too familiar, but it is also irrelevant to the existential question. This scientific view of the natural world and of human life does not establish that the question on the meaning of life is meaningless. To view a phenomenon as natural and as an effect of natural causes is a characteristic feature of scientific explanations that does not predetermine in any way the nature of the phenomenon under study.

Moreover, this particular conception of science has changed radically during the second half of the twentieth century. This led to the return of teleology to the natural sciences, the reintroduction in molecular biology of a teleology free of metaphysical implications, and the adoption of a postulate of cybernetics stating that the logic of meaning should be sought in physical laws.[26] The acceptance of a scientific vision of life is not an acknowledgment that the universe is devoid of meaning. In addition to causal explanations of natural phenomena, there are teleological, or final, explanations that the scientific spirit does not proscribe anymore. They serve as useful tools in our reflection on human life and our search for justifications. Teleological explanations do not supplement causal explanations and are not intended to replace them when they fail to explain. They are simply explanations of a different kind.

The Existential Question and the Feeling of Absurdity

The existentialist thinkers acknowledged that the inquiry into the meaning of life was closely linked to the feeling that life is absurd. Saying that something is absurd is admitting that we do not know what it means, that it does not fit our expectations, that it proves deficient when compared with something that would be appropriate in that context; an absurd thing has nothing to do with anything. The feeling of loss of meaning and the perception of lack of proportion or adequacy are both at the core of the consciousness of absurdity. We can certainly question ourselves about human life without experiencing what Camus called "the incalculable feeling that deprives the mind of the sleep necessary for life."[27] But we can also realize—as I will attempt to show in what follows—that this feeling not only makes the existential question even more urgent but brings us closer to understanding its meaning.

It is a misleading to speak here of a "feeling" of absurdity. A more appropriate term would be "realization," which denotes a particular cognitive state. The anxiety triggered by the feeling of absurdity points to this cognitive state without causing it and without fully capturing its nature. In his essay *The Myth of Sisyphus*, Camus described "the origins of the absurd": the astonishment sneaking in the weariness of living, man's brutal realization that he "belongs to time," the inhumanity of human nature and of its "meaningless pantomimes," as well as the "mathematical," that is, "elementary and final" character of death. Camus considered that the multiple forms taken by the discord between humans and their world bring up the question of the reason for living and create "this strangeness of perceiving that the world is dense," characteristic of the realization of absurdity.[28]

The feeling of absurdity allows us to distance ourselves from our own life. Traditionally, this is expressed through the usual complaints about the shortness of human life, the vastness of the universe, the inescapability of death, or the gradual effacing of memory. Pascal admirably depicted this cognitive state: "When I consider the brief span of my life absorbed into the eternity which comes before and after as the remembrance of a guest that tarrieth but a day—the small space which I occupy and which I see swallowed up in the infinite immensity of spaces of which I know nothing and which know nothing of me, I take fright and I am amazed to see myself here rather than there. There is no reason for me to be here rather than there, now rather than then. Who put me here? By whose command and act were this time and place allotted to me?"[29]

We feel, moreover, that we are strangers to our own life. In a way, we become the spectators of our own existence, as if it were played in front of us. We see it without precondition or familiarity, as the "life stoppage" described by Tolstoy. The ties that bind our mind and emotions to the outside world making it familiar to us gradually loosen. The meaning conditions of our ordinary, familiar world slip away. We find ourselves projected away from our personal viewpoint toward an impersonal one that is either divine or immersed in the material world. The projection is facilitated by our eagerness "to take a point of view outside the particular forms of our lives, from which the seriousness appears gratuitous."[30]

That the feeling of absurdity is first and foremost a cognitive state is made clear by the role of beliefs in its expression. The existential question would not be asked were it not for our beliefs and interests in the world. We constantly nurture a variety of aspirations and desires not only about our actions and their consequences—we make long-term plans, we commit to other people and assume responsibilities in their regard, and we submit to hardships hoping for ulterior benefits—but also about our personality, possible future developments in our life, or the role that others may play in it. And when these beliefs and desires clash with other beliefs about our life that we also hold dear, we experience the feeling of absurdity because we fear that this collision endangers all our decisions and deliberations, depriving our actions of any consequence. For instance, we persist in getting better at tennis knowing full well that sickness may strike us at any moment; we work tirelessly to renovate our house while being aware that a fire may burn it down; we commit ourselves to worthy goals in spite of being self-conscious about our mortality and that of those close to us. There is no guarantee that we will carry out our plans, honor our duties, get a well-deserved return for our efforts, or fulfill what we consider to be our main purpose in life.

This kind of cognitive dissonance reminds us that our conviction in the beneficial outcomes and consequences of our actions seems unreasonable, irrational even, when confronted with what we know of the precariousness of our existence. The limits of human condition and the properties of the world can easily demolish the justification of our beliefs in our actions and prospects. As Camus wrote, "It is essential to consider as a constant point of reference . . . the hiatus between what we fancy we know and what we really know, between practical assent and simulated ignorance which allows us to live with ideas which, if we truly put them to the test, ought to upset our whole life."[31]

The vivid literary and philosophical descriptions of the absurd have been so widely disseminated that, in a way, they prevent us from addressing the mental reality associated with the existential question other than the rhetoric of disorientation and strangeness. One might even surmise that those who have not been exposed to existential literature would express in entirely different terms the mental states experienced in connection with the existential question. Is it not paradoxical to ask philosophy to analyze the absurdity of human life, when it is precisely philosophy that bears the responsibility for closely associating the feeling of the absurd with the current formulation of the existential question?

The answer to this question is negative: while there is no doubt that existentialist literature and philosophy have constantly linked the understanding of the existential question to the exploration of the feeling of absurdity, there is also no indication that this feeling is the product of existentialist literature or philosophy. One does not have to be a philosopher in order to experience this feeling, which seems to be a natural outcome of one's reflection on human life. Even among philosophers, the existentialists were not the first, nor the greatest, to evoke the futility of human life: the Orphic poets were inspired by it, and this sort of lamentation on human existence was common in ancient times. Granted that philosophy had partially shaped existential questions, what would that prove? It would prove only that self-questioning about the meaning of life requires us to reach a certain exteriority, to find a detached viewpoint from which to describe and evaluate human life. Reaching this viewpoint by some sort of bootstrapping does not amount to circular reasoning. It simply happens that such viewpoint is often reached by various people. It matters little whether the revelation comes from the study of existentialist philosophers or Dostoevsky's novels, from a minimal awareness of human existence or a psychological disorder. What matters is to understand—by analyzing the feeling of absurdity—what is the legitimate meaning of the existential question, not what brought this question about.

More often than not, the feeling of absurdity and the associated cognitive effects of remoteness from one's own life and strangeness from the world provide the context in which the existential question begins to make sense. If the question is posed in the abstract or in relation to a third person, it might sound pointless ("Let's talk about X. What is the meaning of his life?"). This might seem to confirm the adepts of philosophical therapy in their belief that the question is nonsensical, but it would do so only in this particular context. In other words, one may be justified in arguing that the existential question is devoid of meaning, but the only ones to be persuaded are those who do not experience the distance and the strangeness provoked by the feeling of absurdity and therefore do not even bother to raise this question. In normal cases, the sense of belonging and familiarity are preconditions of significance. The problem is that the feeling of absurdity disturbs the sensation of familiarity and discredits the sense of belonging. By its very nature, the existential question is therefore deprived of the meaning usually provided by familiarity. But this does not prove that it is devoid of any meaning, especially if it is tied to the cognitive reality of the absurd. Skeptics may counter that the feeling of absurdity always carries some artifice, that distance and strangeness can be aroused more or less deliberately, and that human intelligence better find a remedy to such ill-fated tendencies. Even if the feeling of absurdity were indeed the product of some peculiar, arrogant romanticism of the ego, the problem would still remain unresolved. Once the feeling of absurdity has revealed itself, there is no escape from it. The only course of action left open to us is to use it as an additional resource of reflection on human life.

Reflecting on Human Life and Confronting the Absurd

The feeling of absurdity seems to be the commonest starting point of all reflection on human life. Whether sparked by an inner experience, the shock of an event, or a simple memory, reflection on human life usually evolves from a cognitive state of remoteness and estrangement. The fact that the subject adopts a dissociated viewpoint is the natural effect of his reflexive activity. He moves from the viewpoint of the first person—which reveals the value that the subject sees in his material existence and his strong identification with his goals—toward a viewpoint situated above him or in a third person, wherefrom his existence appears detached from himself.

The discrepancy between these viewpoints is the specific trait of the feeling of absurdity. According to Nagel, the absurd results from the special capacity that humans have "to step back and survey themselves and the lives to which they are committed, with that detached amazement which comes from watching an ant struggle up a heap of sand. Without developing the illusion that they are able to escape from their highly specific and idiosyncratic position, they can view it *sub specie aeternitatis*—and the view is at once sobering and comical."[32] Insofar as this discrepancy stimulates the reflection that helps us to confront, distance from or transcend the feeling of absurdity, it allows us to perform a rational activity that, to a certain extent, contains and reduces absurdity. By concomitantly providing us with an internal and an overhanging point of view, the feeling of absurdity becomes a permanent background feature that simultaneously triggers two complementary effects: a clear evidence of the absurd and a way to overcome it through reflection.

In *The Myth of Sisyphus*, Camus advances a thesis that is more radical and more restricted than Nagel's: the absurd is not tied to the common reflection on existence but brought about by our particular expectations of intelligibility with respect to our life. The feeling of absurdity comes from the fact that our approach to the world is guided by an expectation of unity, affinity, and suitability and by our aspiration that the world will belong to us and resemble us. Unlike Camus though, I think that there is no indication of the feeling of the absurd being tied to a strong and precise expectation of elements that give meaning to life such as appetite for unity, thirst for the absolute, or longing for familiarity. Furthermore, Camus repeatedly suggests that if the world were different, if it could satisfy our expectation of unity, clarity, and likeness, then we would not experience anymore the feeling of the absurd: "If man realized that the universe like him can love and suffer, he would be reconciled."[33] This is doubtful. One might as well argue the contrary, namely that even though we may have reason to believe that the feeling of the absurd is unjustified, this feeling would not disappear. Camus also argues that if the world were different, that is, endowed with different factual realities, we might not experience this feeling anymore. His conviction that we have strong, subjective expectations of meaning that could be fulfilled in a better world, leads him deliberately to confuse the feeling of absurdity with the conviction that life is absurd. Actually, these are distinct and apart: one can experience absurdity—as the cognitive condition previously described here—without concluding that life is meaningless.[34] He claims that the absurd "depends as much on man as on the world," but he does not say whether the divorce opposes humans to their world or takes place within the same person, who cannot avoid holding two opposing viewpoints.[35] In fact, the specificity of the feeling of absurdity resides not in being brought about by a state of the world, but in a consciousness closely associated with reflection on life. We do not experience this feeling for contingent reasons, but as a natural product of reflection through self-distancing, adoption of another's outlook, and self-overview.[36]

Camus asks whether there is a "direct connection" between the certitude that life is absurd (which he identifies again with the feeling of absurdity) and "the longing for death." In other words: does the absence of a reason for living constitute a reason for dying?[37] If there were a connection, and because human actions are linked to beliefs, then the suicide would be the only answer to the certitude that life is not worth living. "The question is how to escape the absurd, through hope or suicide. This is what must be clarified, hunted down, and elucidated while brushing aside all the rest. Does the Absurd dictate death?"[38] It would be indeed irrational to continue acting, and because it is impossible to live without action, it would be preferable to put an end to this fair of vanities. Suicide suppresses the incoherence that governs our beliefs, as well as its unpleasant consequences. Actually, Camus does not discuss the connection between absurdity and suicide, but examines the consequences flowing from the realization of absurdity. He strongly argues that to sense the absurd means to accept it. Suicide is therefore not a solution, because it denies the absurd instead of acknowledging it. To put and end to one's life is to abolish the absurd by dragging it into one's own death, while to accept the absurd is to use it as a sign of conscious rebellion, inspired by utter hopelessness, refusal to yield, and deliberate dissatisfaction.

According to Camus, "What counts is not the best living but the most living: breaking all the records is first and foremost being faced with the world as often as possible," choosing the way of life that brings us closer to our humanity: "my revolt, my freedom and my passion. By the mere activity of consciousness, I transform it into a rule of life."[39]

Camus asserts that one has to confront the intellectual task of upholding the absurd without compromising one's lucidity and without "intentional mutilation of the soul." This excludes, on the one hand, "the extreme rationalization of reality," which for some reason Camus identifies with Husserlian philosophy, and, on the other, "its extreme irrationalization which tends to deify it," which negates "the humiliated reason."[40] However, Camus does not say anything about one's limits or how to define them. And although he insists on the need to preserve the expectations of intelligibility, he also claims that our common justifications in life lose their reason for being once the absurdity of life is experienced. In other words, there is no sense anymore in wondering what our actions mean.

I strongly object to this interpretation of the relationship between the sense of the absurd and the work of rationality. The consciousness of absurdity comes from the reflection on human life, and as such it is closely related to the search for justifications that give meaning to life. The absurdity of life is a philosophical and intellectual problem rather than a psychological or moral one.[41] If by asking the question of the meaning of life we seek to know to what extent we can establish justifications on this subject, then we will still know nothing about what kind of justifications we should be seeking. The appropriate justifications should take into account the particular aspects of our life, which means that the search for life's meaning should also aim at particular aspects. The justifications we would be seeking in order to grasp the meaning of life would not resemble those used in other contexts or situations. In fact, attempting to answer the question of the meaning of life by searching for justification is a way of coming back to the feeling of the absurd. The feeling itself is the trigger for reflection. And, as such, it is the polar opposite of Kierkegaard's paradox, which abolishes itself in a direct justification.[42]

The existential question shares certain traits with what Stephen Toulmin called "limiting questions."[43] A limiting question does not have a literal meaning. It cannot have an answer based on the usual meaning suggested by the words composing it or by its grammatical structure. "How did this happen?" and "Why must one do what is right?" are limiting questions. They express not only surprise (as in reaction to a scientific explanation), but astonishment, even disarray, that such is the case. Nevertheless, such questions are not out of the bounds of rationality; they initiate a search for reasons. Acknowledging their importance only reinforces Pascal's warning: "Two errors: 1) Taking everything literally, 2) Taking everything spiritually."[44]

The existential question initiates the search for reasons and justifications. Obviously, when Pascal anxiously asks the question: "Who put me here? By whose command and act were this time and place allotted to me?,"[45] he is not expecting a literal answer. The very effort of searching the information needed to answer would prevent one's grasping the meaning of what is asked. Is it to say that that the only acceptable answer would have to be put in terms of attitude, reaction, approval, or choice? Not at all, because this would mean dismissing too hastily the rational activity that lies at the heart of the existential question. It does not merely ask what reality or fact would give meaning to life or what general attitude is to be taken toward life; it rather breaks a vast and fertile ground for reflection on what gives meaning to life. When, after an unfortunate event that obliterates one's efforts of many years, one cries out, "Why did this happen?" one does more than express disarray in the face of a stroke of fate; one strives to place this event relative to one's past and future decisions. When we are asking this type of questions, we are engaging in the difficult intellectual work of making the event commensurate to other events and decisions in our life, of fitting it into our reasons and adapting it to our patterns of understanding our life. Usually, such questions exact a strenuous intellectual effort of rationalization, evaluation, and consistency.

Reason often switches from one aspect of the question to another. The question "Why did this happen?" is progressively reformulated as "What will be the effects, on myself, of this having happened?" Moreover, the most common answer to the existential question is not to adopt an attitude (declarative knowledge) but to find a rule (procedural knowledge) that would encapsulate some wisdom or know-how about life.[46] A rule does not provide procedures applicable to all decisions. It is not based on true propositions, nor is it inferred from metaphysical axioms, but it does allow us to establish the significance of our ulterior behavior. Thus, Tolstoy describes life-changing events that affect some of his novels' characters. In the last pages of *War and Peace*, Pierre Bezukhov's state of mind changes profoundly—not into a conversion or adherence to a certain truth, nor an acknowledgment of a fact, but into a newly acquired "tranquility of spirit and inner harmony that he had been so impressed to notice in the soldiers fighting at Borodino." Similarly, in *Anna Karenina*, Levin experiences a feeling of relief and reassurance after his marriage to Kitty: "My whole life, apart from anything that can happen to me every minute of it, is no longer meaningless as it was before but it has an unquestionable meaning of the goodness which I have the power to put into it."[47] In both cases the meaning of life is not revealed by the discovery of a fact or by a factual proposition, which could prove true or false; it is not the result of new attitudes, emotions, or preferences that would entail no rational response. Rather, it is tied to the formulation of a rule or know-how about life that links the obvious with a form of reason.

In logical terms, it is impossible to give a literal answer to the question on the meaning of life whether by means of an identifiable concept or proposition. This does not mean that this question's only content is of an attitudinal or emotional nature because, in formulating it, human beings consent to a serious effort of elaboration and justification. And the only acceptable answer to this question would be one shaped as a search for justifications. Such justifications would not be merely subjective because their legitimacy is not based exclusively on the subject's attitudes and reactions. They will not have a propositional form either. The answer suggested by existential justifications will be closely related to the subject without being subjective. It will not be propositional, yet it will have a rational justification and enjoy a certain form of objectivity.

The reflection on human life is conditioned by constraints that explain the particularity of existential justifications. These constraints concern the invariants of human life, the goods and values that govern our reasons for acting. Their presence justifies the aspiration to objectivity that permeates our reflection on human life. Thus, the elaboration of existential justifications reveals the deepest meaning of the Socratic injunction: "The unexamined life is not worth living" (Plato, *Apology*).

CHAPTER 5

The Invariants of Human Life

Scratching beneath the varnish of philosophers' answers to the existential question, one discovers that all they do is, at best, repeat the question and, at worst, display a sign much like the one in Kierkegaard's secondhand shop. Having philosophical expertise does not entitle one to impose rules or prescribe ways of life. A philosopher's advantage is simply rhetorical: generally, he is abler than most to prove his point. How then, can I explain my coming to the defense of the philosophical reflection on human life as I did at the beginning of this book? What can philosophy hope to achieve by being on its guard against preaching wisdom or limiting itself to the minimalism of philosophical therapy? Many of us are obsessed with the existential question because it persists as a search for intelligibility and justification. Thus, if philosophers are indeed the ones to teach us how to become aware of reality, then they better not ignore it.[1]

"Most Living" through Reflection

The existential question is strongly connected to the feeling of absurdity, which has been analyzed here mainly in cognitive terms. This feeling occurs as soon as we start either to reflect on human life or to seek justifications for it, and it creates an impression of inescapable strangeness and remoteness. We experience it as an effect of the imperfect superposition of multiple perspectives on our lives: we cannot but adopt all those perspectives and be pained by their lack of convergence. It is in this sense that the feeling of absurdity signals the beginning of the reflection on human life.

Human beings are deeply committed to the ideas of rationality and justification. Reflection on human life is supposed to increase our understanding of life, make us more transparent to ourselves, and give us more control on events. While being rooted in the feeling of absurdity, reflection manages to contain and overcome it. But our awareness of this feeling subsists nevertheless in the back of our minds: it renders useless our search for reasons and justifications for human life, and it makes a vain pretense out of our drive for clarity. How can it be tackled? What are its consequences?

Our awareness of absurdity could make us think that it might be preferable to stop reflecting on our existence because it appears that no reflection would ever succeed in making our life intelligible to ourselves. Reflecting on our reasons to act is certainly useful but in a very limited sense. This is illustrated by Aliosha's declaration to Ivan in *The Brothers Karamazov*: "It's a feature of the Karamazov, it's true, that thirst for life regardless of everything; you have it no doubt too. . . . I have a longing for life, and I go on living in spite of logic."[2] Taking over our life is not the result of a justification or comprehension process but originates in the act of living itself. To live our life would not consist in refining our reasons to act, reflecting on our decisions or weaving some sort of meaning into our life; rather, it would mean plunging into action, standing for life, and justifying our stand at least in part based on our interests, aspirations, and commitments.

Some existentialist thinkers have adopted this injunction as a meaning-yielding affirmation. Such is Camus's call to "most living" in *The Myth of Sisyphus*:[3] he binds us to embrace the consciousness of absurdity, to go further by imposing our choices, commitments, and values on it by constantly defying "world's irrationality." The meaning of life must come only from projects we proclaim to be ours. Our responsibility is to maintain the absurd by expressing anew our strong demands for meaning and to deepen it by superimposing our own decisions on it. Camus believes that we are constructing the meaning of our own lives and that we are more or less deliberately molding our lives in a fitting shape by refusing to believe that only transcendent goals can generate meaning. The meaning thus created by us, resists the evidence of the fact that our life does not pursue any general purpose. Above all, the meaning we give to our life does not have to be univocal, verifiable, or predetermined; it may be intentionally ambiguous and uncertain. "To declare that existence is absurd is to deny that it can ever be given meaning; to say that it is ambiguous is to assert that its meaning is never fixed, that it must be constantly won."[4]

The idea of Camus and de Beauvoir that, in an absurd situation, meaning is somehow decided by the imposition of goals, commitments, and decisions raises many legitimate questions. To begin with, the general configuration of Camus's injunction of "most living" is problematic. Its opaqueness and intrinsic difficulty had already been signaled in Schopenhauer's analysis of *Existenz*. Schopenhauer does not use the phrase "absurdity of life," but the theme at the core of his thinking is close to it. According to him, the blind impulse, the unconscious, indistinct will to live is deeply ingrained in all reality, as is the uncontrollable drive to procreate and perpetuate life.[5] The will evolves from inorganic nature, to the vegetal and animal kingdoms, and further to the human brain, where it acquires self-consciousness. The human being becomes thus aware that

reality is but an illusion and that life is essentially suffering. Schopenhauer's terminology of pointless suffering, of the chimerical quality of all
passion, the vanity of all reality, and the futility of all human action comes
quite close to what Camus calls the absurdity of life.

Realizing the senseless cruelty of their condition, human beings face a
dilemma and, according to Schopenhauer, they must choose between the
following options. On the one hand, one may say no to the will acting
within oneself and put a stop to all effort and suffering. In this case, one
would find in one's surroundings only nonmotives for action, appease-
ments, and impediments; one would deny the will to live, recognize the
fundamental identity of all beings, and thus free oneself from individuation (*principium individuationis*). Schopenhauer explicitly links this path
of self-denial to the freedom theme of Indian philosophical schools—a
freedom rooted in knowledge (knowing that all is nothing) and nonaction.[6]
On the other hand, one may choose to affirm the will to live, to assert the
reality of one's individuality and the solid existence of phenomena, thus
preserving the world's suffering.

> Affirmation of the will-to-live, the phenomenal world, diversity of all beings,
> individuality, egoism, hatred, wickedness, all spring from *one* root . . . the
> existence of the plant is just such a restless, never satisfied striving, a ceaseless
> activity through higher and higher forms, till the final point, the seed, becomes
> anew a starting-point and this is repeated *ad infinitum*; nowhere is there a
> goal, nowhere a final satisfaction, nowhere a point of rest. . . . everywhere the
> many different forces of nature and organic forms contest with one another
> for the matter in which they desire to appear, since each possesses only what
> it has wrested from another. Thus a constant struggle is carried on between
> life and death. . . . It presses and urges in vain, yet by reason of its inner nature
> it cannot cease; it toils on laboriously until this phenomenon perishes, and
> then others eagerly seize its place and its matter.[7]

The absurd—or what Schopenhauer terms reality's endless suffering—
is tied to the striving of the will to live to take over an individual and
pretend, through him, that the world is the reality. In spite of appearances,
suicide is not a solution, only a false way out. More than anything, it is a
passionate affirmation of the will to live.[8]

Camus's call to "most living" clearly represents the second option: the
strong assertion of the will to live, human beings' taking charge of world's
absurdity. But if the absurd is indeed suffering, nonconciliation, and discord, how then could its strong assertion change its very nature? How
could "most living" remedy the suffering that is life itself? If our awareness
of absurdity is somehow the result of our search for meaning, then the
very idea that an intensified search would open new life possibilities is
contradictory. This objection in no way implies agreement with Schopen-

hauer's philosophy; simply, it reveals the intrinsic weakness of a solution that praises the "quantity" of life, while disregarding the rational resources that could enable us to give meaning to life's challenge. Above all, it makes the intellectual dimension of the feeling of absurdity disappear under the weight of countless decisions and commitments. Because I fully disagree with such a view of the absurd, I would like to show that the absurd should not be simply *reaffirmed* but also *understood* in the light of the justifications we use in our lives. Rational reflection on human life leads to a resolution of this contradiction.[9]

The feeling of absurdity is closely linked to the manner in which we seek meaning in life, and to the particular kind of justifications we use in so doing. Despair and defiance are no doubt necessary for our coexisting with absurdity but they cannot make its conceptual content accessible to us. Rather, they risk blurring our thoughts and preventing us from realizing why the feeling of absurdity remains at the core of the reflection on human life. Existentialist proclamations of defiance, disdain, commitment, and even retreat with respect to human life share the view that the answer to the meaning of life has nothing to do with intellectual efforts, and especially with the search for reasons: human intelligence can only help with the description of the world as is (or with the prediction or definition of the means for action), but must leave the task of dealing with the meaning of life exclusively to acts of will, attitudes, decisions, and choices. In this view, only a look from outside in can claim objectivity and only the will is entitled to give meaning to life—a meaning attached exclusively to the first-person view of the subject.[10]

To me, this view seems wrong: I think that the first-person view of the world and the effort to see it from a third-person perspective are joined together; their mutual link is essential to the consciousness of absurdity. Also, the individual's effort to understand human life from a personal perspective is not necessarily subjective nor is it arbitrary. Reducing it to an attitude, a standpoint, or a set of decisions is to deliberately discard a truly cognitive resource for the reflection on life. Lastly, even if decisions and choices were imposed on life in order to give it meaning—be it to love life, to fulfill our commitments, or to posit values—this would still not exempt us from the deliberate intellectual effort of reflection, proof, and evaluation. More importantly, if we truly want to challenge life and justify this point of view, we cannot dispense with the search for reasons.[11]

Our inner justifications for our life are closely linked to our feeling of absurdity. Their formal features allow us to explain the persistence of this feeling. If we agree that the search for justifications is somehow tied to an injunction such as "One ought to live," then we have to recognize that the latter is also an intellectual challenge. Rousseau might have been overwhelmed by his nostalgia for some sort of immediacy when he declared:

"I dare almost affirm that a state of reflection is a state against nature, and that the man who meditates is a depraved animal."[12] He is certainly right to the extent that the human species does belong to the animal kingdom, but it is hard to see how people could dispense with reflecting on their lives when, as Socrates said, those are human lives.

I would like to defend a definition of the meaning of life that would enhance the concrete texture of justification.[13] Reflection on our life is subject to constraints related, on the one hand, to the general and invariant features of the human condition (analyzed in this section) and, on the other hand, to goods and values (dealt with in chapter 6). Behavior rules that can be defined in terms of life's invariants and goods are an important step toward reaching objectivity in our reasons to act and our efforts to justify our lives. I believe that the distinctive features of existential justifications explain to a great extent our self-consciousness of absurdity, which lingers in the back of our minds.

Existential Justifications and Self-Reflection

The fact that the search for the meaning of life leads to a process of rational justification becomes clear as soon as we examine the familiar activities through which we compare our lives, criticize or evaluate them, and look for conditions or circumstances that could have made them more consistent and more rational. When questioned about the basis of this kind of reasoning, we have no difficulty in answering. Comparing human lives, possible lives, or lives lived in different circumstances makes sense to us because we assume to have implicit criteria that guide our reflection on life. Among those criteria are an appreciation for the significance of strong commitments or momentous decisions that have lifelong consequences; the insight that the reasons for our decisions and actions may prove false under certain circumstances (as is often the case with faulty beliefs, self-delusions, or insincerity); a capacity for making ourselves recognized as subjects of our lives and not allowing events or other people's desires to upset us; the requirement to invent our own life instead of following some model; the ability to fend off the strokes of fate and to institute new configurations of meaning; faithfulness to previous choices and commitments; and the ability to reconsider and criticize past choices. In part, such efforts to ponder and evaluate human life are driven by moral factors, but most of the criteria mentioned here are intellectual and their formulation conforms to the requirements of rationality and coherence. Those same criteria guide our judgments on life narratives and define the rules followed by most autobiographical narratives. More often than not, they are structured around a crucial event whose significance makes life intelligible.

Are our reasons and justifications for living commensurate with the expectations of intelligibility that the simple fact of living gives rise to? I intend to show that, insofar as reflection shapes the rationality of the self, the search for commensurability and the determination of reasons and justifications are subject to formal constraints linked to the invariants of human life. One of the reasons that the self-consciousness of absurdity persists during the very process of reflecting upon oneself is due to the fact that the existential justification is neither strict nor very orthodox and that we are unable to shake off our dissatisfaction with the forms of intelligibility it offers. Here are a few examples. The existential justification is clearly dependent on a privileged relationship with the human subject, which strengthens its claims to rationality. Also, the reflection on the explanatory reasons of our most important decisions and commitments does not simply stop when a decision is made. Our justifications become susceptible to the influence of ulterior events and, if so, would it not be an abuse of language to still call them justifications? What kind of rationality could be rightly called justification when it is caught in a temporal dimension, and when its reasons can be proved either true or false depending on ulterior events? How can we deal with a time-dependent justification? How can a justification be included into the search for unity? In such conditions, assigning meaning to life amounts to obeying constraints that would render rational justifications impracticable.

All these objections seem perfectly valid, yet their conclusion will not stand. True, the existential justification obeys very peculiar conditions. The philosophical challenge is to show that, whatever their peculiarity, it remains a justification nevertheless. A detailed analysis of the formal constraints that frame the process of justification will help us better understand what it is to assign meaning to life, and why the sensation of absurdity lingers in the back of our minds when we are reflecting on human life.

Generally speaking, there are two methods for reflecting on one's life.[14] The first method consists in producing thoughts that inform us on our desires and beliefs. The second method is to consider which ones of our desires and beliefs fit best in the set of mental states, mental dispositions, and activities that we are attributing to ourselves. Both methods are required during our examination of ourselves through reflection and justification.[15] The two methods correspond to the cognitive aspects of the reflection on selfhood, and their conclusions are fallible. By reflecting and deliberating on selfhood, the self relates to what it knows of itself and furthers its knowledge of itself. However, relating to oneself is not a simple matter because reflection leads us to see ourselves from the outside, as if we were only partly attached to ourselves, without however placing us in a fully impersonal position. Reflection follows the same rules and principles that we follow when we acquire our beliefs; it allows us to grasp the reasons for these beliefs and thus realize their normative scope. We attribute reasons and beliefs to ourselves in order to explain what we have observed about ourselves. This intellectual effort is not a vision, nor is it a trivial observation of ourselves, much less a form of knowledge devoid of observation or inference.[16] None of these descriptions would provide any grounds for the claims to objectivity originating in the reflection on selfhood. However, the concept of "attestation" introduced by Paul Ricoeur in his hermeneutics of the self does suggest a normative perspective. The attestation is a "belief-in" not a "belief-that," and it is close to a "testimony of memory alone." When I become the object of my reflection, I am attesting my commitment to respect the implications of what I will discover.[17] Hannah Arendt's remarks on the cognitive power of imagination are highly relevant in this context. She notices that the imagination sustains intellectual efforts to the extent that it allows one to look at oneself from nowhere in particular, to be simultaneously a world spectator and an actor to oneself, and "to take one's distance from oneself by reaching into the other.[18]

The reasons found through self-reflection are the product of deliberation on our actual beliefs and desires, and they correspond to the "internal reasons" of modern philosophy; the subject calls them "internal" because he posits that it is always possible to find a deliberative path that links them to the set of its motivations.[19] It is precisely because such reasons are the product of deliberation that they can be used for self-insight. However, this does not mean that they are reducible to personal psychology. The reasons and justifications obtained from the reflection on oneself are not psychological in the sense that they would exist because one believed or wished to have them; their discovery is independent from the path leading to them.[20] Our internal reasons—those which the reflection on ourselves reveals by interpreting our beliefs—are related to our desires and motivations, but they are not subjective because they are independent of what we think of them. In this kind of reflection, the effort of rationality consists in discovering reasons established from our beliefs and desires, the general expectation being that they will be recognized as such by all. Only on this condition can it be said that normative expressions (of the form "X has a reason to do this or that") can be true or false. Individuals tend to represent everything they consider justified, as an objective truth; and they think that everybody will grasp and acknowledge their reasons. The conditions in which the process of reflection takes place allow each individual to reach a certain form of objectivity.[21]

Philosophers have often emphasized a major difficulty with self-reflection. The self cannot but modify itself by being the object of reflexive knowledge; its malleability seems to indicate that the reflection on the self has—in addition to its cognitive aspect—what Charles Larmore terms "a practical dimension," whereby the self relates to the part of itself engaged in self-interpretation.[22] This practical dimension leads the self to take charge of itself or, in Sartrean terms, "to recover its being."[23] In this sense, reflection "is a recognition rather than knowledge."[24] The reasons for action are not only known but acknowledged by the self because they engage it to interpret itself accordingly. This means that reflection imposes on the self a set of reasons and beliefs that may be the source of deceit or self-deception. In *Remembrance of Things Past*, the main character Marcel, who is also the first-person narrator of the story, prevents Albertine from getting off the train in Parville after she mentions incidentally her being a friend of Miss Vinteuil. It is this passing mention that makes him aware of her homosexuality: listening to her he cannot chase the image of the passionate embraces he had witnessed in Montjouvain between Miss Vinteuil and one of her girlfriends. At the same time, he discovers that Albertine is part of him, that he loves her. At this reflection stage, the narrator feels the imperative desire to marry Albertine and finds that the situation justifies discussing this marriage with his mother. Later, when Albertine moves in with him, becoming, in a way, his "captive," the reasons that justify his relationship with her come back to haunt him. Does he really love Albertine? Can he truly recognize love in his feelings for her? The viewpoint of the narrator, that is, the viewpoint of the first person, has particular authority in this context: his interpretation of what he truly thinks comes in second to what he claims he thinks.[25] The role that Marcel's idea of love plays in his reflection becomes recognizable as the examination progresses. His idea of love is very much shaped by his jealousy, his expectations, and his readings, which explains why he believes that he loves Albertine. His belief goes so far as to dissimulate his genuine desires to himself. He is doubly engaged as to his reasons: first toward the reasons produced by his idea of love; second, toward the reasons produced by his difficulty in living with Albertine. His reflection attempts to elaborate some kind of compatibility between these reasons, which would gradually help him better understand who he is.

The Personal Perspective

When I ask myself: "Why have I acted this way?" "How else could I have acted?" "Would my life have been different, had I taken that decision?" my demands for intelligibility are closely related to a particular individual: myself. My justifications for my acts are by no means impersonal; they follow directly from what I am. In all likelihood, my reasons for acting in a certain way or for making this or that decision are not those that another person would have taken in the same circumstances. In this sense, the existential justification is characteristically dependent on the agent who elaborates it.

There is a very important philosophical distinction between agent-relative and agent-neutral reasons.[26] An agent-neutral reason can take a general form without reference to the precise person that holds it. For instance, if an agent x has a reason to want a better world, we can safely suppose that the same reason would do for y or anybody else. However, if x has a reason to do something because it serves his self-interest or it is right for him, then that is an agent-relative reason. Agent-relative reasons are not exclusively self-concerned; they can also be other-regarding. There is nothing to preclude third-parties from being involved in such reasons.[27]

Nor does the relation to the agent render a justification necessarily subjective. The agent-relative reason takes its significance from what the agent is, but this does not mean that it depends on the agent's satisfactions or preferences. This has only the appearance of a paradox. Relating reasons to agents follows from the fact that reasons are *for* somebody—but *for somebody* is not necessarily equivalent to *from the viewpoint of somebody*, which would refer to what is desired or known by an agent. When the poet and philosopher Lucretius Carus attempts to argue that death is not an affliction because there is nobody to attest it—if somebody says it is, then he is not dead yet; and if he is dead, he cannot say or be aware of anything—he means that the subjective interpretation of "affliction for somebody" is the only interpretation possible. However, the fact that we cannot be aware of something does not prove that it is not an affliction for us. For instance, I may be stricken by misfortune unknowingly, and somebody may cause me harm without my being aware of it.[28] More generally, a justification is not rendered subjective by the single fact of being tied to personal factors. Also, an agent-relative reason can be objective if it can be seen, recognized, or affirmed as properly belonging to the agent when considered from a viewpoint external to that agent. The reference to a particular person does not weaken the rationality of a justification, nor its objectivity.

A primary consequence of the requirement for the existential justification to be agent-relative is that this justification cannot be impersonal. I can reflect on the life of human beings in general, but I certainly cannot reflect on my own life impersonally. Reflecting on my life would not make any sense if I placed myself in a world in which I had not been born. I can say about a world of which I am not a part that it is better to live in it for a longer time, but what would my own reason be for preferring a longer life in it, if I were not in it? At best, I could engage in impersonal reflections about the interest *for that world* of my presence or absence.[29] When in

Sophocles' tragedy *Oedipus at Colonus*, the hero laments that the greatest misfortune is to be born, he means that this is the case for those who have been born, because the unborn cannot deplore being born. Lord Byron's injunction troubles us for the same reason: "Count o'er the joys thine hours have seen / Count o'er thy days from anguish free / And know, whatever thou hast been / 'Tis something better—not to be."[30] For whom is it better not to be in a world in which he would not exist? The old Jewish answer, "How many have this chance? Not even one in ten thousand," properly reveals the absurdity of a complaint that wants to be taken impersonally when the only thing that gives it any meaning is the relativity to its agent.

In Frank Capra's movie *It's a Wonderful Life*, James Stewart plays George Bailey—a ruined, suicidal man, whose guardian angel takes him to a world identical to the one he wants to quit, with one exception: George has never existed and does not exist in it. The intended lesson is to make George aware of reality and realize the value of being alive. Its practical effect is to show him the absurdity of desiring to quit a world in which he desires nevertheless to be somebody. If I have a reason not to be in this world, that reason cannot deal impersonally with a particular state of affairs in it. A person's death is an affliction in a given world—the one in which that person lives; and his death is an affliction only if he has been born in it. No agent-relative reason can make any sense in a world in which that agent does not exist. The existential justification is agent-relative in the sense that the relation to the agent is part of it. And it is neither impersonal nor indifferent to the existence or nonexistence of the agent in the world in which this justification operates.[31]

The question that comes immediately to mind is: what does the personal element of justification consist of? Because discussing human nature requires a concrete element of determination and individuation, the personal element of justification does not pertain to common human nature. Nor can agent-relative traits of existential justifications refer to a typical individuality, identified by certain qualities of soul and personality, as is the case with Aristotle's *phronimos* (person of practical wisdom). Neither can this personal element consist of a human exemplar related to a typical condition in life (such as that of the fighter, the hero, the king), or to a dramatic hero such as represented in tragedy or comedy.[32] Whatever intelligibility this sort of schematization might yield, such prototypical agents are not involved here. The agent involved in the existential justification is not a human type identifiable by status or obvious differences; it is not defined in itself or through relations; and it is not characteristic, or exemplary.

It does not seem possible to conceive of agent-relativity in terms of personality or traits of character. Personality is not independent of the actions it causes, nor is it detached from the justifications that explain such actions. It leads to actions that might change it in return. Besides, asserting the identity of a character rests on the unlikely assumption that personalities do not change. A person is not characterized by a cluster of desires, intentions, and actions, nor can a person's individuality be defined in terms of character. Moreover, it is rather doubtful that character alone could give the agent reasons to act that it could instantly recognize as justified. It is even more doubtful that these reasons to act—if they existed—would be strictly agent-relative. The concept of agent-relativity does not rely on the stable particularities of a person; rather, it shows how reasons are affected by individual, malleable elements of a personality.[33]

The need to link the individual perspective to existential justification goes therefore farther than the abstract and general necessity of linking justification to an individual with a well-defined character. Agent-relativity can affect the content of deliberations on—or the search for—justifications to the extent that, in the background, the reflective mind continues to ask questions such as: "What does it mean to have a life for myself?" and "What traits in a life would make me recognize it as my own?" Even so, how can the reference to individuality modify the process of practical reasoning and justification? In what way can the fact of knowing who is deliberating have an impact on the process of justification? There is an inherent randomness in me being who I am, with my character and desires; and, if this particular set of personal determinations can influence my justifications and reasoning about my actions, then my reflection and much of my reasoning would very probably be tainted with arbitrariness. But if so, would that not mean that the need for individual reference undermines the rational character of justification? Granted that the nature of justification is profoundly affected by the necessity of such individual references, this still does not disprove the claim that justification is rational and objective.

Individual references have a similar impact on moral deliberation. In principle, the judgment concluding a moral deliberation should not depend on the personal traits of the deliberating agent. Like existential justification, the rationality of moral deliberation must clearly follow the implicit "universalizability rule," which states that a man who thinks that a given action is the right one for him to perform in certain circumstances should logically think that the same action would be right for anyone else in relevantly similar circumstances, that is, that the procedures and conclusions of moral deliberation should be entirely neutral as to the identity of the deliberating agent.[34]

Peter Winch shows both the usefulness and the limits of this rule in moral reasoning, and suggests that—in critical deliberations involving a concerned agent—a special position of primacy should be conferred to "agent's viewpoint" or to "a certain class of first-person moral judgments

. . . as not subject to the universalizability principle."[35] Winch reveals the need for primacy by analyzing the deliberation presented in Herman Melville's *Billy Budd, Sailor*. Billy Budd is a foretopman on board HMS *Indomitable* during the Napoleonic Wars—a hard time for the British navy. Billy Budd is the embodiment of sweetness and beauty; his only imperfection is a stutter that worsens in moments of agitation. He is hated and persecuted by the satanic master-at-arms Claggart.[36] In his campaign to destroy Billy, Claggart falsely accuses him before Captain Vere of inciting the crew to mutiny. Transfixed by this horrible accusation, Billy cannot utter a word in self-defense, and when Claggart touches him, he shots his arm out unwillingly striking Claggart, who falls on the deck, hits his forehead and dies. At the drumhead courtmartial, Captain Vere overcomes his compassion for Billy and—given the recent unrest in the fleet—opts for enforcing the Mutiny Act in the death of an officer. Billy is sentenced to death and hanged on the ship.

Reflecting on this tragic story, many of us would feel that we would not act in the same way as Captain Vere. *I myself* could not have condemned Billy—not for reasons having to do with rejection of authority, lack of courage, or unhealthy compassion—but for purely moral reasons, that is, the moral impossibility *as an agent* facing this situation to take the decision of putting Billy to death. He had no intention to kill. The falseness of Claggart's accusation is exceedingly prejudicial to him. The goodness of his heart attests that his blow came almost unwittingly, in a reaction that his inability to speak without stuttering rendered violent. However, from Captain Vere's external and impersonal standpoint, the sailor Billy Budd acted in a way that, although unintentional, was the direct cause of an officer's death. Vere considers that in these circumstances, he must apply the Mutiny Act immediately and without reservation by ordering the sailor's execution.[37] The story shows Captain Vere to be a good man, of great inner righteousness. One may sincerely believe that the reasons justifying his decision are moral and essentially in harmony with the kind of person that he is. Upon entering the service, the captain had taken a pledge to enforce applicable regulations; he had always acknowledged the validity of martial law; he is personally responsible for the proper functioning of the ship; he cannot do anything that would slacken discipline; and he knows that the slightest indulgence would embolden sailors to mutiny. His finding is important to a morally formed narrative, but so is the concern generated by his swift punishment.

The dilemma presented in this story is not just a conflict between irreconcilable systems of moral reasons. The tragic quality of the situation does not reside in the tension between a morality of intention or compassion and a morality of written law, but rather in the fact that both Captain Vere and the holder of an opposing view would justify their deliberation and decision on moral grounds that they both would recognize as valid. The questions raised by this type of situation can be stated as follows: is it possible that in identical circumstances C, an agent A would think—based on what he is—that he should do Y, while an agent B would think—based on what he is—that he should not do Y (supposing that the abilities, obligations, and commitments of both A and B are fixed)? We can discard at least two false solutions claiming to explain this agent-relativity problem. A purely subjectivist interpretation of agent-relativity that would justify the particularity of deliberation by the preferences and standpoints of a given agent should be discarded because it misses the essential point that the moral reasons invoked by A and B are objective and mutually acknowledged. Also to be discarded is the pseudosolution that considers the traits of character of A and B to be an integral part of the circumstances of deliberation, in which case these circumstances would not be identical because those related to A would include the personality of A and those related to B would comprise the personality of B. The reason for discarding this solution is, as Joseph Raz stated: "The question is not, given my moral character, what shall I do? To put it thus is to foreclose the possibility of a change in one's personal perspective and to deny the self-determining, self-creating aspect of decision and action."[38]

Once these pseudosolutions are abandoned, the only valid path is to assume the existence of a particular factor that would have meaning only in relation to an individual agent (to its character, personality, predispositions, and moral sensibilities). This factor should not be taken as a given that preexists the agent's action or decision, but should be revealed later by the agent's decision or justification through a process of self-discovery and autodetermination initiated by the agent himself.[39] This factor plays a crucial role in making sense of the reasons relative to the agent but should not be confused with them because it is not given beforehand. It is not determined by the justification, yet it is included in the elements relating the justification of the agent. I readily concede that it is difficult to define precisely or to formalize adequately this agent-relative factor.[40] Peter Winch maintains that "what one *finds out* is something about oneself, rather than anything one can speak of as holding universally. . . . What a man *finds out* about himself is something that can be expressed only in terms of the moral ideas by consideration of which he arrives at his decision."[41] My main objective here is not to identify the nature of this particular factor but to show that it exists and that it has an effect on the search for justifications.

Does agent-relativity weaken existential justification's claims to objectivity? Many objective elements can be detected in the deliberation of existential justifications, such as the moral pros and cons invoked by either side; each side's right to explain why they could not act differently; and a third party's attestation of the validity of each side's reasons. While rationally elaborating these justifications, the agent deliberates, envisions counterfactual scenarios, modifies available parameters, evaluates plausible consequences, infers the possible effects of individual decisions, and so forth. This rational effort can reasonably claim to be objective, especially because of its implied search for best reasons. The legitimate claim to objectivity notwithstanding, the particular orientation of the existential justification remains indeterminate to the end, even if its legitimacy becomes obvious once the moral personality of the agent is revealed. It is as if agent-relativity were keeping the justifying structure open to change depending on the identity of the agents, and the completed justification were determined by the presence of a particular individuality.

We encounter a similar difficulty when trying to justify our feelings of love or friendship. When a passionate lover tells himself, "Why do I love her? Because it is her (and nobody else)," it does not mean that he has taken leave from rationality or objectivity, only that he is expecting a particular individuality to give him the reason that justifies his love. Clearly, if such reference to the beloved can play this role, it is not because the personality of the loved one "explains" love by inspiring it, but rather because *she and no one else* being loved is revealed by love itself.[42] Also—by asking "How could I do this? Because I could not do anything else" or answering with Sophocles' Oedipus: "I did not do this"—we are in fact simply presenting a particular individuality that is supposed to intervene in the search for justifications.[43] Such an element is far from compromising the rationality of justification. It is its absence that would seem inconceivable.[44]

Agent-relativity is not limited to a first-person viewpoint. While reflecting on our own life, we always dissociate between an external viewpoint and our inner voice.[45] After her encounter with Vronski with whom she falls in love at first sight, Anna Karenina reflects on her life and her unloved husband: "Have I not tried, tried with all my might to find a purpose in my life? Have I not tried to love him, tried to love my son when I could no longer love my husband? But the time came when I understood that I could no longer deceive myself."[46] By placing herself in the external perspective of a third person, Anna recognizes the relevance of her inner feelings. The inevitable simultaneity of these seemingly opposed viewpoints does not preclude them from throwing light upon each other.

Until now, I have abstained from pointing to a particular conception of the self or of individuality.[47] While I acknowledge the importance of individuality for existential justification, I do not think that the individual can be isolated from all that is not his own self. Knowing how the individual defines himself based on his relations with other people is an issue that has both conceptual and empirical aspects. Hannah Arendt emphasizes its importance thus: "A life without speech and without action, on the other hand—and this is the only way of life that in earnest has renounced all appearance and all vanity in the biblical sense of the word—is literally dead to the world; it has ceased to be a human life because it is no longer lived among men."[48] At the same time, self-interpretation and its role in existential justification are far from contingent. Our reflection on life is like a web forever spun, never completed. In it we see "the unconscious need that everyone has: the need to come to terms with the blind impress which chance has given him, to make a self for himself by re-describing that impress in terms which are, if only marginally, his own."[49]

Events in Human Life

Much of our justification efforts to understand, predict, or plan our life seem pointless when we think of the irrepressible part that events play in affecting it as a whole. By "events," I do not mean only random events—an accident, an illness, an encounter—or purely physical ones, but also psychological events—an obsession, a sudden rejection—as well as events caused by our own decisions, resolutions, and commitments. To the extent that such events not only happen, but happen *to* the agent, they are bound to have an effect on justification efforts. The challenge such events pose sometimes to the search for meaning stimulates our spontaneous examination and reflections on our life. We aim to accommodate such events and to incorporate them—with various degrees of success—into the web of justifications that help us find the meaning of our lives.

Events provide focal points for reflection, not only on human life but also on life narratives. They help the search for meaning to sort itself out and reevaluate already acquired intelligibility. An event can be a critical point signaling a change in meaning that may affect an entire life. When such a pivotal event has taken place, we often say that nothing will be the same again. However, as a break point, an event can also occasion a reaffirmation of the subject's identity. To the extent that the subject remains unchanged and what happens to him is very close to what he already is or to what he has already experienced, the subject can either be greatly affected by the event or discover the source of a new life. In *Anna Karenina*, after Levin has seen Kitty, he thinks that "In the whole world there was only one being able to unite in itself the universe and the meaning of life for him. It was Kitty."[50] This reflection shows a certain activism because it tends to present what follows as depending on a new meaning situation created by the event. The statement "This gave a new meaning to my life" initiates a whole new program for reflection. In the same vein, encountering Anna triggers in Vronski a similar mental process, whereby he looks from a new perspective at what had been until then the meaning of his life: "he had told her the truth: that he would go were she went, that all the happiness of life and the only meaning of life for him now was in seeing and hearing her."[51]

The events described here, although not entirely predictable, have a close connection with the momentous decisions in one's life, thus—it can be safely assumed—requiring a sustained justification effort. Such events might not have occurred at all, occurred as predicted, or occurred differently. But they are not miraculous because they represent a possibility that the agent could have recognized as plausible in the aftermath of a pivotal event in his life. Any thinking person pondering the consequences of a momentous personal decision cannot but envision a set of events that would validate his decision, show it to be unfounded, or disprove it. Their occurrence may well be due to good luck or bad; however, their connection to the decision maker is not at all random.

In order to determine the effects of such events on existential justification, I present here, from my own perspective, Bernard Williams's well-known example on this topic. A painter by the name of Gauguin decides in midlife to leave for Tahiti because he strongly believes that only there will he find inspiration for his future work. To accomplish this, he abandons his family.[52] Some may think that his decision is immoral, but at this point I just want to know if Gauguin's decision is justified and, if so, on what terms. Gauguin sees his departure as a necessary condition for painting the masterworks he carries within. The essential element that gives him reason to act is the envisioned success of his plan. From that point on, several scenarios may unfold, one of them being Gauguin's success and his becoming the painter we all know. In this scenario, the justification of his act through his success becomes available only after his decision is taken.

Now, let us imagine that, on its way to Tahiti, Gauguin's boat sinks with everybody on board. In this scenario, Gauguin's decision is thwarted. The story ends tragically with an event that has nothing to do with Gauguin's decision. The relentless search for the justification leading to Gauguin's momentous decision is suspended permanently. Still, it cannot be said with certainty that this tragic end proves his decision to have been unwarranted. Let us further imagine that the painter seriously injures his hands during the trip, which would make impossible his project of painting in Tahiti. In this scenario, the cause of failure is still external to his project, although it seems more closely tied to his determination to paint, because it has to do with powerlessness—a threat intrinsic to all creation. If Gauguin's life project fails because his ship sinks or because he loses the use of his hands, he would never know whether his decision was justified: in both cases the failure is extrinsic to it. Taken in themselves, those tragic events cannot show that, by deciding to leave, Gauguin was mistaken about himself, his life, and his talent.

Lastly, let us imagine a scenario in which Gauguin arrives safely in Tahiti but manages to produce only mediocre paintings. This time, his failure is intrinsically tied to his project; the causes of powerlessness are traced back to Gauguin; they are entwined with his being, with his hope of becoming a great painter, with the reasons that made him believe that he will be such a painter, with his lack of perceptiveness on those reasons, and with his self-delusion on his talent. In this scenario, events only reveal either what was in himself from the start, that is, his hopelessness as a creator, or what took place in him as a result of his decision, that is, a difficulty to paint that only worsens with each reaffirmation of his decision. Such hopelessness is eventlike to the extent that it might have not taken place. It too depends on bad luck, but this time the bad luck is intimately tied to Gauguin's own self. He might have had good reasons to think that he will become a great painter and his justifications for his decisions might have not been self-deceptive. Evidently though, those justifications were incomplete in this case, because their validity or lack thereof could be ascertained only after the end result became known (i.e., whether the project has succeeded or failed, and whether the success or failure was intrinsic or extrinsic).

There are two things to be learned from the Gauguin stories. First, our life's crucial decisions remain somewhat underjustified, as if the temporality created by each decision is such that the events occurring in it could modify the decision's meaning. Such ulterior events—that were neither real nor predictable at the time of deliberation—could thus reactivate, reorient, or alter justifications conceived for past decisions and deliberations. Second, at least some of those events can either confirm or infirm the justifications we use to explain or legitimize our deeds. A well-thought-out justification remains unchanged but is retrospectively deprived of its scope. This is not only because those elements that were uncertain at the time of decision could have a retroactive effect on justification by coming true or not. In my view, this story's events and its momentous decision are more closely linked than is usually assumed: these events depend not only on Gauguin's particular decision but also on the particular beliefs, hopes, and fears that form the substance of his decision.

These remarks support the idea that justifications related to crucial decisions in one's life might remain incomplete until ulterior events reveal their true scope. The justifications that Gauguin brings in support of his decision cannot come true before time has taken at least part of its course; their validity or lack of it will be known only *ex eventu*. In this case, the possibility of justification is not tied to a third party's indictment of Gauguin for having taken a decision that later revealed itself to be useless to him and harmful to others; rather, it is tied to what Gauguin may reasonably think of himself.

The possibility of such justification may be objected to on the grounds that the validity of deliberation is independent of the course of events. Strictly speaking, a decision is considered justified if it is supported by the information available at the moment it is being taken and nothing else; the justification ought to be complete, regardless of how things turn out. The only elements to be considered in order to justify a decision are whether the reasoning is consistent, the evaluation of probabilities is rational, and the prioritizing of options is optimal. If the agent is deliberating badly, he may decide to improve the way he does it. If he is deliberating properly but things turn out badly, he can defend the rationality of his deliberation even if he might perhaps have preferred to make a different decision. Even if his competent deliberation leads to catastrophe, the agent cannot choose to deliberate differently. But the justifications related to crucial decisions seem to require something else. In this case, the after-the-fact acknowledgment and evaluation of the rationality of deliberation acquires a particular meaning. The specificity of an ulterior evaluation of the subject would depend on whether the place from which he reflects on life is situated in a sequence of events whose possibility and importance follow in great part from this decision.

Anna Karenina quits her husband and son for Vronski, but the social opprobrium and her own guilt are such that her love project collapses. Her hopes are dashed not by an external event—such as say, Vronski's accidental death—but by the life-style brought about by her decision. When this happens, Anna cannot think of what she has done or of the pain she has inflicted on others without realizing that her decision and her justification of it have been, as it were, rebutted from inside. If she feels regret, it is not at what has happened but at what she has done, or rather at the chain of events triggered by her intentional acts, even without her will. She does not feel regret just because she has failed (if we suppose that her idea of her project is unchanged), and in any case feeling regret after the fact does not mean that initially she would or could have acted differently. If, at the moment she realizes her failure, she were told that her initial decision was rational and justified, that ulterior events have no impact on the reasons of her deciding the way she did, and that her regrets are therefore irrational, there is every reason to think that such talk would still not lessen her disarray. "The perspective of deliberative choice on one's life is constitutively *from here*. Correspondingly, the perspective of assessment with greater knowledge is necessarily *from there*, and not only can I not guarantee how factually it will be, but I cannot ultimately guarantee from what standpoint of assessment my major and most fundamental regrets will be."[53]

My remarks are not intended to advance a general theory of justification but only to underline a relevant particularity of justifications related to crucial decisions and existential deliberations: the way people judge their own decisions is at least in part determined by what really happens to them beyond their control. Human lives seem to be a web of tightly knitted justifications, some of them being less well determined than the rest, and some others remaining incomplete until ulterior events occur that, at the moment of deliberation, nobody knows whether they will occur or what they will be.

The Boredom of Living Forever

The inevitability of death has no paralyzing effect on justification efforts.[54] Many philosophers have stressed that the perspective of death can help give meaning to life and expressed a rather vague hope that our certainty of dying can influence our reflection on our lives. Given the finite character of our existence, our decisions and projects have by definition a limited scope. Without going so far as to think that everything we do is tainted by futility, the fact remains that our awareness of our mortality does influence the ways we orient and adapt our choices and decisions. We are therefore confronted with some sort of paradox: the certainty that our life will end one day—and that our life is the only one we will ever live—naturally confers some value on it, thus making our search for reasons and our reflection on it even more valuable. On the other hand, that same certainty enhances the precariousness of our justifications or at least reduces their intelligibility by afflicting them with an inherent incompleteness.[55] We strive to justify our projects to ourselves, but this web of justifications that we cannot stop weaving will, one day, completely disintegrate.

That the finitude of life makes the existential justification even more pertinent does not mean that biological life has an optimal length, much less that its end naturally coincides with the moment at which our justification effort loses its meaning. Rejecting immortality does not mean abandoning any complaint about the shortness of human life. And it would be hard to produce an argument showing that human life always ends at the right moment that would not implicitly rest on the very conclusion it wants to refute. In a much quoted passage of *De Rerum Natura*, Lucretius attempts to show that a long life is not necessarily preferable to a short one because there is no instance in which dying is a bad thing. Indeed, whether one dies young or old, one is dead indefinitely. Once dead, the duration of deprivation from what one enjoyed in life is the same regardless of the duration of the enjoyment.

The fear Lucretius attempts to dispel is caused by the widespread representation of death as some sort of subsistence whereby we would still be vaguely aware of things in spite of loosing everything. This is a spurious argument: the idea that death is not a bad thing for anybody because, regardless of how long we live, we will all be indefinitely deprived of life's benefits, implicitly assumes that life's benefits are really good things. Consequently, enjoying those benefits is better than not enjoying them, and enjoying them longer or being aware of their longer enjoyment is preferable to a shorter enjoyment of them or to the awareness of a shorter enjoyment. Therefore I would inevitably infer that the longer I will enjoy life's benefits the better, and, if so, then I would rather be alive than dead. It is entirely reasonable that when one desires something, one's implicit assumption is to be alive.[56] The lamentation on the shortness of life is not due to mental confusion. Surely, when we say that a dead person "does not exist anymore," we have a different understanding of the concept "nonexistence" than when we refer to a "person" not yet conceived by its parents. In the former, nonexistence is a loss; in the latter, it is a negation. Death is not comparable to nonexistence before birth because death is a loss not based on the particular characteristics of what is lost but on the desirability of such characteristics.

To appreciate the effect the perspective of death has on existential reflection, one must adopt the *casus difficilior* hypothesis that there is no life after death, that life goes on without decline or suffering, that decrepitude is not a reason for dying, and that one's personality does not change with age but remains at its best (because one can imagine that an anxious or depressive person would happily welcome death). Granted all that, what credence should we give the idea that reasons other than misfortunes, old age, and personality decay make an excessively long life unhappy and put an end to the search for justifications to live?

Existential reflection is tied to practical rationality and based on the presence of desires. Again, any desire presupposes my desire not to be dead. There is no doubt that one's desires depend on one being alive even if while desiring one does not necessarily think of the precondition to be alive. We may therefore be allowed to think that the most ardent desires that we experience in life and that often determine its course are conditioned by an even most basic desire—to stay alive. Miguel de Unamuno has described the force of this desire in terms that differentiate it radically from the need for bodily gratifications or the aspiration to abstract, disembodied immortality: "I do not want to die—no; I neither want to die nor do I want to want to die; I want to live forever and ever and ever. I want this 'I' to live—this poor 'I' that I am and that I feel myself to be here and now—and therefore the problem of the duration of my soul, of my own soul, tortures me."[57]

The idea of an absolute desire to live can be objected to on several grounds. First, the desire to die may represent a real desire to not be alive anymore. Schopenhauer thought that suicide is a passionate "affirmation of the will-to-live."[58] Nevertheless, if it is clear that the act of ending one's life may sometimes reaffirm the will to live, it is much less clear whether the desire to die can be consistently restated as a will to live. The desire of annihilation is not foreign to human beings. Certain desires make us aspire to realities and values that we never want to abandon, even if this abandonment alone would keep us alive. In such cases, we believe that we would rather renounce life itself than those values. If we admit as a contingency of human psychology that people can desire some things more than life, then it is conceivable that eternal life is not necessarily one of those things. The reasons that we may have to stay alive cannot be reduced to a pure desire to live. Rather, our efforts of justification and rationality with regard to our lives may lead us to consider such a desire to be relative and conditional.[59]

The existential justification elaborates and evaluates reasons that may also be reasons to live. Human desires, especially those tied to crucial choices in one's life include an element of risk to the self that is confusedly expressed by saying that one would rather die that renounce a crucial choice—or that one would surely die if one renounced it. The sincerity of a desire linked to such choices could thus be measured by its capacity to put life itself at risk. On the other hand, one can see that if a desire for life eternal were fulfilled and we became immortal, it would conceivably deprive all desires of their significance and cause us to renounce desire itself. This is so because of what Bernard Williams called "the tedium of immortality." If indeed there are categorical desires over and above life, they will likely lead us to desire that life be not prolonged beyond a certain limit. I would think that, when reaching that limit, I would have already encountered everything of significance in my life, provided that my personality, character, dispositions, and memories would remain the same. If, on the other hand, I were to change continuously and never be bored, how could it be proved that I remained the same person rather than becoming an eternal succession of different selves in the same body? This precondition of relative personal stability does limit the number of possible life scenarios, relationships, and configurations of interactions and events. Unless one accepts the idea of diminishing consciousness, such scenarios are doomed to continuously repeat themselves, provoking inevitably the cognitive reaction of boredom.

Bernard Williams makes these remarks in an analysis of Leo Janacek's opera *The Makropulos Affair*, based on a play published by Karel Capek in 1922.[60] In it, Elina Makropulos, alias Emilia Marty, alias Ellian Mac-Greggor, and many other names—all bearing the initials E.M.— is a 342-

year-old woman born in the sixteenth century. Her physician father had experimented with an immortality elixir when she was 42 years old, which means that she lived at this same age for 300 years. Overwhelmed by the boredom and lassitude of living, she stops taking the elixir and finally dies. Her reasons for living depend on her desires, which, unchanged in time, gradually lose intensity and grow indifferent to events. The dullness and stultifying repetitiveness of living gradually kills all desires, and her wish to live is replaced by the categorical desire to end her life. Elina dies for having had enough of herself.[61]

It therefore seems that the characteristics of human desires and the particularities of justifications meant to explain them are all framed by a time-limited life. Human desires can evolve, provoke deliberation, or incite a search for reasons only if human life is bound in time by death arriving neither too soon nor too late. Often the desire for immortality is more a desire to live a longer and more interesting life than to live forever. The existence of a reasonable life limit—a difficult balance to strike between living too long and not living enough—seems to be a possibility condition for existential justifications. True, not knowing when we will die undermines our planning efforts, without, however, changing the nature of the search for justifications. On the other hand, it does seem that having a life that is either too long or too short fully precludes the possibility of achieving a certain type of justifications. Generally, death is an object of affliction, but there is every reason to believe that, without it, the reflection on life would not have the same scope.

Living Life Forward and Understanding It Backward

It is quite true that Philosophy says that life must be understood
backwards. But that makes one forget the other saying: that it must
be lived forwards. The more one ponders this, the more it comes to
mean that life in the temporal existence never becomes quite intelligible, precisely because at no moment can I find complete quiet to
take the backward-looking position.

—*The Diary of Søren Kierkegaard*[62]

The task of understanding human life is certainly a cognitive one, but it also affects the actions of the individual; it compels one to act according to reasons that, upon reflection, one recognizes as legitimate. Also, existential justifications are crafted in a time-limited life, a life destined to end, an irreversible, time-directed life. As life advances, the past becomes a fixed reality; and, as Aristotelian philosophers know, "God himself cannot undo what has been done." As soon as one starts reflecting on one's own life, by definition one has a past to reflect on. What are the effects of the "temporality" of human existence on the existential justification?

Our anticipation of the effects of our decisions and plans directs our reflection on life toward the future, but it is in our past that reflection finds the criteria for what is important, possible, or desirable in our life. We quite probably entertain an official view of our past that is acceptable, presentable, and useful in our efforts of remembrance, introspection, and analysis. Its constant background presence in our reflection on life helps us identify our reasons for action and to identify with them. It is by their ties to our past that we recognize such reasons as our own. "Only insofar as he thinks, and that is insofar as he is ageless—a 'he' as Kafka so rightly calls him and not a 'somebody'—does man in the full actuality of concrete being live in this gap of time between past and future."[63] We need to know whether the past remains unchanged in its content and in the criteria it provides to our efforts for existential justification. To what extent can we consider the past to be given once and for all?

Given the fact that reflection on the past is always somewhat "interested," it is hard to believe that the continuous connection to the past would not entail a deformation factor. Contemplation is by definition posterior to events, always occurs from a certain viewpoint, and is influenced by revived feelings, complementary information, or intelligibility expectations that are not necessarily rooted in the past. The feelings that stir up memories of regrets or nostalgia have a cognitive dimension inasmuch as they help us understand the past and learn from it, but this cognitive target is sometimes missed because of the unreliable nature of remembrance.[64] In existential meditation, the past is always summoned to answer, so to speak. There is a reciprocal influence between the interpretation of the past and the explanation of the present. The past simultaneously constrains and orients existential reflection, and it gives the subject a certain sense of reality and personal identity; in return, the past is put into a new perspective by reflection and even changed by it. The counterpart of the power we hold on the past is its power over us, a power that we gave it. This is our way of consenting to the tyranny of the past. Proust reminds us that, however long our list of possessions, that is not where our riches lie. In parallel to the real course of events, we cannot but continuously represent to ourselves several possible scenarios that tell us what could have happened had this or that event been different. The meditation on life sometimes carries along all those possible pasts and involves temporalities clumsily fitted together, as if the countless possibilities of the past ceaselessly surged into the present.

The omnipresent past constantly orients us in time. However forceful our drive to rearrange the past, it has its limits: it could never change the succession of events, because what happened first cannot be made to happen last. Moreover, the reflection on the past is inevitably initiated by a self that has been subsequently shaped by, and encumbered with, all that has happened in the interval stretching from the past under consideration to its aftermath. It is because our past has a real causal effect on what we are that it leaves its mark on us. We are always older than the past we are looking into: our old desires seem less appealing, and our previous expectations seem a little worn. The wear and tear of the past is not due to our diminishing capacities of thinking, acting, or hoping, but to the narrowing range of potentialities on which we exert our capacities. In its march forward, life constantly rearranges these potentialities, and we fear that, as it does so, it might cross a threshold beyond which they would become almost as fixed as the past left behind. This intense anxiety is aptly expressed by Lieutenant Drogo in Dino Buzzati's *Tartar Steppe*:

> Up to then he had gone forward through the heedless season of early youth—along a road which to children seems infinite, where the years slip past slowly and with quiet pace so that no one notices them go. We walk along calmly, looking curiously around us; there is not the least need to hurry, no one pushes us from behind and no one is waiting for us. . . . So the journey continues; we wait trustfully and the days are long and peaceful. The sun shines high in the sky and it seems to have no wish to set. But at a certain point we turn around, almost instinctively, and see that a gate has been bolted behind us barring our way back. Then we feel that something has changed. The sun no longer seems to be motionless but moves quickly across the sky. . . . Then we understand that time is passing and that one day or another the road must come to an end.[65]

At this juncture, the past stops being seen as the time when many other things were possible beside those that happened and becomes the moment that paved the way for them not to be possible anymore. This zooming effect of a dilating and contracting past is a distinctive feature of the existential justification.

The reflection on life cannot be reduced to an accounting of past satisfactions (nor can it be constrained by a single utility function) precisely because it is rooted in the past as much as in the present or the future. Even if satisfactions were the main criterion for assessing success in life, we would still need an independent yardstick for their allocation. For instance, the order in which satisfactions occur in the course of one's life usually makes a big difference. In order to accumulate a certain measure of contentment in one's entire life, one may experience happy moments in one's youth and unhappy ones in old age, start life unhappily and end it happily, or experience an equal amount of happy moments throughout one's life. Most people would rather move from unhappy circumstances to happier ones rather than conversely, even if the total amount of satisfactions remained the same in both cases. This is why a life of invariably deteriorating circumstances is commonly seen as a sad failure regardless of the excellence of its initial conditions.

This way of evaluating our lives is obviously determined by the rational character of our life plans, which are rational precisely because they look forward to circumstances that are better than past ones. It is also determined by our psychology, which derives our satisfaction or lack thereof not only from what happens but also from our previous experiences and wishes. Its main reason though, is the time irreversibility of our human condition: the later in life our failures, misfortunes, and deteriorations occur, the less time we have left to make things right. Another reason for which the reflection on life cannot use satisfaction requirements as an exclusive evaluation criterion for a successful life is that—given equal amounts of life's satisfactions—most of us would prefer a life rich in various experiences and pleasures to one in which pleasure, however great, only comes from one source and is always of the same kind. Our gratification increases with the variety and distinctiveness of our activities.

Since antiquity, philosophers considered the search for unity as the first task of reflection on human life. The random events in our life, the certainty of life's end, the requirement that reflection on life continually lean back on a past that is either all-intrusive or evasive, and, most importantly, the sense that—as life advances—one ought to find new, diversified reasons and justifications for living all contributed in ancient times to the formulation of a strong requirement concerning the connection between reflection on human life and the search for unity.[66] The same idea can be found in the work of many contemporary philosophers. To live one's life means to reflect on the coherence of one's past in order to reduce, if possible, the collision of our desires, our good deeds, and our highly held values.[67] It can even be said that existential reflection is rational precisely because it is dedicated to the search for unity. In Jaspers's view, internalizing our experience brings cohesiveness and harmonization to our life's goals. Unity appears thus to be a higher-order requirement whose absence would make justification impossible.

In spite of all that, one is tempted to ask: "What is the nature of the unity requirement as related to the exercise of reflective abilities?" Clearly, it is not *logical* because it is hard to see what conceptual definition of "unity of ends" would account for the ends pursued along an entire human life. It is also hard to see how such a requirement would naturally come under a *psychological* heading. True, the satisfaction we feel when we recall the various episodes, events, surmounted obstacles, and crucial decisions of our life does include an element of conscious reflection and appreciation for a life we see as cohesive and unified, a life whose choices we would rather remember as having been as little affected as possible by contradiction and conflict. But this does not mean that the wish to achieve unity corresponds to a definite psychological need that we would have to satisfy. In fact, it is a matter of contingency (involving either the particularities of human nature or those of a particular individual) whether a representation of our life as unified would render us happy or not. Nor is the nature of this requirement *prescriptive* in the sense that the individual would be expected to incorporate his plans in a unified whole. The nature of the requirement for unity of existential reflection seems to be essentially *normative*: more precisely, it functions not as a norm for action (it does not call to act in order to unify a life) but as a norm for reflection—a norm according to which reflection is engaged and practiced.[68]

Existential reflection is not reducible to a net balance of satisfaction and cannot be put in the same category as "the deliberative rationality of life plans," a topic that is often discussed in contemporary philosophy. For Josiah Royce, "a person may be regarded as a human life lived according to a plan." He attempted to bring together the rational consideration of life and the requirement of unified goals, and he thought that a person's plan of life does indeed bring together the desires and goals that make this person the creator of a cohesive, unified life, that is, a life having a dominant theme.[69] John Rawls also spoke of "dominant ends" and defined a "rational life plan" as a plan that a person prefers to others based on a purely rational deliberation for being "consistent with the principles of rational choice when these are applied to all the relevant features of his situation, and that would be chosen by him with full deliberative rationality, that is, with full awareness of the relevant facts and after a careful consideration of the consequences." A plan adopted with deliberative rationality is one that "best organizes our activities and influences the formation of our subsequent wants so that our aims and interests can be fruitfully combined into one scheme of conduct" based on criteria of means, effectiveness, inclusiveness, and strong plausibility.[70] In order to define a decision procedure for such plans, Rawls used Sidgwick's idea that the future good of a person—seen as good on the whole—corresponds to what that person would have desired or sought "here and now" had he been able not only to visualize precisely and correctly the consequences of each option available to him now but also to imagine himself reiterating his choice at any other moment of his life. In this view, the rationality principles that guide deliberation dictate that we maximize the net balance of satisfaction—in other words, that we adopt a plan that has the best chances of fulfilling our most important aims and aspirations. Deliberative rationality takes into account the demands of our future selves and the interests of others. The counting principle of rational choice requires that we manage to always protect our deeds against criticism from our future selves. Rawls saw happiness as a psychological effect of a successfully carried through life plan.[71]

The view that rational deliberation encompasses one's entire life seems implausible psychologically and offers a distorted image of the reflection on human life. The assumption that there is a continuous disposition for rational deliberation—directed toward a life plan in which life's moments are all equally important—makes life look like a rectangle shown all at once to be optimally filled in; it also considers any modulation caused by remoteness in time to be less important. The model is wrong: the size of my life's rectangle is up to me; the life I lead affects—at each of its moments—my ulterior desires and judgments.[72] And because all reflection on life proceeds from the viewpoint of the self, no rational deliberation could ever hope that its conclusions will be more substantive than the premises of which it is a part, that is, no rational deliberation can hope to free itself from its dependency on a particular moment in time. In living my life, I do not choose from a fixed set of options presented to me time and time again. My ability to judge is also due to my being the product of my previous choices: if my options were fixed, if they were unaffected by my previous choices, they would be to me abstract options, wholly detached from my life. The ability to insert externalities into deliberation presupposes that the whole life be considered at once, rather than just what remains of it at a given moment. Existential justification cannot be looked at in the same way as the rational deliberation of life plans.

This model for deliberative rationality suggests that we have full control over our lives and that the individual does not change over time. Many authors have, long ago, strongly rejected it. Kierkegaard's concept of paradox introduces a quite different relationship to our life time whereby we renounce the whole temporal realm in order to gain eternity. The motion of repetition is linked to the search for time lost that ends with time remembered (i.e., recollection), whereby a new dimension of existence takes shape and temporality transmutates.[73] Nothing is more opposed to the idea of rational deliberation on life plans than Kierkegaard's requirement for "justification by the result."[74] While his justification is different from what I call existential justification, he takes seriously the time constraints on justification and tries to abolish them in order to escape the realm of time. Kierkegaard acknowledges the failure of his attempt, but this does not affect the critical virtues of his thinking. Besides, the failure is inevitable if one considers that the requirement for justification is rooted in an aspiration whose meaning is undermined by the will for immediacy. This "intuition of us as absolute beings," which is discovered in a "psychology of time," is precisely what Proust was also seeking in *time regained* and in the unpredictable and quasi-miraculous qualities of creation: "one has knocked at all the doors which lead nowhere, and then one stumbles without knowing it on the only door through which one can enter—and it opens on its own accord."[75]

At this point I would like to suggest a comparison between the different standpoints examined here. I started with the constraints imposed on the existential justification, trying to show that the reflection on life is not an account of satisfactions, nor is it a deliberation on a life plan. Existential justifications are subject to conditions related to the general features of human life: a time-limited, directional existence, narrowing potentialities, and irreducible and irreversible events. Such constraints have a normative dimension; they are requirements that existential justifications must satisfy in order to improve our understanding of life. Interestingly enough, such constraints are close to those used by Franz Brentano to define the unity of intrinsic values. An intrinsic value is a reality whose value is independent of context or its consequences, and of any relations to something else. This value belongs only to itself. It does not depend on a summation of goods but on an organic principle of unity that is constitutive of its being good. This principle relates to a rule on the composition of goods, distinct from all summation. In his essay *The Origin of Our Knowledge of Right and Wrong*, Brentano maintains that the importance we give to norms about order and disposition is also found in the definition of organic unity. The order-related rules are the rule of retribution and compensation (not necessarily the same), the rule of differentiation (there is more value in a differentiated whole than in a unified whole), and the rule of improvement (going from worse to better helps to acquire a good greater than one obtained by going from better to worse).[76] The comparison I am suggesting here is the following: the definition of the order and unity of life, as well as the repartition of goods in time, seems to follow rules that are very similar to those established by Brentano for defining the organic unity principle of intrinsic values, that is, the norms of equilibrium, variation, and progression.[77]

CHAPTER 6

The Good in Human Life

Morals and Existential Justifications

IN THE PRECEDING PAGES I have attempted to define the formal constraints on the invariants of the human condition that affect our justifications and reasons for action. I have also mentioned their normative scope and connection to values, which will come under closer examination in the following pages. The objectivity of our existential justifications is partly due to the fact that we justify our decisions by relating them to goods and values. There is a natural affinity between the rationality of existential justification and the definition of human life's goods and values. What are these goods? What kind of objectivity do they display? Considering their place in our life, there is reason to believe that they are not simply added to it, but that they follow a particular order. This is why it seems to me that, without postulating the existence of a meta-good—a second-order good or a formal good, the normative aspect of human life's goods is much harder to grasp.

Let us posit that reflection on human life requires access to a kind of good that is more than a sum of goods and values, much like a category of goods. Such a formal good is closely linked to the defining norms of existential justification and, specifically, to the requirement for unity, to the requirement subjecting justifications to the irreversibility of time, and to the diversity requirement.[1] The formal good I am looking for does not refer to any sort of essentialism and displays no undetermined neutrality because it obeys real constraints.

It is sometimes said that the need to find immanent justifications—that make no reference to an external reality or good—leads to the subjectivity or arbitrariness of the very values supposed to give meaning to human life. This is an issue that often caused criticism of the more modern forms of existentialism. The objectivity of morals, the reality of values and their ordering, would be inconceivable in the sort of existence that finds in itself the only source of its justification. Such criticism hardly qualifies as a valid argument, in my view. That the access to values and goods is tied to the presence of immanent justifications does not make them at all the object of arbitrary decisions or definitions. Justifications are guided by the search for best reasons; they obey norms and therefore may refer to objective goods, indisputable obligations, or impersonal rules that are independent of anybody's decision or will. Moreover, the rationality effort brought about by such justifications is sustained by reasons whose validity comes from a critical reflection the pertinence of which is easily verifiable.

When we qualify a human life as being good or successful, we undoubtedly mean to qualify its moral value, but not only that. Most of what is good in human life is closely linked to morality without being reducible to it. It would be more accurate to say that the goods and the values found in existential reflection include and exceed morality. Surely the existential justifications and deliberations require the same kind of reasons as strictly moral justifications and deliberations. However, not all distinctive traits of existential justifications are always present in moral justifications. For instance, the agent-relative constraint applies to certain types of impersonal moral deliberations.[2] In addition the moment at which a moral decision is taken does not necessarily affect the content of that decision. In fact, a moral justification is mainly related to someone else's interests (considered in abstract terms), to our duties, or to considerations of impersonality and universality. Such purely moral reasons do not occupy a central place in an existential justification precisely because the justification concerns a particular person. Besides, moral deliberations seek general traits and impersonal prescriptions, which cannot be the case for existential justification.[3]

Existential justifications and moral deliberations share however a concern for rationality; also, their reasons exhibit a clear connection to goods and values. Their relationship could be defined in two complementary ways: the existence of *moral* justifications depends on the prior existence of simple justifications. This is an argument a fortiori: in order for a decision to be morally justified, it must be first justified, period. If there is no justification, that is more reason not to have a moral justification. It is precisely in this sense that the elaboration of existential justifications has a real effect on moral deliberations, even if all existential justifications are clearly not moral justifications as such. In addition, the reflection on the various kinds of goods that are defined in the course of a lifetime recognizes as valid some justifications that are not necessarily related to moral goods and do not primarily count as moral justifications. At times, existential justifications and moral justifications are overlapping; at other times, they are clashing. This unusual configuration is due to the unique place reserved to "moral good" among all human goods, when it is defined strictly as tied to someone else's interests and to the defense of impersonal and universal duties.

Gauguin abandons his kin, breaks his commitments toward those who depend on him, and causes their ruin. The moral condemnation is unequivocally justified by his broken promise and the harm done unto others. On the other hand, his aspiration to create masterworks is not seen as insignificant or valueless, even from a strict moral viewpoint. Nobody would think that "Gauguin could have been a great painter, but he renounced it out of duty toward his family, and that is good." A verdict of "that is good, period" would be shocking because it would counter our ideals of human achievement and a successful life. It is no doubt "good" to abandon pleasure for duty; but is it good to renounce everything that gives meaning to life? Nobody would forget that such renunciation would cause irreplaceable loss to personal achievement. At the very least, it would be a restrictive, almost caricatured conception of morality to pretend that this is not a situation of conflict.

The strangest feature of such a conflict is that it appears only once Gauguin becomes a great painter. Only then could it be known what would have been lost had Gauguin opted for duty instead. Had he been killed in an accident or failed as a painter, the judgment would have been easy: "What this man Gauguin has done by quitting his family is bad, simply bad." Why? Because he would have been unable to justify his deed to himself! There would be no existential justification to counter the sense that his decision was morally wrong—at least not a valid existential justification, that is, one that could be linked to any good. True, knowing that Gauguin has become a great painter, we may still think of his decision as morally deplorable, but we would be faced with a more complex moral situation. We would face, on the one side, a morality strictly defined by impersonal duties and, on the other, a more complex morality that requires the realization of human perfection and the fulfillment of personal abilities. This moral conflict provides two concurrent types of justifications, both equally related to real goods, both having a moral dimension, some differences in nature and degree notwithstanding. Moral judgment is concerned with the value of duty, commitment, and the harm done to others, whereas existential justification deals with the goods and values rising from the blossoming of personal talents and from individual human accomplishment.

This clash of justifications and goods occurs however at a moment when it can have no effect on Gauguin's decision: even if his decision to abandon his family were justified in the end by his masterworks and by all the good that his new life allowed him to accomplish, the life of his family is still ruined. His existential justification was incomplete at the time his decision was taken; and when—*ex eventu*—is seems finally complete, confirmed, or falsified, the effects of his decision have already taken their toll. Such clashes seem therefore to present a particular profile: either the justification of an existential decision is still undetermined or incomplete and the moral judgment—however valid and true—falls flat for having found nothing to oppose; or the justification is complete, but—in spite of its concomitance with the moral judgment—has no effect on the formulation of the latter because it has already been verified. The ensuing clash between the goods and values involved also presents a particular configuration: the goods and values prevailing in moral judgments are goods in any circumstances—if they need mentioning, it is because they must be taken into account. The goods and values to which the existential justification refers in such cases show their nature as goods only at the end of life, once it has had its share of hardships and randomness.

Notwithstanding their differences, strictly moral justifications and existential justifications are both the product of the same effort of rationality. Both refer to goods and values that may clash in spite of their common nature as goods; and both are linked by an element of conditionality. The question whether Gauguin's ambition to become a great painter also has a moral dimension can be asked only after Gauguin has become one. Only then could we ask whether his ambition can be contrasted to his strict duty, without any prejudice to the answer. Before his success, the judgment of his deed as immoral cannot be revised. Gauguin's existential decision must be completely justified to himself before we can even appreciate the nature of his conflict with moral obligations.

We need not go any further into the nature of this conflict. I will simply attempt to show how postulating a formal good could help to better understand such a conflict. The concept of formal good corresponds indeed to the category of human goods, and postulating the existence of such a category helps to define the conflicts among different goods. Before explaining why I deem it necessary to postulate the existence of a formal good, I will start by describing the different kinds of goods present in human life, with their shared and distinctive features.

Happiness and the Subjectivity of Human Good

First and foremost, the human good has a subjective significance. We could not even speak of "good" without assuming the existence of a feeling of happiness. But what does this feeling consist of? When do we experience such a feeling? Is it in every instance of our life? This would be hard to believe, especially because the memory of some misfortunes caused by past happiness might still linger in our minds. Do we experience happiness when we look back at our entire life? This must surely be the happiness of contemplating one's life, not the happiness of life itself. Do we experience happiness just before dying? To expect it at that precise moment would seem somewhat paradoxical, would it not?

Many authors consider that—defined subjectively—happiness is tied to an indisputable psychological reality: the feeling of satisfaction with our life up till now and with the expectation that it will continue this way.[4] To this we may add the presence of an activity allowing us to attain previously chosen objectives, or at least to toy with the idea of future plans. It is an open question whether this is a logical condition (because the definition of happiness includes conceptually the realization of such plans) or a causal condition (because the realization of such plans creates a mental state that could be identified with happiness). These conditions would be valid only if there were nothing of an essential nature in our life that we would have preferred never to have happened or to have happened differently.

Happiness cannot be dissociated from justification. We would be indeed surprised if someone declared himself to be steadily and permanently happy without being able to give one single reason for his happiness.[5] Being able to justify one's happiness is, however, not enough for separating happiness from subjectivity.[6] Several objections come to mind against this idea of happiness as a subjectively experienced good. The first is concerned with false happiness. Sometimes a false belief may be a source of happiness (for instance, x is happy because she believes to be loved when she is in fact cheated on). The counterobjection would state that discovering that a past happiness was based on a false belief would not compromise its past reality or, more generally, that it is impossible to be wrong about one's own happiness. Indeed, when I declare "I am happy because . . .," it seems impossible that falsifying the reason given by me would abolish my happiness. Is this indeed the case? Yes, it is, if my happiness consisted mainly in physical satisfactions. No, it is not, if my happiness was grounded in a belief. For instance, if my happiness came from the belief that I did a good thing to somebody but in the end this perceived good proved to do great harm to that person, thus falsifying the belief that justified my happiness, then how could I still say that I was truly happy when I believed to be doing a good thing for him? The only riposte to this objection is strictly epistemological: there can be no false happiness.

A purely subjective conception of human good has another weakness: the attempt to find reasons for justifying happiness could never be limited to a summation of desires and satisfactions; it would also have to show how particular projects and desires were organized in a person's life. In order to secure the ability of justifying the satisfaction experienced with respect to an entire life, one must go beyond the first-order desires and needs by assuming the existence of related desires and needs of a higher order that make it possible to regulate the first-order ones.[7] Our desires are always fulfilled in a context of relatively scarce resources and capacities, and of concurrent projects and goals; at times our short-term desires may clash with the long-term ones, and at other times some of our desires may be distinctly self-destructive. The satisfaction experienced with respect to human life is therefore tied to an element of reflection designed to show that the intended goals have been achieved and that they are well put together.[8] This kind of satisfaction relates to a formal property that cannot be properly accounted for in a strictly subjective conception of human good.

Objective Human Goods

The hypothesis of the objectivity of human goods corresponds to the intuition that a person could legitimately say that another person is happy—that it is therefore possible to evaluate happiness based on relatively stable criteria by adopting the viewpoint of a third person. Listening to a life narrative whereby plans are realized and goods are effectively accomplished, one could say: here is a truly accomplished human life. This kind of judgment aspires to a form of objectivity that is not limited to giving reasons, because even subjective goods can be justified. Likewise, listening to a person's life narrative, one can conclude that such a life is an abject or miserable failure, regardless of that person's judgment on his own happiness. There are also life-styles that—whatever the satisfaction achieved—it would be a stretch to call happy, precisely because of the limited capacity for action and feeling that is involved. Could we speak of a slave's happiness based on the subjective feeling of happiness that he may experience when small mercies and derisory pleasures acquire an immense significance in the emptiness of his life? Could we speak of happy lives—even in the presence of satisfaction—when horrible life-styles are involved or when individuals' first-order desires are conflicting or impossible to fulfill or when their frenzied desires bring a considerable satisfaction that breeds dissatisfaction? Not every satisfaction qualifies as happiness.

Several philosophers have emphasized the propositional aspect of happiness. Happiness is not only the fact of "being happy"; it is "being happy about x, y, z," where the part "x, y, z" (i.e., the things that make one happy) is essential to defining the reality of that happiness. Happiness is real if it relates to states of things that can be described by verifiable propositions. This explains why we can experience satisfaction with something that does not lead necessarily to our own happiness, but to somebody else's happiness, such as a loved one. Likewise, when we wish our loved ones happiness, it is in the sense not only that they experience satisfaction but, most importantly, that their happiness be grounded in objectively good states and things. In this view, it is not enough to say that people feel happy and consider themselves to be happy in order for them to be considered so in the strict sense of the term. Feeling happy is a necessary condition but it is not a sufficient one because the feeling may be experienced for the wrong reasons or be grounded in a false belief. It is therefore difficult to speak of happiness when it cannot be related to human goods that apply to an entire life, realize human potentialities, and lend themselves to external appreciation. It is also conceivable that such objective goods could be present in a person's life without any accompanying satisfaction; still this would not prove that happiness can be reduced to satisfaction. A simpleton or a lobotomized individual could be perfectly happy (in the subjective sense) to count grass blades. Yet very few people would consider him so in view of the derisory quality of his occupation as compared to truly good things for human beings, which bring objective happiness. And they would not change their minds even if such an individual could explain very well why he experienced such pleasure in counting grass blades.[9] Again it is not enough for a subjective good to be justified in order for it to be associated with objective goods. The idea of objective happiness satisfies a deeper need than a mere epistemological rejection of a subjective conception of happiness.[10]

Human Goods

These considerations suggest that the feeling of satisfaction ought to be grounded in real goods. As objective referents of happiness, human goods are not limited to material goods; they include talents, intersubjective relationships, self-esteem, the quality of the connection to another, and many personal goods such as the ability to reflect, the sense of beauty, the richness of experienced feelings, one's psychological resources, and a good character. Those things are all good in themselves and, as such, they are desirable and deserve to be sought as ends in themselves.

The objectivity of such goods is initially defined in prudential terms. A life-style, an activity, a certain good, can all be qualified as objectively good if one could not but desire them or if one could not be happy without them. What confers them an objective status is the justified and universal quality of their appeal to us. They correspond to generic and universal objects of desire, their universal desirability having become a quasi-intrinsic characteristic—and, as such, they are not conditioned by actual desires and attitudes.[11] Another, much stronger definition of objectivity, uses substantial terms. Goods are justifiably desired realities that make people really happy. Not everybody wants them but they deserve to be desired for prudential reasons. Such goods are intrinsic values, and their best illustration is Kant's notion of goodwill.[12] It is inconceivable that any individual who sought happiness in harming others would have access to the slightest objective good. Thus, a person who had committed a vile act (eliminating a troublesome rival, betraying one's friends), regrets it, and then chooses to ingest a pill that makes him forget his guilt and be happy would never be considered by a third party to be really happy.[13]

The definition of objective human goods raises epistemological questions. Is it possible to establish identity criteria for such goods independently of the prevalent favorable bias toward them? The general idea is that these goods correspond to the necessities of our intellect and not to contingent psychological tendencies.[14] Often though, the justification process turns out to be circular because of the ties linking identity criteria to judgments about goods.[15] Other difficulties lie with the ways in which practical rationality deals with conflicting goods.[16] On this subject, I will simply say that the diversity of goods does not threaten practical rationality; rather, it is practical rationality that helps shape this diversity.

Good Life and "Human Flourishing"

The third form of human good is a good life. The concept of "the good life" ranks among the most frequently used among philosophers and also by the general public. The English term is an adaptation from the Greek *eu zein* (to live well). Introduced as a borrowing from ancient ethics, the concept has mainly served the critique of prevalent moral theories in the English-speaking world.

Primarily, "the good life" means a happy, accomplished, successful life. In this sense, the term is used synonymously with "human flourishing," from the Greek *eudaimonia*. Unlike the Greek term, however, "human flourishing" comes from modern philosophy. Specifically, it first appeared in an article entitled "Modern Moral Philosophy," published in 1958, in which Elisabeth Anscombe severely criticized modern moral thinking. In it, Anscombe reminds us that modern moral philosophy—whether consequentialist or of Kantian inspiration—rests on the concepts of obligation and duty, that is, on *ought*. The specific moral signification of these concepts is but a relic of a legalist ethical interpretation grounded in the belief of divine law. It belongs to the past and must be replaced with the concept of "what is ethically required in a situation."[17] The definition of what the human being needs in order to prosper and reach his full potential has a decidedly normative bent and is as verifiable as any empirical statement. It leads to saying, for instance, that—in order to best exert his human capacity for choice and action—the human being needs instructions for action called virtues. It was in relation to this kind of understated, minimally moral understanding of the concept of duty (in the sense of what is required) that Anscombe introduced the concept of human flourishing:

"essentially, the flourishing of a man *qua* man consists in his being good
(e.g., in virtues); but for any X to which such terms apply, X needs what
makes him flourish, so a man needs, or ought to perform, only virtuous
actions." Virtuous action is a duty because it is what a good human being
needs—or what the normative concept of human being needs—for human
flourishing.[18] This article launched the notion of human flourishing, and
its pages became the philosophical success story of the recent decades.[19]

From the start, the concept of human flourishing is opposed to the subjective definition of happiness as justified satisfaction, while preserving its
conceptual distinctiveness from the idea of objective happiness based on
prudential and substantial goods. Human flourishing is an existential
mode, a human norm with objective designs defined by intrinsically good
activities, talent development, and perfectibility. Happiness and human
flourishing refer to two distinct ontological categories: one is a state of
mind, the other a way of life. The concept of human flourishing is defined
by the possession, the pursuit, or the practice of goods, such as contemplation, richness, wisdom, or virtue. The concept of happiness is defined by
the mental states produced by the possession of such goods. This is why it
can be said of a particular person's life to have reached accomplishment
regardless of that person's opinion on the subject, and why it cannot be
said of someone that he is happy regardless of how he feels.[20] The concept
of human flourishing refers to an objective norm defined according to what
is required for the optimal development of the human being.[21]

Current theories of human flourishing are normative theories involving
many substantial assertions. Starting with the difficult to define normative
concept of human being, these theories make the idea of optimal human
development into the ultimate purpose of our actions, and use it as foundation to a theory of normative reasons for acting.[22] They want to elaborate
a theory of human good grounded in a definition of human development
that is objective—that is, independent of desires and attitudes—and that
makes the reasons for action depend on what is required for humans to
flourish.

This conception of human good raises several questions. First, the
meaning of what Anscombe calls the *"ought to, need to,* and *require to,"*
is rather imprecise and difficult to explain in the context of human actions
and choices that have no direct link to human "flourishing." Regardless of
the development criterion, the meaning of "human-specific normativity"
remains underdetermined. Second, it is hard to see how the statements
about "what is required for human flourishing" would translate in terms
of duty and obligations to be fulfilled and thus establish our duties toward
others. Moreover, how are we to justify our duty to ensure our personal
fulfillment? Granted our duties to ourselves, why should our duty to

"flourish" be the most important one?[23] Lastly, the claim about the objectivity of the concept of human flourishing rests on a definition of human good as substantially "good functioning" of human beings; but it is still dependent on a form of *essentialism* supported by a culturally determined idea of man.[24] The judicious connections established by Anscombe between "ought" and "need" are conceptual connections, and, as such, their validity should not depend on the hypothesis of an unchanging human nature. Moreover, the new interpretation of duty (presented to us) as a norm of human beings focuses on *ought to be*, not on *ought to do*. It cannot claim to represent a duty to act, an injunction, or a norm for action. And such a conception of human good is questionable because it involves a philosophy of psychology and a self-contained theory of rationality that have yet to be designed.

The Good in Human Life: Formal Good and Philosophy

Contemporary theories of human flourishing claim to be the only existing philosophies of human good. I reject this claim. The concept of human flourishing relates to a theory of human good that is far from unique and that, as far as I can tell, is not even a theory of goodness. To speak of "the good life" remains confused if the kind of goodness that is involved is not specified. A good life is not only an accomplished life; it may also be one that is guided by a principle of goodness, a goodness fitted to the scale of human life.[25]

The good in human life is not reducible to subjective good, objective good, or human flourishing. The need to distinguish human good from human flourishing fulfills several requirements. First, it fulfills the requirement to guarantee a form of normativity that is linked to the reflection on human life. To simply consider happiness and human flourishing does not allow normative questions about human life (its dissatisfactions, incoherence, self-delusions), nor does is facilitate comparisons between lives. Indeed, happiness and human flourishing are both reducible to natural properties, whereas the norms that guide us in formulating judgments fitted to existential justifications are not natural. In addition, the formal constraints of compatibility and consistency that give meaning to the concepts of happiness and human flourishing can be much more easily justified by assuming the existence of a higher-order good.[26] Lastly, the hypothesis of a human good distinct from human development fulfills the requirement to dissociate between two different kinds of reasons to act. The reasons to act that are provided by considering my own development are tied to a particular psychological reality. In contrast, those related to the good in human life are related to the order of goods and values, and also to the kind of intelligibility I am seeking in life and the kind of justifications I am elaborating. The second kind of reasons pertains to the norms that guide my reflection on my life. Questions such as "How ought I to live?" and "What kind of person should I be?" can only be asked based on a close examination of my own life.[27]

The previously mentioned distinctive traits of existential justification are helpful in outlining the concept of formal good. It represents the set of norms governing justification and determining whether human life can have meaning or not. These norms concern the search for unity and consistency, the obligation to take into account the progress in time, and the imperative to relate reasons for action to the subject so as to secure its ability to act and affirm the integrity of its personality. Existential reflection starts from the hypothesis of a good that guides the search for existential justifications, structures them, and gives them unity.

The hypothesis of a formal good or of an order of goods signals a psychological issue that cannot be ignored. The reasons for action draw their normative force from the values and goods related to them. But once recorded in the existential justification, they must obey the same constraints that frame the existential reflection itself. These constraints concern the general characteristics of life and take into account the ways in which goods are being shared, combined, and differentiated in the course of life. Consequently, it becomes necessary to find a principle, a kind of formal good that would justify the reference to the ordering of goods, to their disposition in time, and to their consistency, their plurality, or their hierarchy. It is only in relation to such a principle of order that we could determine the place of compelling duties and obligations toward human beings, among all other goods.

A further need that justifies the hypothesis of a formal good is that of postulating a nonsubstantial good, that is, a good that would not be vulnerable to the critique of the good life. For my part, it is in order to challenge the essentialism of goods at the root of the ideology of the good life that I support the postulate of a formal good. In my view, the formal good cannot be conceived as a kind of model or rule. Contrary to conventional wisdom, the ancient thinkers, and Plato in particular, can help us with the definition of a formal good. Plato confers a fundamental role to "good"; and although the platonic good is evidently not a substance, Plato emphasizes the fact that his good is "beyond substance." The comparative reading of Plato's *Republic* and *Philebus* gives us a better idea of the scope of a definition of formal good. Plato conceives of good as an impersonal prescriptive principle and, at the same time, as a principle of an incorporeal order. Plato explains how—at the moment of reincarnation—every soul must choose a life, and how each life, whether that of a hero or a peasant, is shown as a whole made of events, hopes, expectations, and reasons related to goods. He then stresses that, after choosing a life, every soul must make it in his own image; but that, before being chosen, all lives exhibit a formal principle of good, an incorporeal order. Even the last soul to choose a life will get one with a formula for good as real as that embodied in the life chosen by the first soul in line. Finally, each person will live his life as his own and make what sense he can of it.[28]

The third reason in support of the "formal good" postulate concerns the need to define the constraints of ordering and cohesiveness that apply to all human goods. By postulating the existence of these constraints on all goods, I am objecting to two seemingly contrary views grounded in a common prejudice. The first view belongs to the extremist defenders of current theories on virtue and states that all philosophy of good must refer to a properly identified substantial good. This view represents a form of essentialism. The second view is found in Hobbes and in the defenders of rational choice, including Rawls, and states that the definition of good does not include any intrinsic characteristics, be they as formal as the principle of organic unity; it also states that good is but an object of preference and, as such, is neutral or undetermined. Their common prejudice is the refusal to consider good as a formal normative order. In fact, good is not a substantial reality defined once and for all, nor is it an undetermined place. It represents certainly a formal principle, but one that inspires and sustains a strong aspiration to the rationality of values and their objectivity.

In antiquity, the reflection on human life was focused on the rational principles of life that help actions follow rationality and, therefore, assist human beings in keeping a certain distance from themselves. Today, the status of reflection is altogether different. What constitutes the object of reflection is rarely political and contemplative life. Contemporary thought most often focuses on private, nonheroic life. Our knowledge of ourselves is not guided anymore solely by the requirement to separate passions from reason and from affectivity, because psychotherapeutic and psychoanalytical introspection heightens our sensitivity to semantic shifts and transfers of meaning as ceaseless reconfigurations of our psyche. On the topic of the exemplar quality of life, antiquity had a few canonical descriptions at its disposal, but for us, after several centuries of fictional explorations of the self, our reflection feeds on multiple life forms borrowed from all times and cultures. Our intelligibility of life does not depend on adherence to myths and other collective significations, but on an individual elaboration; it is not shaped anymore according to a hierarchy of human activities topped by contemplation.

Socrates said that the unexamined life is not worth living. In his view, philosophy was the best means for performing such self-examination.

Now, existential reflection can resort to philosophy not as a stronghold against life or as low-cost wisdom, but as a pattern to apply to life. Philosophy is one of the dimensions of the existential reflection that facilitates the incorporation of reflexive conclusions into one's own life. It is not certain that it could calm passions or improve life, but surely it can contribute to the development of human abilities for rational and autonomous action.[29] Philosophy, like the overture to Mozart's *Don Giovanni*, starts with a minor chord. Yet it is one of the major forms of moral disquiet.[30]

Notes

CHAPTER ONE
ETHICS AND THE CHALLENGE TO MORAL PHILOSOPHY

1. The same could be said of institutions of higher learning such as École normale supérieure, Collège de France, and Centre national de la recherche scientifique (CNRS).

2. This is sometimes called the *reductio ad Hitlerum*. See Leo Strauss, *Natural Law and History* (Chicago: University of Chicago Press, 1965), 42.

3. "Pour la philosophie morale," *Le Débat*, no. 72 (1992): 40–51.

4. See, for instance, my contributions to the series *Philosophie morale*, published since 1993 by Presses Universitaires de France (PUF) under my direction, and to the *Dictionnaire d'éthique et de philosophie morale* [1996], ed. Monique Canto-Sperber (Paris: PUF, 2001).

5. See my discussion in chapter 2.

6. Alain Badiou, *L'Éthique. Essai sur la conscience du mal* (Paris: Hatier, 1993), 5.

7. Ibid., 8.

8. In this, Alain Badiou adopts the confident tone of a prophet: "Ethics defines Man as victim" (ibid., 12).

9. Ibid., 33.

10. In the same vein, see Marcel Gauchet, "Les droits de l'homme ne sont pas une politique," *Le Débat*, no. 3 (1980): 3–21; and "Quand les droits de l'homme deviennent une politique," *Le Débat*, no. 110 (2000): 258–88.

11. Badiou, *L'Éthique*, 29. As for parliamentary politics, "it consists in transforming the spectacle of the economy in a resigned consensus opinion" (30).

12. For a critical view of the facile derision detected in certain humanistic trends, see Luc Ferry, *Man Made God: The Meaning of Life*, trans. David Pellauer (Chicago: University of Chicago Press, 2002), 101–10, 113, 141–43. It argues that a moral commitment does not lose its value simply because it has the support of the media.

13. Charles S. Pierce was referring to the effects of the object of our ideas that can be viewed as having a practical import, in "How to Make Our Ideas Clear," in *Collected Papers of Charles Sanders Pierce*, ed. Charles Hartshorne and Paul Weiss (Cambridge, Mass.: Harvard University Press, 1934), 5:402. William James adds that the significance of an idea can be figured out by determining what conduct it is likely to incite, and this conduct becomes for us the only significance of that idea, in "The Pragmatic Method," in *Essays in Philosophy* (Cambridge, Mass.: Harvard University Press, 1978), 124.

14. Cf. chapter 3.

15. Gilles Deleuze, *Foucault* (Paris: Minuit, 1986), 96.

16. Badiou, *L'Éthique*, 8–9.

17. Ibid., 10.

18. This, despite the fact that the so-called moral grandstanding–which is as hollow as it is pompous–tends to define itself as an attitude of pure protestation, resistance, or defense.

19. Badiou, *L'Éthique*, 45–48.

20. Ibid., 30.

21. Ibid., 16.

22. Ibid., 14.

23. Ibid., 74–75. For those wishing to know more about the past political stances of the man who currently heads the Department of Philosophy at École normale supérieure, see the article he published in *Le Monde* soon after the Vietnamese intervention ended the Khmer Rouge regime in 1979.

24. See examples given in Badiou, *L'Éthique*, 38.

25. Ibid., 40.

26. Ibid., 31.

27. Cf. my discussion of "Pluralism and Objectivity" in chapter 2.

28. Badiou, *L'Éthique*, 31. The quoting of Mao Tse-tung for establishing the truthfulness of pluralism cannot leave indifferent those who know that 2 to 3 million political opponents perished during the Cultural Revolution, or that repression and famine resulted in 65 million victims in communist China.

29. Ibid., 31. This is also a strategy of political debate that Badiou endorses by calling for the adoption of a "situational language." See also ibid., 72–73.

30. Ibid., 9, 21, and 17.

31. Ibid., 52–55.

32. Ibid., 78 and 33.

33. See the strong—if puzzling—statement by Alain Etchegoyen: "what ethics has to offer does not satisfy the demands of morality," in *La Valse des éthiques* (Paris: François Bourin, 1991), 15.

34. Michel Onfray, *La sculpture de soi* (Paris: Grasset, 1993).

35. Gilles Lipovetsky, *Le Crépuscule du devoir* (Paris: Grasset, 1992), 16. The author declares that ethics represents "the reconciliation of the heart with joy and of virtue with interest."

36. Ibid., 61.

37. Ibid., 14; this is the ethics of "sacrificial values" and "hyperbolic imperatives of duties" (15); the ethics of "the supreme obligations of the ideal" and of "maximal duty" (24).

38. Ibid., 200.

39. Ibid., 201.

40. Ibid., 15, defines ethics as social dissolution of a "religious form." See my critique of this definition in "Morals and Religion" in chapter 1.

41. Pascal Bruckner, *La Tentation de l'innocence* (Paris: Grasset, 1995). For a different view, see Onfray, *La Sculpture de soi*.

42. Ferry, *Man Made God*, 20, 37. See also André Comte-Sponville and Luc Ferry, *La Sagesse des Modernes* (Paris: Laffont, 1999), 12: "We do not consider moral norms to be essential. All they do is give orders . . ., forbid things . . . or spell out duties. Who would not prefer instead love and freedom?" By the way, if

morality were entirely negative, it would only contain prohibitions and interdictions, to the exclusion of duties.

43. On this point, see Luc Ferry's objections to Lipovetsky in *Man Made God*, 60–68.

44. Lipovetsky, *Le Crépuscule du devoir*, 192.

45. Ibid., 182–84 and 18–19.

46. Ibid., 17.

47. Ibid., 26.

48. Comte-Sponville and Ferry, *La Sagesse des Modernes*, 13.

49. Ibid., 53.

50. Paul Ricoeur, "De la morale à l'éthique et aux éthiques," in *Un Siècle de philosophie 1900–2000* (Paris: Gallimard, 2001), 103–20; Jürgen Habermas, *Justification and Application: Remarks on Discourse Ethics*, trans. C. Cronin (London: Cambridge University Press, 1993), 82–98.

51. Lipovetsky, *Le Crépuscule du devoir*, 269, 270, 284.

52. Ferry, *Man Made God*, 33–35.

53. Genesis 18:25: "Shall not the judge of all the Earth do what is just?"

54. There is no mention of sacrificial cults, great Jewish celebrations, purification rituals, or the Temple, and only one of Shabbat. See Hermann Cohen, *L'Éthique du Judaïsme* (Paris: Le Cerf, 1994); http://www.jewishvirtuallibrary.org/source/biography/HermannCohen.html.

55. This is particularly the case in *Proverbs* and *Ecclesiastes*. The book of Ezekiel substitutes in chapter 18 the idea of individual retribution justified by one's action for the idea of collective retribution, which is also mentioned in Exodus 20:5: "For I the Lord your God am a jealous God, punishing children for the iniquity of parents to the third and fourth generation of those who reject me."

56. Matthew 5:48: "Be perfect, therefore, as your Father is perfect."

57. Matthew 5:47.

58. In Christian doctrine, the golden rule of universal reciprocity of duties and gifts applies to Christian communities. Such reciprocity, whether positive or hypothetical, is found in Matthew 25:31–43 and 6:12: "And forgive us our debts as we also have forgiven our debtors"; and Luke 6:31: "Do to others as you would have them do to you." For contrasting comments, see Leviticus 19:18: "You shall love your neighbor as yourself," and Rabbi Hillel's Babylonian Talmud T9/1: "Do not do unto others what you do not want them to do unto you," or Shabbat 31a: "What is hateful to you, don't do to others."

59. The Letter of Paul to the Romans 2:14–15: "When Gentiles, who do not possess the law, do instinctively what the law requires, these, though not having the law, are a law to themselves." See also Matthew 15:11, Mark 7:15, and Luke 3:10–14.

60. Luke 17:10. This is why evil is not limited to acts but encompasses intentions as well. Moral fault is defined by its intentional nature.

61. Matthew 5:10, 15:1–9; John 5:45: "your accuser is Moses, in whom you have set your hope"; Mark 7:8: "You abandon the commandment of God and hold to human tradition."

62. For the continuity of pagan versus Christian morality, see Michel Foucault, *Dits et Ecrits* (Paris: Gallimard, 1994), 4:547–54; Peter Brown, *The Body and Soci-*

ety: Men, Women and Sexual Renunciation in Early Christianity (New York: Columbia University Press, 1988).

63. Matthew 25:40.

64. C. Spicq, "The Conscience in the New Testament," *Revue Biblique* (1938): 50–80; Thomas Aquinas, *Quaestiones disputataes de veritate*, 22.5; see also www.nd.edu/~afreddos/translat/aquinas3.htm.

65. Jeremiah, 31:33; Ezekiel, 36:26.

66. Saint Augustine, *The Confessions*, trans. Henry Chadwick, Oxford World's Classics (Oxford: Oxford University Press, 1998), book 10; see also www.sacred-texts.com/chr/augconf/aug10.htm.

67. On the sources of modern rationalism in the Monadism and Theodicy of Leibniz, see Jon Elster, *Leibniz and the Development of Economic Rationality* (Oslo: Oslo University Press, 1975).

68. See Agnès Antoine, *Esprit* (December 1966): 34.

69. Friedrich Nietzsche, *Beyond Good and* Evil, trans. W. Kaufmann (New York: Vintage, 1989), 57.

70. The polemic of Saint Augustine against Pelagius deals precisely with the latter's attempt to reduce religion to morality. In the Christian tradition, one has to obtain forgiveness and grace from God in order to overcome the evil and freely choose the good. Hence, the centrality of conversion, penitence, and humility even though—in Saint Augustine's view—God only asks what he himself gives.

71. William Ockham, *De praedestinatione*, ed. Ph. Boehner (Olean, N.Y.: St. Bonaventure University Press, 1945), 516–17, in *I Sententiarum*, d. 17, q. 3; http://worldcatlibraries.org/wcpa/. See also Luther, *Writings/Oeuvres* (Geneva: Labor & Fides, 1957–93), 7:306–8.

72. Olivier Boulnois, "Les deux fins de l'homme. L'impossible anthropologie et le repli de la théologie," *Les Études philosophiques* (1995): 205–22. See *Basic Writings of Saint Thomas Aquinas*, ed. A. C. Pegis (Indianapolis: Hackett Publishing, 1997); http://godrules.net/library/aquinas/htm.

73. *Gaudium et Spe* no. 36, http://www.ewtn.com/library/COUNCILS/v2 gaulat.htm: "societies and their creations have their own laws and values, which Man must learn how to interpret and organize."

74. Karl Rahner, *Spiritual Writings*; trans. Philip Endean (Maryknoll, N.Y.: Orbis Books, 2004); Richard McCormick, *Notes on Moral Theology* (Lanham, Md.: University Press of America), vol. 1 (1965–80); vol. 2 (1981–84).

75. Paul Valadier, *Éloge de la conscience* (Paris: Le Seuil, 1994).

76. Asking this question means resisting wanton identification of "modernity" with "irreligiousness." Cf. Charles Taylor, "Iris Murdoch and Moral Philosophy," in Maria Antonaccio and William Schweicker, eds., *Iris Murdoch and the Search for Human Goodness* (Chicago: University of Chicago Press, 1996), 24–27.

77. See "Immortality and the Vanity of Human Life" in chapter 4.

78. Leo Tolstoy, *Confessions* [1879] and *The Death of Yvan Illitch* [1886]; Georges Bernanos, *The Carmelites*, trans. Gerard Hopkins (Glasgow: Collins, Fontana Books, 1961). The following excerpt from *Joy* also appears in *The Carmelites*: "Fear is the daughter of God who was redeemed on the night of Good Friday. . . . She is sometimes mocked, sometimes cursed and renounced by all. . . . Yet make no mistake, she sits by every death-bed interceding for mankind (15)."

79. Cf. Émile Durkheim, *Les Formes élémentaires de la vie religieuse, le système totémique en Australie* [1912] (Paris: PUF, 1985). A distinctive feature of Judeo-Christianity is that such prohibitions determine the relation of man to mankind and to God.

80. This contradicts the suggestion made by Elisabeth Anscombe in, "Modern Moral Philosophy," in *Collected Philosophical Papers*, vol. 3, *Ethics, Religion and Politics* (Oxford: Blackwell, 1981), 25–42.

81. Paul Ricoeur, *Oneself as Another*, trans. K. Blamey (Chicago: University of Chicago Press, 1992), 192–94, 236. See also Émile Durkheim, *L'Éducation morale* (Paris: PUF, 1963), 7–8.

82. Ferry, *Man Made God*, 19.

83. See Pierre Bayle, *Pensées diverses sur la comète* [1682] (Paris: Nizet, 1984). Bayle thought that the rational belief in the God of natural theology gives one reason to submit to moral principles. Cf. Jacques Domenech, *L'Éthique des lumières* (Paris: Vrin, 1989).

84. Marcel Gauchet, *The Disenchantement of the World*, trans. Oscar Burge (Princeton, N.J.: Princeton University Press, 1999).

85. Marcel Gauchet, *La Religion dans la démocratie* (Paris: Gallimard, 1998), 14. Gauchet also talks about coexistence between "the end of religion and the reinvention of religion" (20).

86. On this topic, see Pierre Manent, *La Cité de l'homme* (Paris: Fayard, 1994).

87. See "The Myth of Modernity" in chapter 1 for a critique of this concept.

88. Ferry, *Man Made God*, introd.; Axel Kahn, *Et l'Homme dans tout ça?* (Paris: Nil Éditions, 1999).

89. François Dagognet, *Une Nouvelle Morale* (Paris: Institut Synthélabo, 1998); Marcel Conche, *Le Fondement de la morale* (Paris: PUF, 1993); André Comte-Sponville, *Vivre* (Paris: PUF, 1988).

90. Marcel Gauchet, *La Religion dans la démocratie* (Paris: Gallimard, 1998), 106. The author correctly points out that our task is to uncover what morality owes to religion and defines morality as "the capacity to explain to oneself the reasons that guide one's conduct considering the final terms of one's condition and destination."

91. Ferry, *Man Made God*, 31.

92. Ibid., 5: "It is not at all certain that . . . we are really capable of escaping a dilemma often most correctly rendered in caricature. Enlightenment philosophers tried it, and all our progressive thinkers are following them." In fact, if the caricatured aspect of the dilemma is conspicuous, its adequacy is much less so. Religion was not designed so as to increase the acceptance of old age. As for cosmetic surgery, it may render old age easier to bear, but it is far from justifying it.

93. Ibid., 6 and 47.

94. Ibid., 34.

95. Ibid., 61–63, 66. Gilles Lipovetsky defended this idea in *Le Crépuscule du devoir*, 58–83. As for myself, I would say that there is no twilight of duty, at least not in the sense that duty would shine today in all its splendor, but rather that duty lurks today in the same shadows as ever.

96. Ferry, *Man Made God*, 37, 40, 120, 128.

97. Ibid., conclusion, 132.

98. Ibid., 25–27; also "The new transcendence is not less imposing than the older one even if it is imposing in another way" (ibid., 71).

99. In an exchange with Luc Ferry, André Comte-Sponville rightly noticed: "Oxymorons are sometimes a source of reflection but mostly, they remain a diabolical and dangerous temptation" (*Sagesse des Modernes*, 51).

100. Ferry, *Man Made God*, 45, 140.

101. Ibid., 71.

102. Ibid., 138.

103. Ibid., 139.

104. Ibid., 135.

105. Ibid., 135–36.

106. See also Prince Mishkin's narrative in Dostoevsky's *The Idiot*.

107. Ferry, *Man Made God*, 141.

108. Ibid., 136: at least if freedom were the power to act autonomously.

109. See Paul Ricoeur, *Freedom and Nature: The Voluntary and the Involuntary*, trans. Erazim Kohak (Evanston, Ill.: Northwestern University Press, 1966); *Fallible Man*, trans. W. J. Lowe (New York: Fordham University Press, 1986).

110. Ferry, *Man Made God*, 132–35; see also my "Pluralism and Objectivity: The Debate on Human Cloning" in chapter 2.

111. The fact that Luc Ferry chooses love to illustrate the "out of this world" status of such reality (in *Man Made God*, 136–38) renders the thesis even more obscure. Also puzzling is the unexplained assertion that only by marking values outside the world would it be possible to bring individuals together.

112. Ibid., 68.

113. Ibid., 69. That such "transcendental humanism" should be taken to mean here "in tune with current beliefs" is proved by the statement that it has transformed itself in accordance with the limits drawn by modern humanism. On this point, André Comte-Sponville's analysis is again correct: "In fact, this kind of humanism seems to have the same flaws as religion, without the latter's spiritual and human richness. Spinoza would say that transcendental man is a refuge of ignorance as much as God is for believers a mystery that will remain for ever unsolved" (*La Sagesse des Modernes*, 66).

114. Ferry, *Man Made God*, 63, 72. Thus, a morality without transcendence is compensated for by the displacement of divinity.

115. Ibid., 35, 96.

116. Ibid., 134.

117. Ibid., 136, 142.

118. Democracy: where legitimacy is rooted in consent, the rule of law, and equal rights, where the State is distinct and apart from Society.

119. Comte-Sponville and Ferry, *La Sagesse des Modernes*, 13.

120. Lipovetsky, *Le Crépuscule du devoir*, 13.

121. See Luc Ferry, *Qu'est-ce que l'homme?* (Paris: Odile Jacob, 2000), 73; Alain Renaut, *Histoire de la philosophie politique* (Paris: Calmann-Lévy, 1999), 18–43; see also Luc Ferry and Alain Renaut, *Political Philosophy 3: From the Rights of Man to the Republican Idea*, trans. Franklin Philip (Chicago: University of Chicago Press, 1992).

122. Ferry, *Man Made God*, 64–65.

123. Lipovetsky, *Le Crépuscule du devoir*, 200.

124. Ibid., 15.

125. Ibid., 106 and 302.

126. Ferry, *Man Made God*, 64.

127. As Luc Ferry rightly notes in *Man Made God*, 69.

128. Ibid., 36, 62.

129. Lipovetsky, *Le Crépuscule du devoir*, 13, 186; "Moral tradition is by far more continuous than discontinuous" (187).

130. Ferry, *Man Made God*, 38, 48, 61–63, 121.

131. Lipovetsky, *Le Crépuscule du devoir*, 13. For this reason, the author thinks that the appropriate term here should be "ethics of the third kind" (15).

132. Ibid., 163. One is tempted to think that the reason for this claim is to preserve the current sociological nonsense.

133. See the interview in *Esprit* (May–June 2000): 170.

134. See Thomas Nagel, "The Fragmentation of Values," in *Mortal Questions* (Cambridge: Cambridge University Press, 1979); and Charles Larmore, "Reasonable Disagreement and Moral Pluralism," in *The Morals of Modernity* (Cambridge: Cambridge University Press, 1996); and see my discussion on "Pluralism and Objectivity" in chapter 2.

135. See Charles Taylor, *Sources of the Self: The Making of Modern Identity* (Cambridge, Mass.: Harvard University Press, 1989); Isaiah Berlin, *The Crooked Timber of Humanity: Chapters in the History of Ideas* (Princeton, N.J.: Princeton University Press, 1990); Alasdair MacIntyre, *After Virtue: A Study in Moral Theory* (Notre Dame, Ind.: University of Notre Dame Press, 1984).

136. According to both O. K. Bouwsma, in *Wittgenstein, Conversations, 1949–1951*, ed. J. L. Craft and R. E. Hustwit (Indianapolis: Hackett, 1986), XXIII–XXIV, and Jacques Bouveresse, in *Essais I. Wittgenstein, la modernité, le progrès et le déclin* (Marseille: Agone, 2000), 89–124, Wittgenstein disdained the idea of moral progress in history, as well as the notion that in this world we live better than ever before. He regarded the future of humanity with skepticism, paid attention to the daily details in the life of specific human beings, and was unimpressed by humanity and popular movements. As a result, he felt quite close to Kierkegaard and Dostoevsky.

137. For an interpretation of the relationship between concept and event, intellectual history and political history, or between philosophy as "phenomenology" of political life and morality for the past three centuries, see Leo Strauss and Joseph Cropsey, *History of Political Philosophy*, 3rd ed. (Chicago: University of Chicago Press, 1987); and Leo Strauss, *The City and Man* (Chicago: Rand McNally, 1964).

138. See Manent, *La Cité de l'homme*, for an analysis of Machiavelli's writings as a "starting point" of modernity, and for a convincing approach to "backtrack historicism."

139. Ferry, *Man Made God*, 33, 40, 122.

140. Lipovetsky, *Le Crépuscule du devoir*, 15, 18; Ferry, *Man Made God*, 65. Luc Ferry and Alain Renaut wrote in *French Philosophy of the Sixties: An Essay in Antihumanism*, trans. M.H.S. Cattani (Amherst: University of Massachusetts Press, 1990), 65 and 226, that modernity brings to mind the demise of the *subject* described in the first chapter of Deleuze and Guattari's *Anti-Oedipus* as "a floating

space without ties or reference, pure availability." See also Gilles Deleuze and Félix Guattari, *Anti-Oedipus: Capitalism and Schizophrenia*, trans. Robert Hurley, M. Seem, and H. R. Lane (New York: Viking Press, 1977), 1–42.

141. On the distinction between individual and *subject*, see Alain Renaut, *The Era of the Individual: A Contribution to a History of Subjectivity*, trans. M. B. DeBevoise and Franklin Philip (Princeton, N.J.: Princeton University Press, 1999), 10–20. Must we cease to subjectively read the history of modernity in order to see the gradual unfolding of human individuality? While Descartes does not settle the question of the distinction between individual and *subject*, Leibniz provides a strictly individualistic ontology, that is, a monadology integrated in a theodicy. Present-day individualism follows the mainly Nietzschean criticism of all theodicy and arises from the obligation to dissociate individualistic ontology from the hypothesis of an underlying rationality that ensures the coexistence of individuals. Kantian criticism on the other hand, defends an individual's obligation to think autonomously as the only way that would enable him to establish values "that are self-grounded and self-established as norms that humanity waives itself, constitutive of inter-subjectivity, and based on the idea that humanity creates for itself, for its own dignity" (167). Kant's thesis raises strong objections, some of which can be summarized as follows: (1) the contrast between individual and subject is not a matter of fact but of philosophical interpretation, and as such, its legitimacy comes only from interpretation; (2) the philosophical interpretation plays the role of an ad hoc hypothesis from which a conclusion is drawn; (3) criticism of the connection between ontological individualism and a theodicy does not, by itself, make impossible the processes that regulate interaction among individuals (one can think of the combined effect of creating standards of cooperation, internalizing such standards, or adopting self-sacrifice standards); (4) Kantian self-determination is not the only definition of autonomy; (5) the Kantian definition of *subject* is not necessary in order to ground objective values in rationality. Because the writings that are the object of my criticism do not mention the distinction between individual and *subject*, I henceforth use the term "modern subject."

142. Ferry and Renaut, *French Philosophy of the Sixties*, 227.

143. On this point, see Charles Taylor, "Atomism," in *Philosophical Arguments* (Cambridge, Mass.: Harvard University Press, 1997), 130–36, 181.

144. Pascal Bruckner, *La Tentation de l'innocence* (Paris: LGF, 1996), 36. The modern individual claims both his autonomy and his innocence (14–15).

145. Ibid., 271.

146. Lipovetsky, *Le Crépuscule du devoir*, 241–42, 245, 265.

147. However individualistic our societies may appear in their representations of themselves, there is a constant conflict between their image of themselves and the social reality of solidarities, dependencies, and subordinations. Durkheim said that the major challenge of modern times is to understand such a mixture of autonomy and dependence. See *De la Division du travail social, étude sur l'organisation des sociétés supérieures* [1893] (Paris: PUF, 1978). See also, Louis Dumont, *Homo aequalis* (Paris: Gallimard, 1977); *Essais sur l'individualisme* (Paris: Le Seuil, 1983).

148. Unlike Henry Sidgwick, Plato and the early Utilitarians sought to reconstitute morality in its entirety at the cost of psychological implausibility.

149. *Magazine littéraire*, no. 361 (January 1998): 39.

150. To the objection that all those philosophical references cannot be put on the same level because being entirely Kantian carries a certain weight today while being 100 percent Aristotelian or Spinozist carries none, my answer is that although integral Kantianism may be possible today, the more important question is whether it represents a realistic moral view that would satisfy our normative resources. Hegel said that in Kantian philosophy "the coldest, shallowest of deaths has no more significance than cutting off a head of cabbage or swallowing a mouthful of water." G.W.F. Hegel, *Phenomenology of Spirit*, trans. A. V. Miller, (New York: Oxford University Press, 1977), 360.

151. Aristotle sharply opposes Plato on the question of morality (morality does not consist in inquiries about essences or in *theoria* for its own sake) and on methodological issues.

152. There is even a markedly antitheoretic current in contemporary moral philosophy: cf. Stanley G. Clarke and Evan Simpson, *Anti Theory and Moral Conviction* (Albany: State University of New York Press), 1989.

153. See "Morals and Religion: The Misconception That Atheism Is a Prerequisite for Moral Debate" in chapter 1.

154. There is no doubt that this same ignorance of history colors the merciless criticism hurled by some French philosophers at Michel Foucault's last philosophy. Their preconception that the Greeks could not conceive of autonomy disqualifies Foucault's reference to the Greek idea of man as being a Greek-inspired form of surreptitious antihumanism. In other words, proclaiming one's affiliation with "the Greeks" would renew the efforts to undermine the subject. For a defense of rational autonomy in Greek philosophy, see Ferry and Renaut, *French Philosophy of the Sixties*, 120: "From the beginning to the end of his work, Foucault remained consistent with his vulgate. . . . The anti-humanism of 1968 philosophy opens onto barbarism."

155. See Monique Canto-Sperber, "Le Bien de Platon et le platonisme en moralité," in *Les Éthiques grecques* (Paris: PUF, 2001); "Éthiques anciennes et éthiques modernes," in ibid.

156. According to Alain Renaut in *Histoire de la philosophie politique* (Paris: Calmann-Lévy, 1999), 1:18: "Plato and Aristotle discovered the idea of rightness . . . by contemplating nature, which they saw as being itself a kind of order and a hierarchical cosmos." One might wonder about the meaning of this assertion. Could it be a statement of fact? Hardly! Does it make sense conceptually? If it did, then "nature" would have here a totally different meaning from the one given it by the Moderns; therefore, the term itself could not be used in any refutation. See also Ferry and Renaut, *Political Philosophy 3: From the Rights of Man to the Republican Idea*.

157. A project designed by the philosopher Jürgen Habermas as a modern, constructivist, progressivist, and universalist endeavor opposed to the retrograde, obscurantist, and antimodern tendencies of contemporary philosophy.

158. Vincent Descombes, "La rationalité politique," *La Pensée politique*, no. 2 (1994): 148.

159. Luc Ferry and Alain Renaut, *68–86: Itinéraires de l'individu* (Paris: Gallimard, 1987), 42, 71: "If the progress of individualism logically implies the criticism

of traditional values, . . . then such criticism, as well as any new assertion of values, could only preserve their legitimacy through debate; legitimacy must cease being 'traditional' and become 'legal.'" See also Luc Ferry and Alain Renaut, *Heidegger and Modernity*, trans. Franklin Philip (Chicago: University of Chicago Press, 1991).

160. Luc Ferry, *Political Philosophy I: The New Quarrel Between the Ancients and the Moderns*, trans. Franklin Philip (Chicago: University of Chicago Press, 1990); Alain Renaut, *The Era of the Individual*, trans. M. B. DeBevoise and Franklin Philip (Princeton, N.J.: Princeton University Press, 1977); Alain Renaut and Lucas Sosoe, *Philosophie du droit* (Paris: PUF, 1991), 414.

CHAPTER TWO
GOALS OF ETHICAL REFLECTION

1. For example, Christian Dior's line of cosmetics Éthique, or the article "The Ethics of the Gift Package" in *Le Nouvel Observateur* (16–22 December 1999): 31. Other terms, such as "citizen," have been similarly hackneyed. Thus when our leaders talk of "citizens' enterprise" or "citizens' school," they mean nothing in particular and evoke at best a vague idea of what an enterprise or school should be like.

NB. Many thanks to Olivier Mongin, for the permission to reuse here a text previously published in *Esprit*, May 2000.

2. For a critique of the overblown distinction between ethics and morality, and on the alleged ability of ethics to take the place once held by morality, see chapter 1.

3. Onora O'Neill, *Towards Justice and Virtue: A Constructive Account of Practical Reasoning* (Cambridge: Cambridge University Press, 1996).

4. Theoretically, one might admit that such justification is not necessarily infallible, even without seeing what exactly could challenge it. One would, however, expect the challenge to be something other than the discovery of a scientific truth about some form of inequality among human beings, because even then one would still have to justify any inequality in their treatment. Cf. David Wiggins, "La Vérité en éthique," in Monique Canto-Sperber, ed., *La Philosophie morale britannique* (Paris: PUF, 1994), 147–70.

5. Charles Taylor, *Sources of the Self: The Making of Modern Identity* (Cambridge, Mass.: Harvard University Press, 1989); Isaiah Berlin, *The Crooked Timber of Humanity: Chapters in the History of Ideas* (Princeton, N.J.: Princeton University Press, 1990).

6. Hans Jonas, *The Imperative of Responsibility: In Search of an Ethics for the Technological Age* (Chicago: University of Chicago Press, 1984); François Ewald, in *La Responsabilité* (Paris: Sciences Humaines, 1996); Marc Neuberg, *La Responsabilité: Questions philosophiques* (Paris: PUF, 1997).

7. This example is analyzed by John Maynard Keynes (1883–1946), in *The General Theory of Employment, Interest and Money* (Amherst, N.Y.: Prometheus Books, 1997), 403.

8. Jean-Pierre Dupuy, "Philosophical Foundations of a New Concept of Equilibrium in the Social Sciences: Projected Equilibrium," *Philosophical Studies* 100, no. 3 (2000): 323–45.

9. On consequentialism and the responsibility for omissions, see Shelly Kagan, *The Limits of Morality* (Oxford: Oxford University Press, 1989); and Samuel Scheffler, *The Rejection of Consequentialism* (Oxford: Oxford University Press, 1994).

10. Laurence Engel, *La Responsabilité en crise* (Paris: Hachette, 1995); Olivier Beaud, *Le Sang contaminé* (Paris: PUF, 1999), 237–49; Antoine Garapon, "Pour une responsabilité civique," *Esprit* (March–April 1999); Gilles Martin, "Précaution et évolution du droit, " in Olivier Godard, *Le Principe de précaution dans la conduite des affaires humaines* (Paris: MSH/INRA, 1997), 331–50.

11. Paul Ricoeur, *Freedom and Nature: The Voluntary and the Involuntary*, trans. Erazim Kohak (Evanston, Ill.: Northwestern University Press, 1966); *Finitude and Culpability*, vol. 1, *Fallible Man*, trans. W. J. Lowe (New York: Fordham University Press, 1986), and vol. 2, *The Symbolism of Evil*, trans. E. Buchanan (New York: Harper and Row, 1967); *Oneself as Another*, trans. Kathleen Blamey (Chicago: University of Chicago Press, 1995); Gary Watson, ed., *Free Will* (Oxford: Oxford University Press, 1982).

12. In one scenario, a slightly drunk driver goes through a red light. With dulled reflexes, he can only stop three feet inside the crossing line. Because nobody is crossing the line at that moment, his story ends there. In another scenario, a pedestrian starts crossing while the light is still yellow and gets hit by a car. Whatever the extent of driver's guilt, he finds himself plunged into personal tragedy.

13. On accessing intentions, see Elisabeth Anscombe, *Intention* (Oxford: Blackwell, 1957); Donald Davidson, *Essays on Actions and Events* [1980], 2nd ed. (Oxford: Clarendon Press, 2001); Ricoeur, *Oneself as Another*, 322–36.

14. Yan Thomas, "Le sujet de droit, la personne et la nature: sur la critique contemporaine du sujet de droit," *Le Débat*, no. 100 (1998): 85–107. See also Jean Carbonnier, *Flexible droit. Pour une sociologie du droit sans rigueur* (Paris: LGDJ, 1992).

15. It would be more accurate to call it a legal exception to a punishable infraction, rather than decriminalization. At this writing, abortion is legal if performed until the twelfth week of pregnancy.

16. Great Britain offers a telling example in this context. In the United Kingdom it is legal for termination to be carried out up to twenty-two weeks of pregnancy, that is, later than in France, and yet the percentage of abortions per births is lower than its French counterpart. When this book went to print, French statistics were showing circa 200,000 abortions per 700,000 births, that is, more than 25 percent abortions per 100 percent births, which is distressing if not alarming when compared to U.K. statistics. The lack of any direct relation between the liberalism of the law and the number of recorded abortions proves that those who thought otherwise were wrong.

17. From the rich Anglo-American literature on the question of abortion, see Louis Pojman and Francis J. Beckwith, eds., *The Abortion Controversy: A Reader* (Boston and London: Jones and Bartlett Publishers, 1994); William B. Bondeson, H. Tristam Engelhardt Jr., Stuart F. Spicker, and Daniel H. Winship, eds., *Abortion and the Status of the Fetus* (Dordrecht: Reidel, 1983). See also Anne Fagot-Largeault, "Les Droits de l'embryon (foetus) humain, et la notion de personne humaine potentielle," *Revue de métaphysique et de morale*, no. 3 (1987): 361–84.

18. Some may consider late-term abortions to be morally acceptable although the fetus could survive outside the womb. Those people should nevertheless admit that aborting a fetus in these conditions is a form of infanticide.

19. At this writing, the legal limit for abortion is fourteen weeks in Sweden, twenty-two weeks in Great Britain, and twenty-two weeks in Spain.

20. Often, such moral deliberation is restricted, constrained, and filtered by social realities that may hinder the freedom of decision. For instance, a woman may feel forced to terminate her pregnancy for fear of losing her job, for lack of financial means to raise a child, or for preserving her career advancement opportunities. Not to be forgotten are the various social factors that take away the sense of procreative responsibilities from men.

21. Some recently published essays do not seem sufficiently concerned with distinctions between these normative orders, that is, law and morality. Cf. Noëlle Lenoir, "L'Europe sera éthique ou ne sera pas," *Libération*, 17 December 1999; Mireille Delmas-Marty, *Vers un droit commun de l'humanité* (Paris: Textuel, 1996).

22. Blaise Pascal, *Pensées*, trans. A. J. Krailsheimer (New York: Penguin Classics, 1995), 29.

23. Iris Murdoch, *The Sovereignty of Good* [1970] (London: Routledge, 2001); David Wiggins, *Needs, Values, Truth* (London: Blackwell, 1997); Sandra Laugier, *Du Réel à l'ordinaire* (Paris: Vrin, 1999).

24. "Supervenience" is more an attempt to designate elegantly and even metaphorically the manner in which the normative order comes within the natural or descriptive order, than an attempt to explain "in what manner exactly" it comes within. The precise nature of this asymmetrical relationship remains unclear. See Simon Blackburn, "Supervenience Revisited," in *Essays in Quasi Realism* (Oxford: Oxford University Press, 1993), 130–48. A general survey and a bibliography on the subject is found in Ruwen Ogien's contribution ("La Survenance") to Monique Canto-Sperber, ed., *Dictionnaire d'éthique et de philosophie morale* (Paris: PUF, 2001).

25. One could also think of moral persons, or of the persons in the Holy Trinity.

26. On family resemblance, see Ludwig Wittgenstein, *Philosophical Investigations*, trans. G.E.M. Anscombe (New York: Macmillan, 1953). On prototypes, cf. Eleanor Rosch and B. B. Lloyd, eds., *Cognition and Categorization* (Hillsdale, N.J.: Erlbaum, 1978); Mark Johnson, *Moral Imagination* (Chicago: University of Chicago Press, 1993); John Harris, "The Concept of the Person and the Value of Life," *Kennedy Institute of Ethics Journal* 9, no. 4 (1999): 309–24; Edmund L. Erde, "Paradigm and Personhood: A Deepening of the Dilemmas in Ethics and Medical Ethics," *Theoretical Medicine and Bioethics* 20 (1999): 141–60.

27. The distinction between the descriptive and normative aspect of the concept of person is not uniformly received; cf. Lucien Sève, "La personne, concept éthique d'intérêt public," *Laennec, Médecine, Santé, Éthique*, no. 5 (June 1996); the CCNE report, *Recherche biomédicale et respect de la personne humaine* (Paris: La Documentation française, 1987).

28. Charles E. Larmore, *The Morals of Modernity* (Cambridge: Cambridge University Press, 1996); Garrett Cullity and Berry Gaut, eds., *Ethics and Practical Reason: On the Theory of Value and Action* (Oxford: Oxford University Press,

1999); Monique Canto-Sperber and Ruwen Ogien, "La rationalité pratique," in Monique Canto-Sperber, ed., *Dictionnaire d'éthique et de philosophie morale* (Paris: PUF, 2001).

29. John McDowell, *Mind, Value and Reality* (Cambridge, Mass.: Harvard University Press, 1998).

30. See, for instance, Luc Ferry's stand in Luc Ferry and André Comte-Sponville, *La Sagesse des Modernes* (Paris: Laffont, 1999), 58–59; also, Charles Taylor, "La conduite d'une vie et les moments du bien," in *La Liberté des Modernes* (Paris: PUF, 1998).

31. See Christine Korsgaard, *The Sources of Normativity* (Cambridge: Cambridge University Press, 1996).

32. Thomas Nagel, *The View from Nowhere* (Oxford: Oxford University Press, 1986).

33. Franz Brentano, *Vom Ursprung sittlicher Erkenntniss* [1889] (Hamburg: Meiner, 1969); Max Scheler, *Formalism in Ethics and the Non-Formal Ethics of Values* (Evanston, Ill.: Northwestern University Press, 1973); Christine Tappolet, *Émotions et valeurs* (Paris: PUF, 2000).

34. Ruwen Ogien, ed., *Le Réalisme moral* (Paris: PUF, 1999).

35. Thomas Nagel, "The Fragmentation of Value," in *Mortal Questions* (Cambridge: Cambridge University Press, 1979); Bernard Williams, "La cohérence éthique," in *La Fortune morale* (Paris: PUF, 1994); Larmore, *The Morals of Modernity*; Ruth Chang, ed., *Incommensurability, Incomparability and Practical Reason* (Cambridge, Mass.: Harvard University Press, 1997).

36. This argument can be objected to on the grounds that the genome is not a real part of individual personality, but a social construct. Cf. Henri Atlan et al., *Le Clonage humain* (Paris: Le Seuil, 1999).

37. Some catastrophist suggestions turn up in Axel Kahn's book, *Et l'Homme dans tout ça?* (Paris: NIL Editions, 1999); Nadine Fresco, "Le Jardin d'acclimatation," in Henri Atlan et al., *Le Clonage humain* (Paris: Seuil, 1999); Monette Vacquin, *Main basse sur les vivants* (Paris: Fayard, 1999).

38. Unfortunately, the specter of utilitarianism is used to counter and deter any attempt at heuristic investigation of the value of mental states, the concept of well-being, or the value of consequences. It is enough to mention utilitarianism for most French philosophers to scream "No! No! No!" Whatever theoretical criticism one may have regarding utilitarianism—and in my case, such criticism is properly justified—one can only acknowledge admiringly the intelligence and sophistication evidenced by this school of thought, and the worthy perspective that it can bring to the analysis of complex situations. See Catherine Audard, *Anthologie historique et critique de l'utilitarisme*, 3 vols. (Paris: PUF, 1999).

39. Ronald de Sousa, *The Rationality of Emotions* (Cambridge Mass.: MIT Press, 1990); *Critique* (Spring 1999), special issue dedicated to emotions.

40. Ethics has today the fate of those ideas that are perceived as creating a social link, a fantasy world of communication. In our culture, many powerful notions seem to have this role. It is better to be forewarned of this possibility so as to avoid falling for it, if not altogether to cast it aside.

CHAPTER THREE
FRENCH MORAL PHILOSOPHY AND ITS PAST MISFORTUNES

1. In Great Britain, the *Westminster Review* and the *Fortnightly Review*. In France, *Le Journal des Débats*, *La Revue des deux Mondes*, and *La Revue de Paris*. As for Germany, it was the first European country to publish philosophical reviews (with the exception of *La Décade philosophique*, which was published during the French Revolution).

2. There were many other reviews in France at the end of the nineteenth century: *La Revue* (1855); *La Philosophie positive*, founded in 1867 to propagate the ideas of Auguste Comte under the direction of Émile Littré and G. Wyroubof; *L'Année philosophique*, founded in 1867 by F. Pillon; *La Critique philosophique, politique, scientifique et littéraire*, created in 1872 by Charles Renouvier to defend the theory of neocriticism; *La Revue philosophique de la France et de l'étranger*, founded in 1876 by Théodore Ribot, to publish mainly articles on experimental psychology; *La Revue de philosophie*, founded in 1899 under the direction of E. Peillaube.

3. Xavier Léon directed *La Revue de métaphysique et de morale* (*RMM*) till his death in 1935. Élie Halévy was also director until his death in 1937. On the content of *RMM*, see its October–December 1993 issues dedicated to its centenary.

4. *RMM*, no. 4 (1893): 1, foreword. See also Félix Ravaisson, "Métaphysique et morale," reprinted in *RMM*, no. 4 (1993): 435–54.

5. H. Bergson, "Perception et matière," *RMM* (1896): 257–79.

6. G. Sorel, "Y a-t-il une utopie dans le marxisme? " and "L'Éthique du socialisme," *RMM* (1899): 152–75, 280–301.

7. Émile Durkheim, "Représentations individuelles et représentations collectives," *RMM* (1898): 273–302.

8. Gottlob Frege, "Le nombre entier," *RMM* (1895): 73–78.

9. Maurice Blondel, É. Durkheim, and Bertrand Russell were targeted by such criticism. See the review of *L'Action* by M. Blondel, in *RMM* (November 1893). The reviewer of *Les règles de la méthode sociologique* wrote in *RMM* (1895): 1: "Mr. Durkheim's definitions are exclusive and blind, his methodology is abstract and pointless." See also Poincaré's attack on B. Russell's book, *An Essay on the Foundations of Geometry*, in *RMM* (1899): 251–79.

10. In 1893 René Berthelot argued with Gabriel Tarde about an article entitled "Les Transformations du droit"; Louis Weber and Louis Couturat defended opposing views in the article "L'évolutionnisme physique et le principe de la conservation de l'énergie." Another heated debate started in 1893 between Couturat, Russell, Le Chalas, and Poincaré on the principles of geometry. Similar debates on mathematical logic involved Couturat, Peano, Le Roy, and Whitehead.

11. For instance, the obituary of Renouvier notes that, in spite of having been excommunicated from Paris University by Victor Cousin, he remained one of the masters of the "philosophical revival that swayed France for the past twenty years."

12. Élie Halévy and Léon Brunschvicg, "La Philosophie au Collège de France," *RMM* (1893).

13. The shift was spurred by Benjamin Jowett, Master of Balliol College at Oxford, and by the philosopher T. H. Green.

14. In its first issue, the journal states that its purpose is to show "catholicity and impartiality" and to publish articles "which really advance the subject a step further."

15. In the first issue, the editors stated: "It is not American Thought as much as American Thinkers that we want."

16. Just as the ancient Greeks had excelled in philosophy because they were at the center of the world and were welcoming people from everywhere, so the American continent is seen as "a bridge between Europe and Asia," a place where "the Same meets the Other." In their introduction to the first issue of the *Philosophical Review*, the editors declared: "There is every reason to believe that America will be the stage on which the human spirit will perform its next phase of philosophical discovery, interpretation and construction." Four hundred years after Columbus, "America is a land of great promise for philosophy."

17. See Celestin Bouglé's essay, published in 1894 in consecutive issues on "Social Sciences in Germany"; Theodor Ruyssen's essay, on "Morality in Contemporary German Philosophy: Hartmann, Wundt, and Paulsen," published in 1895.

18. For instance, the 1894 issue was dedicated to the philosophy courses taught at Cambridge and in Berlin.

19. Such interest is confirmed by Élie Halévy in his *Formation du radicalisme philosophique*, published by Alcan from 1901 to 1904, long out of stock in France, and republished many times in the United Kingdom. The latest French critical edition, published by PUF, dates from 1995.

20. See the *RMM* issues dated 1894 and 1900.

21. In 1892–93 the review *L'Année philosophique* published numerous reports on debates about William James's theories on emotion.

22. The creation of the *Revue de sociologie* in 1893 under the direction of René Worms was greeted with a critical comment: "The very generality of sociological science is worrisome."

23. Consider, for instance, the following quotation from *RMM* 1897 relating to the future of the philosophical activism in the United States: "The U.S. has spared nothing to structure the teaching of philosophy in America, to embrace new traditions and adopt new ways of thinking: creating grants and subventions, endowing chairs of philosophy, inviting foreign teachers (true, they are German), and calling international congresses and conferences that welcome all metaphysicians and psychologists on Earth. *Nevertheless, the content evaluation of three recently founded reviews is not very persuasive.*"

24. In 1904, the Congress was held in Heidelberg; and in 1912, in Bologna; after a hiatus caused by World War I, it resumed in 1924 in Naples, in 1927 at Harvard, 1930 in Oxford, and 1934 in Prague. During the interwar years, these international meetings lost some of their appeal for French thinkers. After World War II these meetings did not display the ability to advance crucial debates that had singled out the first congresses. The 1900 congress had brought together Bergson, Poincaré, Couturat, Cantor, McColl, Peano, MacFaane, LeVerrier, Houssais, Russell, and MacTaggart. Sidgwick had also been invited but he died a few weeks before its opening.

25. Boutroux was a member of the Institut français, a professor at Sorbonne, president of congress's organizing committee, and author of *De la Contingence des lois de la nature* (1874) and *L'Idée de la loi naturelle* (1894).

26. The minutes were published in the 1901 issues of the *RMM*.

27. See *RMM* (1901): 10–12.

28. *RMM* (1901): 12.

29. Couturat conceded that hoping for an agreement on ideas was unrealistic, but he emphasized the advantage of working together to reach a common agreement on the use of words and on the definition of pending problems. For this reason, only a universal and artificial language could lead to a scientific and philosophical terminology that would be used internationally. After Couturat's death, the first realization of such a project was the publication of the *Vocabulaire technique et critique de la philosophie* under the direction of André Lalande from 1902 to 1923.

30. *RMM* (1901).

31. George E. Moore, *Principia Ethica* [1903] (Amherst, N.Y.: Prometheus Books, 1988).

32. These ideas can be found in Kant's writings and especially in Sidgwick, *Methods of Ethics* [1874] (London: Macmillan, 1965), 27–29, 32, 109.

33. A. Schilpp, *The Philosophy of G. E. Moore* (New York: Tudor Publishing, 1952), Autobiography, 14.

34. Alfred Ayer, *Language, Truth and Logic* (London: Gollancz, 1936); Richard Hare, *The Language of Morals* (Oxford: Oxford University Press, 1952).

35. Moritz Schlick, *Fragen der Ethik* (Frankfurt: Suhrkamp, 1930); *Problems of Ethics* (New York: Prentice-Hall, 1939); *Questions d'éthique* (Paris: PUF, 2000).

36. Charles Stevenson, *Ethics and Language* (New Haven: Yale University Press, 1944).

37. F. C. von Brentano, *Vom Ursprung sittlicher Erkenntnis* (Leipzig: Dunker & Humbolt, 1889). Translated in 1902 as *The Origin of the Knowledge of Right and Wrong*, it was reviewed by Moore in the *International Journal of Ethics* (14 October 1903): 115–23. On Brentano's work, see also Roderick Chisholm, in particular *Brentano and Intrinsic Value* (Cambridge: Cambridge University Press, 1986), and Linda L. McAlister, ed., *The Philosophy of Brentano* (London: Duckworth, 1976).

38. Edmund Husserl, *Logical Investigations* (London: Routledge, 1900).

39. Husserl was a student of Brentano in Vienna from 1884 to 1886, where he took courses on practical philosophy and the sources of ethics.

40. Edmund Husserl, *Vorlesungen uber Ethik und Wertlehre*, 1908–14, in *Husserliana XXVIII*, ed. U. Melle (Dordrecht, Boston, and London: Kluwer, 1988), 114.

41. Alexander Pfänder, *Phänomenologie des Wollens* (Leipzig: Verlag von Johann A. Barth, 1900).

42. *Der Formalismus in der Ethik und die Materiale Wertethik* (1913–16). Later, Scheler's ideas took different paths in the works of Nicolai Hartmann (*Ethik* [Berlin: de Gruyter, 1926]) and Hans Reiner. In French philosophy, there is a slightly different axiological tradition: Eugene Dupréel, *Esquisse d'une philosophie des valeurs* (Paris: Alcan, 1939), and Louis Lavelle, *Traité des valeurs: I. Théorie générale de la valeur* (Paris: PUF, 1951); *II. Le système des différentes valeurs* (Paris: PUF, 1955).

43. Martin Heidegger, *Sein und Zeit* [1927], translated by Joan Stambaugh as *Being and Time* (Albany: State University of New York Press, 1953).

44. Hare, *The Language of Morals*, 1–2.

45. Gabriel Marcel, *Journal métaphysique* (Paris: Gallimard, 1927). See also the work of the German philosopher Paul Ludwig Landsberg, *The Erfahrung des Todes* [1937], translated as *The Experience of Death: The Moral Problem of Suicide* (Manchester, N.H.: Ayer Co. Publishers, 1953).

46. Jean-Paul Sartre, *Being and Nothingness*, trans. Hazel E. Barnes (New York: Philosophical Library, 1956), 628: "All these questions which refer us to a pure and not accessory reflection, can find their reply only on the ethical plane. We shall devote to them a future book."

47. Jean-Paul Sartre, *Notebooks for an Ethics (1947–1948)*, trans. David Pellauer (Chicago: University of Chicago Press, 1992); *Existentialism and Humanism*, trans. Philip Mairet (London: Methuen, 1965).

48. The fact that Sartre qualified Gabriel Marcel's existentialism as Christian is telling in that respect. See *Existentialism and Humanism*, 26.

49. Ibid., 56; *Being and Nothingness*, "Bad Faith," 47–70; "Facticity," 79–83.

50. Jacques Maritain, *Collected Works* (http://www.nd.edu/~maritain/); *Freedom of the Modern World* and *Integral Humanism*, trans. Otto Bird, J. Evans, and R. O'Sullivan (Notre Dame, Ind.: University of Notre Dame Press, 1996), vol. II; *Rights of Man and Natural Law*, trans. Doris C. Anson (New York: Charles Scribner and Sons, 1943), also to appear in vol. 13 of *Collected Works*; Étienne Gilson, *The Spirit of Mediaeval Philosophy*, trans. A.H.C. Downes (Notre Dame, Ind.: University of Notre Dame Press, 1991); http://www.ethicscenter.nd.edu /inspires/documents/Etienne_Gilson.pdf.

51. Emmanuel Mounier, *The Character of Man*, trans. Cynthia Rowland (New York: Harper, 1956).

52. Paul Ricoeur, *Freedom and Nature: The Voluntary and the Involuntary*, trans. Erazim V. Kohak (Evanston, Ill.: Northwestern University Press, 1966); *The Fallible Man*, trans. W. J. Lowe (New York: Fordham University Press, 1986); *The Symbolism of Evil*, trans. E. Buchanan (New York: Harper and Row, 1967).

53. Paul Ricoeur, *Time and Narrative*, trans. Kathleen Blamey and David Pellauer (Chicago: University of Chicago Press, 1990), 3 vols. See also Emmanuel Levinas, *Humanism on the Other*, trans. Nidra Poller (Chicago: University of Illinois Press, 2003).

54. The unexpected exception was the research pursued by neo-Thomist philosophers.

55. John Rawls, *A Theory of Justice* (Cambridge, Mass.: Harvard University Press, 1971); see also *Political Liberalism* (New York: Columbia University Press, 1996).

56. See Max Horkheimer's letter to Theodor Adorno, 14 September 1941, and Adorno's answer to it, 23 September 1941, quoted in Rolf Wiggerhaus, *The Frankfurt School: Its History, Theories and Political Significance*, trans. Michael Robertson (Cambridge Mass., MIT Press, 1994), 505.

57. Jürgen Habermas, *The Structural Transformation of the Public Sphere* [1962], trans. Thomas Burger and Lawrence Polity (Cambridge, Mass.: MIT Press, 1989); *On the Logic of the Social Sciences*, trans. S. W. Nicholson and J. A. Stark.

(Cambridge Mass.: MIT Press, 1990); *The Theory of Communicative Action*, trans. Thomas McCarthy (Boston: Beacon Press, 1985), 1:295–300.

58. See for instance, Ülrich Gähde and Wolfgang H. Schrader, eds., *Der Klassische Utilitarismus* (Munich: Akademie Verlag, 1992); Dieter Birnbacher, *Verantwortung für Zukönftige Generationen* (Stuttgart: Phillip Reclam, 1988); Giuliano Pontara, *Filosofia pratica* (Milan: Il Saggiatore, 1988); Esperanza Guisán, *Manifiesto hedonista* (Barcelona: Anthropos, 1992).

59. See Elisabeth Anscombe, "Modern Moral Philosophy" and "On Brute Facts," in *Collected Philosophical Papers III: Ethics, Religion and Politics* (Oxford: Blackwell, 1981), 26–42 and 22–25; Peter Geach, "Good and Evil," *Analysis* 17 (1956): 33–42; Philippa Foot, "Goodness and Choice," in *Virtues and Vices* (Berkeley: University of California Press, 1978), 132–47.

60. Manfred Riedel, ed., *Rehabilitierung des praktischen Philosophie* (Fribourg-im-Brisgau: Rombach, 1972–74); Hannah Arendt, *The Human Condition* (Chicago: University of Chicago Press, 1958); Hans-Georg Gadamer, *Truth and Method* [1960], trans. Joel Weinsheimer and D. G. Marshall (London: Continuum International Publishing Group, 1994).

61. On this point, see my book *La Philosophie morale britannique* (Paris: PUF, 1994). See also, as a historical document, the 1958 proceedings of the Royaumont Symposium, which brought together French philosophers and mainly British representatives of analytical philosophy, entitled *La Philosophie analytique* (Paris: Minuit, 1962).

62. These trends apply the Hegelian distinction between *Moralität* (abstract and universal rules of morality) and *Sittlichkeit* (community-specific ethical principles) and—in opposition to the liberal tradition—they consider *Sittlichkeit* an accomplished form of morality that paves the way to a superior kind of liberty and autonomy. It is also commonly associated, sometimes abusively, to authors such as Michael Sandel, Charles Taylor, and Albrecht Wellmer.

63. There are very few historical or critical studies dedicated to this period. See Luc Ferry and Alain Renaut, *French Philosophy in the Sixties: An Essay in Contemporary Antihumanism*, trans. M.H.S. Cattani (Amherst: University of Massachusetts Press, 1990); Vincent Descombes, *Modern French Philosophy*; trans. L. Scott-Fox (Cambridge: Cambridge University Press, 1980); François Dosse, *History of Structuralism*, trans. Deborah Glassman (Minneapolis: University of Minnesota Press, 1997), 2 vols.

64. Michel Foucault, *The Order of Things: An Archeology of Human Sciences* (New York: Pantheon Books, Random House, 1970), 387; see 310–12 for his view on classical thought. Foucault points out: "Of course, these are not affirmations; they are at most questions to which it is not possible to reply" (386).

65. Ibid., 328.

66. Gilles Deleuze and Félix Guattari, *Anti-Oedipus: Capitalism and Schizophrenia*, trans. Robert Hurley, M. Seem, and H. R. Lane (New York: Viking Press, 1977), 16.

67. See for instance Alain Badiou, *L'Être et l'événement* (Paris: Le Seuil, 1988); *L'Éthique* (Paris: Hatier, 1993).

68. Friedrich Nietzsche, *On the Genealogy of Morality*, ed. Keith Ansell-Pearson (Cambridge: Cambridge University Press, 1994), 11.

69. F. Nietzsche, *Daybreak: Thoughts on the Prejudices of Morality*, ed. M. Clark and B. Leiter, trans. R. J. Hollingdale (Cambridge: Cambridge University Press, 1997), book III, § 103, 60.

70. It is because Stendhal combines an implacable analysis of moral sentiments with a taste for the energy of noble souls that Nietzsche would say: "Stendhal is one of the fairest accidents of my life," in *Ecce Homo: How One Becomes What One Is*, trans. R. J. Hollingdale (New York: Penguin Classics, 1992), 22.

71. See Nietzsche, *Human, All Too Human: A Book for Free Spirits*, trans. Marion Faber and Stephen Lehmann (London: Penguin Books, 1994); *On the Genealogy of Morality*, 133.

72. Nietzsche, *On the Genealogy of Morality*, 40.

73. There are two exceptions to this: Gilles Deleuze, *Nietzsche and Philosophy* [1962], trans. Hugh Tomlinson (London: Athlone Press, 1983) and Michel Foucault, *Dits et Écrits 1954–1988* (Paris: Gallimard, 1994), vol. 4. See also Philippe Raynaud's enlightening contributions, "La philosophie morale de Nietzsche" and "Nietzsche et le Nietzschéisme dans la philosophie française au XXe siècle," in Monique Canto-Sperber, ed., *Dictionnaire de l'éthique et de philosophie morale* (Paris: PUF, 2001).

74. In the year 2000, the official announcement of Alain Badiou's course at the International College of Philosophy assessed the twentieth century as follows: "In the name of presumed inhuman truths, the antihumanist audacity opposed skeptical humanism. . . . Could it be that the mad dash of communism only served to reinstate the reign of insignificance, the taste for small mercies and family pleasures, or to restore the puerile morality that it is better to be kind than mean."

75. Jean-Pierre Dupuy, ed., *Self-Deception and Paradoxes of Rationality* (Stanford, Calif.: CSLI Publications, 1998).

76. Besides, psychoanalysts would be the first to reject any attempt to consider psychoanalysis the designated heir of moral philosophy.

77. Karl Marx and Friedrich Engels, *The Communist Manifesto* [1848] (New York: Signet Classics, 1998), 63.

78. G. A. Cohen, *Karl Marx's Theory of History: A Defense* (Princeton, N.J.: Princeton University Press, 1980), 216–48; for non-Marxist authors, see Steven Lukes, *Marxism and Morality* (Oxford: Oxford University Press, 1985); John Elster, *An Introduction to Karl Marx* (Cambridge: Cambridge University Press, 1986); and Philippe Van Parijs, *Marxism Recycled* (Cambridge: Cambridge University Press/Maison des Sciences de l'Homme, 1993).

79. George Crowder, *Classical Anarchism: The Political Thought of Godwin, Proudhon, Bakunin and Kropotkin* (Oxford: Oxford University Press, 1991).

80. Jean-Paul Sartre, *Situations*, trans. Benita Eisler (New York: George Braziller, 1965), vol. 4, 287.

81. Sartre's deeply ambiguous views on critical examination, on questioning the motives of actions and challenging established beliefs—which I consider beneficial to moral reflection—come out in his slogan "Not choosing is to have already chosen," in his dispute with Merleau-Ponty on revealing information about Soviets' gulags, and in his argument with Camus after the publication of *The Rebel*.

82. Sartre's militancy in the ranks of the Communist Party increased the popularity of Marxist militancy at a time when Marxists were rather hostile to Sartre's thinking.

83. The same could be said of Sartre's less famous proclamation: "All ethic is both impossible and necessary." Any ethic that does not reveal its impossibility only deepens the alienation and the mystification of men. See *Saint-Genet, Actor and Martyr*, trans. Bernard Frechtman (New York: George Braziller, 1963), 224.

84. See for instance, Jean-Marc Ferry, *Les Puissances de l'expérience* (Paris: Le Cerf, 1991), I and II.

85. Paul Ricoeur, *Oneself as Another*, trans. K. Blamey (Chicago: University of Chicago Press, 1992).

86. See Robert Misrahi, *Spinoza. Un Itinéraire du bonheur par la joie* (Paris: J. Grancher, 1992); Marcel Conche, *Le Fondement de la morale* (Villers-sur-Mer: Éditions de Mégare, 1982); André Comte-Sponville, *The Little Book of Philosophy* (New York: Vintage Books, 2005), and *A Small Treatise on Great Virtues* (London: Metropolitan Books, 2001).

PART TWO
INTRODUCTION

1. Søren Kierkegaard, *Either/Or: A Fragment of Life* [1843], trans. V. Eremita and A. Hannay (New York: Penguin Classics, 1992), 28.

2. Cf. "The Myth of Modernity" in chapter 1.

3. Arthur Schopenhauer, *Gespräche*, ed. A. Huebscher (Stuttgart–Bad Cannstatt: Frommann, 1971), 22; quoted by Rüdiger Safranski, in *Schopenhauer and the Wild Years of Philosophy*, trans. Ewald Osers (Cambridge, Mass.: Harvard University Press, 1990), 105.

CHAPTER FOUR
THE ABSURD AND THE MEANING OF LIFE

1. *Tractatus Logico-Philosophicus*, trans. C. K. Ogden (London: Routledge & Kegan Paul, 1994), 6.521; www.uweb.ucsb.edu/~luke_manning/tractatus /tractatus-jsnav.html.

2. *Tractatus Logico-Philosophicus*, 4.112. Wittgenstein maintains (6. 42) that "there can be no ethical propositions" that a discipline such as moral philosophy would make it its task to clarify. Even so, he admits elsewhere that many sense-endowed statements may contain moral predicates relating to a standard, an end or a purpose. "A Lecture on Ethics," *Philosophical Review* 74 (1965): 3–12; *Lectures and Conversations on Aesthetics, Psychology and Religious Beliefs* (Oxford: Blackwell, 1966); *Lectures: Cambridge, 1932–1935* (Oxford: Blackwell, 1979). Wittgenstein certainly wanted to criticize the idea that philosophy can produce theories on morals, but he thought that questions such as "What is the place of ethics in human life?" or "What is the moral purpose of a philosophical work?" were entirely pointless. See also Jacques Bouveresse, *Wittgenstein: la rime et la raison*.

Science, éthique et esthétique (Paris: Minuit, 1973); Cora Diamond, "Ethics, Imagination and the Method of Wittgenstein's *Tractatus*," in R. Heinrich and H. Vetter, eds., *Bilder der Philosophie, Wiener Reiche 5* (Vienna: Oldenburg, 1991), 55–90; *The Realistic Spirit: Wittgenstein, Philosophy and the Mind* (Cambridge Mass.: MIT Press, 1991).

3. *Tractatus Logico-Philosophicus*, 6.52.

4. According to Wittgenstein, while failing to produce moral theories, moral philosophy as a whole is a testimony to the desire to reach beyond the bounds of sense.

5. At least in spirit, this conforms to the early Wittgenstein's idea of "the right method in philosophy": "To say nothing except what can be said, i.e. the propositions of natural science, i.e. something that has nothing to do with philosophy: and then always, when someone else wished to say something metaphysical, to demonstrate to him that he had given no meaning to certain signs in his propositions." *Tractatus*, 6.53.

6. A. J. Ayer: "The Claims of Philosophy," in *Reflections on Our Age: Lectures Delivered to the Opening Session of UNESCO at the Sorbonne University–Paris* (London: Allan Wingate Publishing, 1948).

7. John Wisdom, "Other Minds," *Mind* 49 (1940): 370.

8. *Tractatus Logico-Philosophicus*, 6.53.

9. Fyodor Dostoevsky, *The Brothers Karamazov*, ed. David McDuff (New York: Penguin Classics, 1993), 585.

10. Karl Jaspers, *Nietzsche: An Introduction to the Understanding of His Philosophical Activity*, trans. C. F. Walraff and F. J. Schmitz (Baltimore: John Hopkins University Press, 1997), 334.

11. Leo Tolstoy, *A Confession* [1879], trans. David Patterson (New York: W. W. Norton, 1996), 27; www.albertarose.org/Christian/Tolstoy/confession/, parts 3–4. Its publication follows that of *War and Peace* [1869] and *Anna Karenina* [1877]. See also *The Death of Ivan Ilych* [1886] at www.online-literature.com/tolstoy/.

12. It is even conceivable that analysis or criticism of the existential question might have as much a calming effect on such emotions, as a stimulating one. The total absence of emotion might, on the other hand, be interpreted as evidence of the trouble that one can experience by asking such a question. Either way, it seems impossible to escape the vacuity of such interpretations.

13. See for instance, Kurt Baier, "The Meaning of Life," Inaugural Lecture Delivered at the Canberra University College, 1957, in E. D. Klemke, ed., *The Meaning of Life*, (Oxford: Oxford University Press, 2000), chap. 11; Kai Nielsen, "Linguistic Philosophy and the Meaning of Life," *Cross Currents*, 1964; Thomas Hurka, "The Well Rounded Life," *Journal of Philosophy* 87, no. 12 (1987): 727–46; Thomas Nagel, "The Absurd," *Journal of Philosophy* 68, no. 20 (1971): 716–27, and *What Does It All Mean? A Very Short Introduction to Philosophy* (Oxford: Oxford University Press, 1987); Robert Nozick: *Philosophical Explanations* (Oxford: Oxford University Press, 1981), and *The Examined Life* (New York: Simon and Schuster, 1989); Owen Flanagan, *Self Expressions—Mind, Morals and the Meaning of Life* (Oxford: Oxford University Press, 1996). These analytical philosophers studied the existential question at the risk of incurring the wrath of their peers, who relentlessly hammered the question "What does that mean?" on everybody taking an interest in something other than the natural world.

14. Charles Taylor, *The Explanation of Behaviour* (London: Routledge and Kegan, 1964).

15. The absence of a dominant goal to life does not preclude the possibility that some particular goal would provide an interpretation rule that would help to better justify the facts of life.

16. Albert Camus, *The Myth of Sisyphus* [1942], trans. Justin O'Brien (New York: Vintage, 1991), 51. See also www.mythosandlogos.com/Camus.html.

17. Nagel, "The Absurd"; Donald Davidson, "A Coherence Theory of Truth and Knowledge," in E. LePore and B. McLaughlin, eds., *Actions and Events: Perspectives on the Philosophy of Donald Davidson* (Oxford: Blackwell, 1986), 307–19.

18. Aristotle, *Nicomachean Ethics*, III-7 and VI-9, trans. W. D. Ross (Oxford: Clarendon Press, 1908), see also www.etext.library.adelaide.edu.au/a/aristotle/nicomachean/; Nagel, "The Absurd."

19. Nagel, *What Does It All Mean?*, 3–8; see also "The Absurd," 717–18. For him, an existential justification is what reveals the meaning of our actions.

20. J.-P. Sartre, *Being and Nothingness*, trans. Hazel E. Barnes (New York: Philosophical Library, 1956), "Freedom and Responsibility," 553–56, "Quality as Revelation of Being," 600–613; Bernard Williams, "The Makropulos Case: Reflections on the Tedium of Immortality," in *Problems of the Self: Philosophical Papers, 1956–1972* (Cambridge: Cambridge University Press, 1976), 82–100. See my discussion on "The Boredom of Living Forever" in chapter 5.

21. Cf. Baier, "The Meaning of Life."

22. On this point, see Nagel's argumentation in "The Absurd."

23. Cf. "Morals and Religion" in chapter 1.

24. Tolstoy, *A Confession*, 57; see also www.albertarose.org/Christian/Tolstoy/confession/, part 8.

25. Friedrich Nietzsche, *The Will to Power* [1888], trans. Walter Kaufmann and R. J. Hollingdale (New York: Vintage, Random House, 1968), book 1-20/Spring–Fall 1887, 16.

26. J.-P. Dupuy, *The Mechanization of the Mind* (Princeton, N.J.: Princeton University Press, 2000), 119–22; Jacques Monod, *Chance and Necessity—An Essay on the Natural Philosophy of Modern Biology* (New York: Alfred Knopf, 1971).

27. Camus, *The Myth of Sisyphus*, 6.

28. Ibid., 13, 15, 14. See also on 6: "This divorce between man and his life, between the actor and his setting is precisely the feeling of the absurd."

29. Blaise Pascal, *Pensées*, trans. A. J. Krailsheimer (New York: Penguin Classics, 1995), 19.

30. Nagel, "The Absurd," 719.

31. Camus, *The Myth of Sisyphus*, 18.

32. Nagel, "The Absurd," 720.

33. Camus, *The Myth of Sisyphus*, 17. Also, on 20: "I am not a stranger to the world."

34. Camus thinks that the phenomenological analysis of the feeling of absurdity opens the way to the absurdity of life, although he concedes that "The feeling of the absurd is not, for all that, the notion of the absurd. It lays the foundation for it and that is all." Ibid., 28.

35. Ibid., 21.

36. Richard Hare, "Nothing Matters," in *Applications of Moral Philosophy* (London: Macmillan, 1972), 281: "When I claim that nothing matters, I do not refer to a state of things, nor do I imply that a different reality would put a different light on the things around me. Rather, I argue that in my present state of mind, I cannot know what it means to acknowledge their value."

37. Camus, *The Myth of Sisyphus*, 6.

38. Ibid., 9.

39. Ibid., 61–62, 64. See also my discussion at the beginning of chapter 5.

40. Camus, *The Myth of Sisyphus*, 39, 47, 48. The term "humiliated reason" comes from Kierkegaard.

41. This contradicts Hume's point of view in "Of the Understanding," in *A Treatise of Human Nature*, ed. D. F. Norton and M. J. Norton (Oxford: Oxford University Press, 2000), book I; see also www.etext.library.adelaide.edu.au/h/hume/section1/html.

42. The realization of life's absurdity is a starting point, not a point beyond which one cannot go. It is unlike other forms of absurdity such as Kierkegaard's absurd tied to the "offense to faith": the absurd becomes God and the impossibility of understanding Being—an impossibility that illuminates everything. The "knight of the faith . . . acknowledges the impossibility, and in the very same moment he believes the absurd" as Abraham believed the absurd. *S. Kierkegaard's Writings: Fear and Trembling*, ed. Edna H. Hong and Howard V. Hong (Princeton, N.J.: Princeton University Press, 1978), 6:47. In his philosophy, the offense and the paradox play a crucial role because the absurd does not lead to any search for reasons and justifications other than an immediate and atemporal one (cf. my discussion at the end of chapter 5). "But if the paradox is *index* and *judex sui et falsi* [the criterion of itself and of the false], then the offence can be regarded as an indirect testing of the correctness of the paradox, for offence is the erroneous accounting, is the conclusion of untruth, with which the paradox thrusts away." *Kierkegaard's Writings: Philosophical Fragments*, ed. and trans. E. H. Hong and H. V. Hong (Princeton, N.J.: Princeton University Press, 1985), 6:51. Also: "The understanding declares that the paradox is the absurd, but this is only a caricaturing, for the paradox is indeed the paradox, *quia* absurdum. . . . When the understanding wants to have pity upon the paradox and assist it to an explanation, the paradox does not put up with that, for is that not what philosophers are for—to make supernatural things ordinary and trivial?" *Kierkegaard's Writings. Philosophical Fragments*, 7:52–53.

43. Stephen Toulmin, *An Examination of the Place of Reason in Ethics* (Cambridge: Cambridge University Press, 1950).

44. Pascal, *Pensées*, 76.

45. Ibid., 19.

46. The distinction between *knowing that* and *knowing how* originates in Gilbert Ryle, *The Concept of Mind* [1949] (Chicago: University of Chicago Press, 2000), chap. 2.

47. See Antony Flew, "Tolstoy and the Meaning of Life," *Ethics* 73 (1963); Leo Tolstoy, *War and Peace*, trans. Rosemary Edmunds (New York: Penguin Classics, 1971), 1197; *Anna Karenina*, trans. Constance Garnett and Mona Simpson, Modern Library Classics (New York: Random House, 2000), 923.

CHAPTER FIVE
THE INVARIANTS OF HUMAN LIFE

1. The philosopher is much like Locke's "under-labourer": "it is ambition enough to be employed as an under-labourer in clearing the ground a little and removing some of the rubbish that lies in the way to knowledge." John Locke, "Epistle to the Reader," in *The Essay Concerning Human Understanding* [1689] (Amherst, N.Y.: Prometheus Books, 1995), XIII; http://humanum.arts.cuhk /Philosophy/Locke/echu.

2. F. Dostoevsky, *The Brothers Karamazov,* trans. Constance Garnett (Houston: Spark Publ., 2004), part II, book V, 214; http://online-literature.com/dostoevsky/ brothers_karamazov/34.

3. Albert Camus: *The Myth of Sisyphus* [1942], trans. Justin O'Brien (New York: Vintage, 1991), 61. See also www.mythosandlogos.com/Camus.html.

4. Simone de Beauvoir, *The Ethics of Ambiguity,* trans. Bernard Frechtman (New York: Citadel Press, 1996), section III: The Positive Aspects of Ambiguity, 5—Ambiguity, 75–155; see also www.webster.edu/~corbetre/philosophy/existen- tialism/debeauvoir/ambiguity-3.html.

5. Arthur Schopenhauer: *The World as Will and Representation* [1819], trans. E.F.J. Payne (New York: Dover Publications, 1969), vol. 1, §20, 106–9; vol. 2, 349–57; see also http://marxists.org/reference/subject/philosophy/works/ge/ schopenh.htm.

6. Arthur Schopenhauer, *The World as Will and Representation,* trans. E.F.J. Paine (New York: Dover Publications, 1969), vol. 2, suppl. to book III, chapter 25 on § 57, 321: "There is really only one being; the illusion of plurality (Maya) re- sulting from the forms of external objective apprehension, could not penetrate right into the inner, simple consciousness; hence this always meets with only one being."

7. Ibid., vol. 1, book IV, § 56, 309; and vol. 2, supplement to book IV on §§ 56– 68, 610.

8. Unlike Schopenhauer, Camus considers that suicide cancels the absurd be- cause it abolishes the will to live.

9. On mankind's metaphysical needs, see Schopenhauer, *The World as Will and Representation,* vol. 1, book I (First Aspect), 1–92, book IV, § 69, 398–402, and appendix (Second Aspect), 415–534; vol. 2, supplement to book II, chapter XVII.

10. David Wiggins, "Truth, Invention and the Meaning of Life," in *Needs, Values, Truth: Essays in the Philosophy of Value* (Oxford: Clarendon Press, 1998).

11. For Wiggins's critique of "non-cognitivist accounts," see ibid., 98–101.

12. Jean-Jacques Rousseau, *Discourse on the Origin of Inequality,* trans. Mau- rice Cranston (London: Penguin Classics, 1984), part I, section I, 85.

13. This would exclude justification of the type: "This is justified because logical condition X is satisfied."

14. On the reflexive tradition, see Jean Nabert, *Éléments pour une éthique* (Paris: Aubier, 1971), and *La philosophie réflexive* [1957], reprinted in *L'Expérience intérieure de la liberté* (Paris: PUF, 1994), 397–411; see also Paul Ricoeur, *Freedom and Nature: The Voluntary and the Involuntary* [1950], trans. E. V. Kohak (Evans- ton, Ill.: Northwestern University Press, 1966).

15. Richard Wollheim, *The Thread of Life* (New Haven: Yale University Press, 1984), 167–68, 170: "introspection proposes and interpretation disposes." Wollheim emphasizes the two types of relations that link mental states to mental dispositions. For instance, the fact that Anna Karenina notices the ridiculous way her husband has of putting his hat on reveals to her the hypocrisy of their relationship: she notices her mental state and infers a mental disposition from it. The opposite may also happen: a mental disposition may point to a mental state. On this, Wollheim mentions Bertrand Russell's famous testimonial: "I went out bicycling one afternoon, and suddenly, as I was riding along a country road, I realised that I no longer loved Alys. I had had no idea until that moment that my love for her diminished." *The Autobiography of Bertrand Russell* (London: Allen & Unwin, 1967), 1:147. Here, the mental state informs the subject of the existence of a mental disposition.

16. Elisabeth Anscombe, *Intention* (Oxford: Blackwell, 1957), §§ 28–32; see also Ernst Tugendhat, *Self-Consciousness and Self-Determination: Studies in Contemporary German Social Thought* [1979], trans. Paul Stern (Cambridge, Mass.: MIT Press, 1986).

17. Paul Ricoeur, *Oneself as Another*, trans. Kathleen Blamey (Chicago: University of Chicago Press, 1995), 126, 129, 193, 238, 348–51.

18. Hannah Arendt, *Lectures on Kant's Political Philosophy* [1977], ed. Ronald Beiner (Chicago: University of Chicago Press, 1982), 44, 62, 94.

19. Bernard Williams, "Internal and External Reasons," in *Moral Luck* (Oxford: Oxford University Press, 1981), 101–13. For a critique of internal reasons, see John McDowell, "Might There Be External Reasons?" in J.E.J. Altham and Ross Harrison, eds., *World, Mind and Ethics: Essays on the Ethical Philosophy of Bernard Williams* (Cambridge: Cambridge University Press, 1995), 68–85; *Mind and the World* (Cambridge, Mass.: Harvard University Press, 1996). In McDowell's view, external or categorical reasons exist regardless of desires.

20. Reasons do not share the psychological status of beliefs, nor their content. Beliefs become normative reasons only after having been tested, weighted, and evaluated. For a reason to be bad, it is not enough that it be grounded in a faulty belief; it must also be the case that the faulty belief cannot justify that reason, which amounts to a double condition.

21. In the last few years, several empirical studies have dealt with the mental processes involved in our interpretation of life's events and in our ways of making sense of our experiences. See, for instance, Gary T. Reker and Kerry Chamberlain, eds., *Explaining Existential Meaning: Optimizing Human Development across Life Span* (Thousand Oaks, Calif.: Sage Publications, 2000).

22. More than terminology, we owe part of our own analysis to Charles Larmore, *L'Authenticité* (Paris: PUF, 2002). Before him, Henri Bergson suggested the existence of practical reflection in *La Pensée et le mouvant* (Paris: PUF, 1938), 183, and in *Essais sur les données immédiates de la conscience* [1888] (Paris: PUF, 1927), II and III. Similar suggestions are found in Sartre's *Being and Nothingness*, trans. H. E. Barnes (New York: Washington Square Press, 1993), 19: "To support passively . . . is a conduct which I assume and which engages my liberty." See also his distinction between pure and impure reflection (218–23).

23. Charles Larmore explains the difference between cognitive and practical reflection by suggesting that practical reflection engages the uniqueness of the indi-

vidual, while the cognitive reflection aims to reveal the universal intelligibility of the self. Sartre, *Being and Nothingness*, 172.

24. Sartre, *Being and Nothingness*, 219.

25. Donald Davidson, "First Person Authority," *Dialectica* 32 (1984): 38; Hilary Putnam, "The Meaning of Meaning," in *Philosophical Papers* (Cambridge: Cambridge University Press, 1975). For an opposing point of view, see Gilbert Ryle, *The Concept of Mind* (Chicago: University of Chicago Press, 1984), chap. 6.

26. This distinction is also referred to as between subjective and objective reasons. Thomas Nagel was among the first to suggest it in his ground-breaking book, *The Possibility of Altruism* (Princeton, N.J.: Princeton University Press, 1970), part 2, Subjective Reasons and Prudence, 25–32; part 3, Objective Reasons and Altruism, 77–82. Because of the ambiguity of the term "subjectivity," Derek Parfit proposed to replace Nagel's distinction with the currently prevailing one, between agent-relative and agent-neutral reasons. See D. Parfit, *Reasons and Persons* (Oxford: Clarendon Press, 1984), 143; see also Thomas Nagel, "Agents and Victims," in *The View from Nowhere* (New York: Oxford University Press, 1986), 180–88.

27. An agent-relative reason may involve the actions of a third party. If my enemy x' has an interest in me not doing something, then he has an agent-relative reason for me not to do it.

28. One may certainly be betrayed without being aware of it or, as Madame de Sévigné said: "On ne devine pas . . . ne laissez point vivre ni rire des gens qui ont la gorge coupée et qui ne le sentent pas. Il faut parler aux gens. . . . (People cannot guess. . . . Never let live and laugh happily, those who do not know that their heads will roll. They must be told.)" Madame de Sévigné, *Correspondence* (Paris: Gallimard, 1974), vol. 2 (July 1675–September 1680), letter dated 18 September 1679. Lucretius's argument can be found in *De Rerum Natura*, trans. William Ellery Leonard (New York: Dover Publications, 2004), book 3, "The Soul Is Mortal" and "Folly of the Fear of Death," 66–99; http://classics.mit.edu/Carus/ nature_things.3.iii.html. Deploring now what we will miss by dying makes no sense because, once dead, we will not be here to lament the loss of the benefits of being alive, much less to endure any pain for being dead.

29. Bernard Williams, "The Makropulos Case: Reflections on the Tedium of Immortality," in *Problems of the Self: Philosophical Papers, 1956–1972* (Cambridge: Cambridge University Press, 1999), 82–100.

30. Lord Byron, "Euthanasia," in *Complete Poetical Works*, ed. Jerome J. McGann (Oxford: Clarendon Press, 1980), vol. 1, no. 172, 352–54.

31. Schopenhauer had clearly made this point by saying that renouncing to reflect on one's self (including the formulation of agent-relative reasons) in favor of totally depersonalized compassion is a categorical prerequisite for abolishing individuality: "Sympathy is to be defined as the empirical appearance of the will's metaphysical identity through the physical multiplicity of its phenomena. In this way a connexion shows itself; and this is entirely different from that which is brought about by the forms of the phenomenon, and which we comprehend under the principle of sufficient reason." Schopenhauer, *The World as Will and Representation*, vol. 2, supplement to book IV, chapter 47 on § 67, 602.

32. In Aristotle's *Poetics* the literary genres of tragedy and comedy are defined according to the human models represented in them. This kind of identification was widespread in antiquity.

33. In an impersonal or Kantian conception of morality, the character and the personal dimension are morally neutral. The personal element I am referring to here is close to what Hannah Arendt calls the *daimon* that she associates with "having proven oneself in life," in *Men in Dark Times* (Fort Washington, Pa.: Harvest Books, 1970), 73, 71; also in *The Human Condition* (Chicago: University of Chicago Press, 1998), 7–17.

34. Sidgwick states this rule of equity as follows: we cannot judge whether the same action is good for agent A and bad for agent B if—in their nature or circumstances—we cannot find differences allowing us to determine that they reasonably justify their different duties. "Whatever I judge reasonable or unreasonable that another should do for me, that by the same judgment I declare reasonable or unreasonable that I should *in the like case* do for him." Henry Sidgwick, *The Methods of Ethics* (London: Macmillan, 1907), 384–85; http://www.la.utexas.edu/research/poltheory/sidgwick/index.html.

35. Peter Winch, "The Universalizability of Moral Judgments," in *Ethics and Action* (London: Routledge and Kegan Paul, 1972), 159; Joseph Raz, "The Truth in Particularism," in *Engaging Reason: On the Theory of Value and Action* (Oxford: Oxford University Press, 2000), 218–47. See also David Wiggins, "Truth and Truth as Predicated of Moral Judgments," in *Needs, Values and Truth: Essays in the Philosophy of Value* (Oxford: Blackwell, 1997), 166–84.

36. Herman Melville, *Billy Budd, Sailor* (Oxford: World's Classics, 1997), 312: "What recourse is left to it [Claggart's nature] but to recoil upon itself, and, like the scorpion for which the Creator only is responsible, act out to the end the part allotted it." See also the libretto by Foster in Britten's homoerotic opera: "Oh beauty, o handsomeness, goodness! Having seen you, what choice remains to me, but to destroy you?" (act 1, scene 3).

37. Or that he cannot postpone the immediate enforcement of the *Act* by waiting to reach shore and convene a martial court. See Wiggins, *Needs, Values and Truth*, 173.

38. Raz, "The Truth in Particularism," 245.

39. Compare this to Sartre's "We may say that there is a human universality, but it is not something given, it is being perpetually made. I make this universality in choosing myself; I also make it by understanding the purpose of any other man, of whatever epoch. This absoluteness of the act of choice does not alter the relativity of each epoch." *Existentialism and Humanism*, trans. P. Mairet (Brooklyn: Haskell House, 1977), 24; see also http://www.cis.vt.edu/modernworld/d/Sartre.html.

40. This thesis has a philosophical equivalent in Sartre's idea that existence preexists essence and that choice determines character: "There is no question here of a freedom which could be undetermined and which could pre-exist its choice. We shall never apprehend ourselves except as a choice in the making. . . . The structure of the choice necessarily implies that it be a choice in the world." *Being and Nothingness*, 616–17. Henri Bergson thought before Sartre that possibilities do not preexist choices but are produced retroactively by them.

41. Winch, "The Universalizability of Moral Judgments" 168; see also Raz, *Engaging Reason*, 245: "The question leaves the possibility however unlikely, that my response will surprise me; that it will not confirm my own previously formed idea of myself." It is in this sense that we are the makers of our character.

42. On this point, see my entry "Love," in Monique Canto-Sperber, ed., *Le Dictionnaire d'éthique et de philosophie morale* (Paris: PUF, 2001), 34.

43. This is correct provided that it is not an expression of self-indulgence or complacency.

44. Raz, *Engaging Reasons*, 243: "It is right for people to act as their moral character tells them to act. But their reason is not that this is what they are disposed to do, or that that is more consistent with their past decisions. It is that they can do no other." See also Sidney Shoemaker, *The First Person Perspective and Other Essays* (Cambridge: Cambridge University Press, 1996).

45. We experience dissociation when we ponder the consequences of our actions or the value of a deed, when we structure all our choices in time by their weight, when we define our priorities and choose our models.

46. Leo Tolstoy, *Anna Karenina*, trans. Louise Maude and Aylmer Maude (Oxford: Oxford University Press, 1995), part III, 292.

47. Richard Wollheim, *The Thread of Life* (New Haven: Yale University Press, 1984).

48. Arendt, *The Human Condition*, 176.

49. Richard Rorty, *Contingency, Irony, Solidarity* (Cambridge: Cambridge University Press, 1989), 43.

50. Tolstoy, *Anna Karenina*, part III, 277. In contrast, before committing suicide, Anna tells herself: "I want love, and it is lacking. So everything is finished!" (737).

51. Ibid., part I, 104.

52. See "Morals and Existential Justifications" in chapter 6.

53. Bernard Williams, *Moral Luck: Philosophical Papers, 1973–1980* (Cambridge: Cambridge University Press, 1981), 35; see also Jonathan Baron, *Thinking and Deciding* [1988] (Cambridge: Cambridge University Press, 1995), chaps. 18 and 24.

54. See "The Impossibility of a Final Justification" in chapter 4.

55. W. B. Yeats, *The Collected Works*, ed. W. H. O'Donnell (New York: Scribner, 1999), 3:108: "When I think of all the books I have read, wise words heard, anxieties given to parents . . . of hopes I have had, all life weighted in the balance of my own life seems to me a preparation for something that never happens."

56. Lucretius, *De Rerum Natura*, book 3: "The Soul Is Mortal" and "Folly of the Fear of Death," 66–99, also found at http://classics.mit.edu/Carus/nature_things.3.iii.html; Williams, "The Makropulos Case: Reflections on the Tedium of Immortality," 82–100; Thomas Nagel, "Death," in *Mortal Questions* (Cambridge: Cambridge University Press, 1991), 1–10.

57. Miguel de Unamuno, *The Tragic Sense of Life* (Princeton, N.J.: Princeton University Press, 1962), 60.

58. Arthur Schopenhauer, *The World as Will and Representation* [1886], trans. E.F.J. Payne (New York: Dover Publications, 1996), vol. 1, 392–402, § 69; vol. 2, chapter XLV, 568–72 and chapter XLVIII, 603–34.

59. Bernard Williams calls them *categorical desires* as opposed to *conditional desires*. See, for instance, "Persons, Character and Morality," in *Moral Luck*, 1–19.

60. B. Williams, "The Makropulos Case: Reflections on the Tedium of Immortality," 82–100.

61. Only an intellectual contemplation devoid of any personal dimension would have offered an escape from such a fate. Plato thought that the satisfactions brought by studying timeless and impersonal topics are themselves timeless and impersonal.

62. *The Diary of Søren Kierkegaard* [1843], trans. Gerda M. Anderson, ed. Peter Rohde (London: Owen, 1960), part 5, section 4, no. 136.

63. Hannah Arendt, *Between Past and Future* (New York: Viking Press, 1968), 11.

64. On the epistemology of remembrance, see Paul Ricoeur, *Memory, History, Forgetting*, trans. Kathleen Blamey and David Pellauer (Chicago: University of Chicago Press, 2004).

65. Dino Buzzati, *Tartar Steppe* [1945], trans. Stuart C. Hood (Manchester: Carcanet Press, 1985), 42–43.

66. Julia Annas, *The Morality of Happiness* (Oxford: Oxford University Press, 1993), introd.

67. Karl Jaspers, "The Philosophical Life," in *Way to Wisdom: An Introduction to Philosophy*, trans. Ralph Manheim (New Haven: Yale University Press, 2003), 120: "If our lives are not to be diffuse and meaningless, they must find their place in an order. In our daily affairs we must be sustained by a comprehensive principle, we must find meaning in an edifice of work, fulfillment and sublime moments, and by repetition we must gain in depth." See also Charles Taylor, "La conduite d'une vie et les moments du bien," in *La Liberté des Modernes* (Paris: PUF, 1997), 297–306, and *The Ethics of Authenticity* (Cambridge, Mass.: Harvard University Press, 1992).

68. Elisabeth Anderson, *Value in Ethics and Economics* (Cambridge, Mass.: Harvard University Press, 1993); H. R. Arkes and C. Blumer, "The Psychology of Sunk Cost," in T. Connolly, H. R. Arkes, and K. R. Hammond, eds., *Judgment and Decision Making* (Cambridge: Cambridge University Press, 2000), 97–103.

69. Josiah Royce, *The Philosophy of Loyalty* (New York: Thomas Crowell, 1936), lecture 4, section 4; John Rawls, *Theory of Justice* (Cambridge, Mass.: Harvard University Press, 1971), § 63, 407–15.

70. Rawls, *Theory of Justice*, § 63, 408, 410–11.

71. Ibid., § 64, 416–21.

72. Williams, *Moral Luck*, 12–13.

73. Søren Kierkegaard, *Fear and Trembling*, in *Kierkegaard's Writings*, ed. and trans. E. H. Hong and H. V. Hong, vol. 6 (Princeton, N.J.: Princeton University Press, 1978), 49. See, in the same volume, *Repetition: A Venture in Experimenting Psychology*, 220–21 and 304: "Is there not then a repetition? Did I not get everything double? Did I not get myself again, and precisely in such a way that I may have a double sense of its meaning? Compared with such a repetition, what is a repetition of worldly possessions, which is indifferent toward the qualification of the spirit? Only his children did Job not receive double again, for a human life cannot be redoubled that way. Here only repetition of the spirit is possible, even though it is never so perfect in time as in eternity, which is the true repetition."

74. Kierkegaard, *Fear and Trembling*, 62–63.

75. Marcel Proust, *Remembrance of Things Past: Time Regained*, trans. C. K. Scott Moncrieff, T. Kilmartin, and A. Mayor (New York: Random House, 1982), 3:898.

76. Franz Brentano, *The Origin of our Knowledge of Right and Wrong*, trans. Roderick Chisholm and Elisabeth Schneewind (London: Routledge, 1969); Roderick Chisholm, *Brentano and Intrinsic Value* (Cambridge: Cambridge University Press, 1986).

77. This is not unlike William James's idea that a life may acquire new meaning through assembly, rearrangement, synthesis, and integration of variations into unity—also known as "the recurrence of dealing with *maybes*." William James, "Is Life Worth Living?" in *The Will to Believe and Other Essays in Popular Philosophy* (New York: Dover Publications, 1956), 59.

CHAPTER SIX
THE GOOD IN HUMAN LIFE

1. Owen Flanagan considers that the good is defined in human life by the search for an identity and by the means to express it, but I doubt that self-expression would accomplish that. O. Flanagan, *Mind, Morals, and the Meaning of Life* (Oxford: Oxford University Press, 1996).

2. Those were specifically discussed in the pages dedicated to Melville's *Billy Budd* in the section "The Personal Perspective" in chapter 5.

3. Moral deliberation applies the principles of impartiality, veil of ignorance, and agent-neutrality analyzed by Derek Parfit in *Reasons and Persons* (Oxford: Oxford University Press, 1984).

4. There is a particular kind of pleasure derived from one's activities and experiences that can be called "enjoyment." In this case, the pleasure is not tied to any previous need but to the very nature of the enjoyed activity.

5. On the other hand, one may very well feel upbeat or in good spirits for no particular reason.

6. A prescriptivist philosopher can recognize subjective evaluations based on universalizable reasons.

7. The distinction between first-order and higher desires and needs comes from Harry G. Frankfurt's "Freedom of the Will and the Concept of a Person" [1971], in *The Importance of What We Care About* (Cambridge: Cambridge University Press, 1988).

8. Cf. chapter 5.

9. See Robert Nozick, *Philosophical Explanations* (Oxford: Oxford University Press, 1984), 410; and *État, anarchie, utopie* (Paris: PUF, 1988), 64–67. A similar effect would be obtained by ingesting a powerful drug like *soma*, the hypnotic, mind-altering antidepressant described by Aldous Huxley in *A Brave New World*.

10. This is true to the extent that one cannot seriously defend the epistemological thesis claiming that false happiness does not exist or that a feeling of satisfaction is always and necessarily justified.

11. Georg Henrik von Wright, *The Varieties of Goodness* [1957] (London: Routledge and Kegan Paul, 1963), 99. This objectivity of goods is not easily defin-

able: it means independence from desires and attitudes, but at the same time such desires must be recognizable as justified and legitimate. Cf. David Gauthier, *Morals by Agreement* (Oxford: Oxford University Press, 1986); James Griffin, *Well Being* (Oxford: Oxford University Press, 1986).

12. This objectivity of goods may very well be contingent on the way human nature operates.

13. Conversely, we can imagine that a person, unable to see himself as happy, can very well be considered happy by a third party, because of all the objective goods that he enjoys. In this case, though, the person would be able to acknowledge both his inability to enjoy those goods and the fact that they should make him happy.

14. Are these goods objects of intuitions as G. E. Moore saw them in his preface to *Principia Ethica*? Should they be identified by a form of transcendental deduction (showing that we cannot but consider certain things to be good for their own sakes) or by causal relation (things are good if they are related to something else which is itself good and provides a basic ethical judgment, such as the "distinctive endowment of a human being" offered by John Stuart Mill)? See *On Liberty* [1859] (London: Routledge, 1991), 90. For Kant, such goods help promote humanity as an end in itself based on perfectible abilities. See I. Kant, *Fundamental Principles of the Metaphysics of Morals* [1785], trans. L. W. Beck, Library of Liberal Arts (Indianapolis: Bobbs-Merrill, 1959), 17–18. For Aristotle, such goods can be spoken of in two ways: some may be goods in themselves, others—by reason of these. See *Nicomachean Ethics*, trans. W. D. Ross (Oxford: Clarendon Press, 1908), book I, 6. See also http://etext.library.adelaide.edu.au/a/aristotle/nicomachean.

15. Few philosophers have sought to justify epistemologically "their list of things that must be good." Among them: Aristotle, *Rhetoric* (Whitefish, Mont.: Kessinger Publishing, 2004), 19; J. S. Mill, *On Liberty*, http://etext.library .adelaide.edu.au/m/mill/john-stuart/m6450/; and G. E. Moore, *Principia Ethica* (Cambridge: Cambridge University Press, 1903), http://fair-use.org/g-e-moore/ principia-ethica/.

16. Joseph Raz, *Engaging Reasons* (Oxford: Oxford University Press, 1999), 399–407, 422, and 433–39, where the collision of expected goods with achieved ones is included in deliberative rationality. Their incompatibility is examined by practical reason when dealing with goals and relationships that are either *other-regarding* or *self-concerned*. See his chapter 13 "The Central Conflict: Morality and Self-Interest," 302–32.

17. G.E.M. Anscombe, "Modern Moral Philosophy," in *Philosophy* 33, no. 124 (1958); reprinted in *Ethics, Religion and Politics: Collected Philosophical Papers*, vol. 3 (Oxford: Blackwell, 1981), 26–47.

18. Anscombe, *Ethics, Religion and Politics*, 41. The conceptual clarification of *ought* involves analyzing the human faculties, abilities, and dispositions whose development represents human flourishing. This explains why Anscombe insisted that philosophy return to psychology.

19. In what follows, I attempt to extract this concept from the Aristotelian bath in which it is often immersed. The reference to Aristotle often serves only as a transhistorical backing of the typically modern concept of *human flourishing*. On this point, see Monique Canto-Sperber, *Les Éthiques grecques* (Paris: PUF, 2001).

20. Conversely, if it were said of somebody "he is happy, but he squandered his potential and achieved nothing of what he should have," this statement would create uneasiness without being contradictory, for juxtaposing an assertion about one's satisfaction with life on a finding that is independent of it. A drug addict may declare to be happy, but it can be said of him that he is not happy in exactly the same sense that the addict intended (not in the sense of, say, *fortunate* or *admirable*).

21. Cf. David Ross, *Foundations of Ethics* (Oxford: Oxford University Press, 1930), 257–58, on the distinction "good on the whole" versus "good through and through."

22. This is what Thomas Hurka calls their "teleologism" in *Perfectionism* (Oxford: Oxford University Press, 1993).

23. W. G. Maclagan, "Self and Others: A Defence of Altruism," *Philosophical Quarterly* 4 (1954).

24. On this point, see Bernard Williams critique in *Morality: An Introduction to Ethics* (Cambridge: Cambridge University Press, 1972).

25. Alasdair MacIntyre bases his definition of human good on the cohesiveness of traditions, and on the concepts of exemplar life and narrative order; he speaks of virtue, not *eudaimonia*. In their writings, Bernard Williams, Stuart Hampshire, and Iris Murdoch also avoid mentioning *eudaimonia* and dissociate goodness from happiness. I have attempted to show that a normative theory of morality is indefensible within ancient moral philosophy as long as the concepts of good and *eudaimonia* remain associated. Only by dissociating them can the formal, impersonal, and prescriptive elements of ancient ethical philosophy be treated fairly. See Canto-Sperber, *Les Éthiques grecques*.

26. This assumption allows us to speak of a soul's goodness, when it would be problematical to speak of a soul's happiness.

27. For Kant, goodwill is a good in itself, but this does not mean that it is our ultimate purpose, to which everything else is secondary. It is even nonsensical to declare oneself in pursuit of goodwill. On the other hand, Kant's thesis may very well mean that whatever the values of an individual, if he has goodwill, he owns an unconditional good. This thesis is close to the Stoics' hope: they claimed that virtue is the only good that one can never lose; it is also close to the assertion that, if there be a good for everybody, it could only be virtue.

28. Plato, *Republic*, trans. Benjamin Jowett, http://classics.mit.edu/Plato /Republic.html, book X, 619e–621b; see also the printed version, trans. G.M.A. Grube and C.D.C. Reeve (Indianapolis: Hackett Publishing, 1992), 290–92. See Plato, *Philebus*, trans. Benjamin Jowett, http://classics.mit.edu/Plato/Philebus.html , 64b; see also the printed version, trans. Seth Bernadete (Chicago: University of Chicago Press, 1993), 240.

29. Aristotle, *Nicomachean Ethics*, trans. Roger Crisp (Cambridge: Cambridge University Press, 2000), 38, 45, 141; http://classics.mit.edu/Aristotle /nicomachean.html; *Politics*, trans. B. Jowett (New York: Colonial Press, 1900); and http://classics.mit.edu/Aristotle/politics.html.

30. Arthur Schopenhauer, *The World as Will and Representation* [1886], trans. E.F.J. Payne (New York: Dover Publications, 1966), vol. 1, book 2, § 17, 95–99.

Index